The Evaluative State, Institutional Autonomy and
Re-engineering Higher Education in Western Europe

Issues in Higher Education

Titles include:

Jürgen Enders and Egbert de Weert (*editors*)
THE CHANGING FACE OF ACADEMIC LIFE
Analytical and Comparative Perspectives

John Harpur
INNOVATION, PROFIT AND THE COMMON GOOD IN HIGHER EDUCATION
The New Alchemy

V. Lynn Meek and Charas Suwanwela (*editors*)
HIGHER EDUCATION, RESEARCH, AND KNOWLEDGE IN THE ASIA-PACIFIC
REGION

Thorsten Nybom, Guy Neave and Kjell Blüchert (*editors*)
THE EUROPEAN RESEARCH UNIVERSITY

Guy Neave
THE EVALUATIVE STATE, INSTITUTIONAL AUTONOMY AND RE-ENGINEERING
HIGHER EDUCATION IN WESTERN EUROPE
The Prince and His Pleasure

Mary Ann Danowitz Sagaria
WOMEN, UNIVERSITIES, AND CHANGE

Snejana Slantcheva and Daniel Levy
PRIVATE HIGHER EDUCATION IN POST-COMMUNIST EUROPE

Sverker Sörlin and Hebe Vessuri
KNOWLEDGE SOCIETY VS. KNOWLEDGE ECONOMY

Voldemar Tomusk
THE OPEN WORLD AND CLOSED SOCIETIES

Issues in Higher Education
Series Standing Order ISBN 978–0–230–57816–6 (hardback)
(*outside North America only*)

You can receive future titles in this series as they are published by placing a
standing order. Please contact your bookseller or, in case of difficulty, write to
us at the address below with your name and address, the title of the series and
the ISBN quoted above.

Customer Services Department, Macmillan Distribution Ltd, Houndmills,
Basingstoke, Hampshire RG21 6XS, England

The Evaluative State, Institutional Autonomy and Re-engineering Higher Education in Western Europe

The Prince and His Pleasure

Guy Neave
CIPES, Matosinhos, Portugal

palgrave
macmillan

First published 2012 by
PALGRAVE MACMILLAN

Palgrave Macmillan in the UK is an imprint of Macmillan Publishers Limited,
registered in England, company number 785998, of Houndmills, Basingstoke,
Hampshire RG21 6XS.

Palgrave Macmillan in the US is a division of St Martin's Press LLC,
175 Fifth Avenue, New York, NY 10010.

Palgrave Macmillan is the global academic imprint of the above companies
and has companies and representatives throughout the world.

Palgrave® and Macmillan® are registered trademarks in the United States,
the United Kingdom, Europe and other countries.

ISBN 978–0–230–34803–5

This book is printed on paper suitable for recycling and made from fully
managed and sustained forest sources. Logging, pulping and manufacturing
processes are expected to conform to the environmental regulations of the
country of origin.

A catalogue record for this book is available from the British Library.

A catalog record for this book is available from the Library of Congress.

10   9   8   7   6   5   4   3   2   1
21   20   19   18   17   16   15   14   13   12

Printed and bound in the United States of America

To
Bob and Adele
Unsurpassed in scholarship, inspiration and friendship

Contents

Foreword

In many European countries, a number of recent reforms to increase the efficiency of higher education institutions and promote their responsiveness towards society's needs and demands are in hand. A few countries are engaged in creating more stratified higher education systems by strongly investing in a limited number of research universities to increase their capacity to compete in a globalized world. These reforms present some common trends – increasing institutional autonomy, reinforced power of central administration, decreasing collegiality and changing quality systems from improving accreditation to diversifying funding sources. New public management plays an increasing role in the public sector, including higher education. Markets (or quasi-markets) are increasingly used as instruments of public policy: by the European Commission, through the implementation of the Bologna Process and the Lisbon strategy, and by the OECD, through influencing reforms at a supranational level.

At a 'macro' level, convergence by higher education systems is clear. It may be seen as a response to globalization and to emerging neoliberal policies. However, at a micro level, pronounced local and national characteristics persist and are seen as holding out against uniformity, despite the fact that internal reforms to the higher education system are legitimated, at least rhetorically, by the nation's need to assert its place in an increasingly globalized world. National specificities are mediated by the acts of the state, which paradoxically ramp up the state's regulatory powers. The contradiction between the external weakening of sovereignty and the internal strengthening of the state stands at its most clear with the implementation of the Bologna Process. National interests mask the European political objectives as each country returns to a national logic to meet national objectives.

Guy Neave analyses recent changes in Portuguese higher education from a comparative perspective, setting them both as part of and against a broad European backdrop and by placing them against the corresponding policy dynamic in French and Spanish higher education. What is fascinating in Neave's analysis is the use of the interplay of national developments with the concepts of autonomy and the Evaluative State in comparing the three countries. He brings the two paths of institutional autonomy and the rise of the Evaluative State to bear on the specific Portuguese context, while at the same time placing this same context within the perspectives and trends, similarities and differences that derive from a broader canvas that Western Europe is turning out and which, occasionally, find an echo in Portugal itself.

In France, the Evaluative State emerged as a pre-conditioner for autonomy. France assumed a pioneering role in the development of the Evaluative State. It did so while remaining faithful to the deeply embedded notion of Republican values. Unlike developments in other countries, such as the UK and the Netherlands, where the market and New Public Management showed a strong hand in developing quality systems, in France the Evaluative State 'aimed primarily at making public service more efficient and better able to cope with the rising numbers of the Student Estate' without in any way challenging the position of the university as a public service, 'independent of any hindrance whether political, economic, religious and ideological'.

Only recently has France veered towards the more overtly ideological overtones of neoliberalism, under the guidance of President Sarkozy and his former Minister of Higher Education and Research, Valérie Pécresse. The establishment of a new evaluation agency in the shape of an agency of public purpose, institutional contractualization, reinforcd powers of the university president, increased authority, responsibility and the curtailment of both participant democracy and collegiality are all components of the new policy. A careful timing of the phases of the presidential elections in universities, of evaluation, contract negotiation and terms of office has given muscle to this policy while the Academic and the Student Estates were outflanked and presented as placing their own interests above those of the nation in their refusing the offer the Prince held out.

In Spain, a very different logic was involved. Construction of 'the Evaluative State followed on from the prior definition of autonomy rather than serving as an instrument for laying out the conditions under which institutional autonomy subsequently emerged, as had been the case in France and the Netherlands'. Emerging from a dictatorship, the new Spanish Constitution of 1978, which marked the return to democracy, created the autonomous regions and nationalities as a first level of government for the institutions located within them. Only more than a decade later was the Evaluative State initiated and developed, supported not by a single national agency but by a national agency in conjunction with regional agencies envisaged for each autonomous region.

The Spanish approach was not without its tensions, particularly between the new regional authorities, eager to assert their new power and authority, and an Academic Estate that saw the control of its activities moving from the distant capital to the more proximate Junta de Gobierno. The 2001 *Ley Organica Unversitaria* (LOU) sought to ease the tensions between academic and political autonomy by separating one from the other. The University Coordination Council was divided into two national coordination bodies, one more political which brought together those responsible for higher education in the regional Juntas de Gobierno, and the other more academic which brought university rectors together. And the setting up of a National Agency for Assessment and Accreditation aimed at ensuring rapid convergence with the Bologna agenda.

In 2007, the LOU was modified. The University Coordination Council was closed down, but two separate coordination bodies – political and academic – were retained, thereby giving 'further emphasis on the basic bicephalous structure – political/administrative versus academic'. The new law also reinforced the decision-making power of senior academics over academic matters, although it committed the accreditation agency to the task of evaluating academic staff.

However, Spanish legislation did not subscribe to the neoliberal credo, as was the case in other countries. The Spanish approach, which aimed at developing a strategy of internal participation in Spanish universities, created tensions with the degree of political autonomy wielded by the Autonomous Communities. As Guy argues, this has changed the role of the Social Council from representing external interests in academe into 'representing university interests to the private sector and very particularly that of fundraising for the university'.

For Guy Neave, the Portuguese case is seen in terms of exceptionalism. It follows neither the French pattern, where the emergence of the Evaluative State was a precondition for autonomy, nor the Spanish pattern, where institutional autonomy preceded the emergence of the Evaluative State. In Portugal, 'by contrast, the two tasks of reconstructing higher education are pursued simultaneously. The one interacts with the other'.

In Portugal, taking advantage of what can be considered as a weak state and of the opportunities opened up by the passing of the University Autonomy Act in 1988, the university rectors assumed the role of what Guy Neave interprets in terms of the Party of Movement, especially in areas such as quality assessment and financing. The strategy of the Party of Movement included setting up the Foundation of Portuguese Universities to serve as a think-tank to produce reports and policy documents which enabled rectors to keep one step ahead of the ministry and to influence national policies accordingly. The Foundation was also used to launch an experiment on quality assessment that later served as the model for the Quality Assessment Act.

However, the energies of the Party of Movement waned and in the first half of the first decade of the new millennium, the initiative passed to the Party of Order. By hiring the OECD to produce an overall evaluation of the Portuguese higher education system (2006), the government embarked in a reform that would reflect both the ethic and justification, of neoliberalism and that the thrust of reconstruction would fall in with the canons of its main administrative and operational template – New Public Management. At about the same time, the European Association for Quality Assurance in Higher Education (ENQA) was asked to evaluate and make recommendations for the Portuguese quality assessment system. Its report led to the decision to close the old system down and to replace it with an agency of public purpose which closely corresponded to European standards and guidelines laid out by ENQA.

In Neave's words 'far from seeing the universities as part of the solution, which had been the implicit assumption of the "Party of Movement", the OECD Review Team held the universities to be part of the problem. Thus, distrust migrated from focussing on Central administration, and instead latched on to higher education as the *causus malorum*'.

Neave draws our attention to two additional singularities of the Portuguese system. The first is to be seen in the structure of the 2007 Higher Education Guideline Law that establishes a general legal framework, 'allowing the institution to fill in the details', opening 'the path up to what may be regarded as "organic restructuring", driven from within the higher education system and subsequently recognized – or rejected – by the ministry'. This characteristic 'is not found in parallel enactments elsewhere', making the Guideline Law 'a practical example of institutional autonomy in action'.

The second singularity is the possibility for universities to request the ministry to permit them to become a foundation university under private law. For Guy Neave, even if some may argue that the legislator in no way saw foundation universities explicitly as 'hot houses' for innovation of a financial and an administrative nature, that is what lies in store for them.

The new Portuguese Higher Education Guideline Law involves a dualism in higher education policy that relies on increased institutional autonomy to promote 'self-adjustment' from beneath to the law, while 'system wide, macro decisions for shaping higher education from above nevertheless continue to figure as part of central government's reserve powers'.

To conclude, Guy Neave has been extremely successful in accomplishing his objectives of establishing a synthesis, an overview of higher education policy as it has unfolded in Portugal around the issues of autonomy and the Evaluative State, and then placing the dynamic thus revealed within a broader, comparative perspective. In the final chapter he offers an exploratory view of possible future developments in higher education, the evolution of the Evaluative State and the possibility of the resurrection of the long-established guardian relationship between universities and government – but only for a few high-performing elite research universities.

Alberto Amaral
Director General
Agencia do Avilacão e Accreditacão do Ensinho Superior
Lisbon

Preface

Though the study of higher education often prides itself on addressing 'problems', and consultants, with no less hubris, devise 'solutions' of varying degrees of originality and predictability, very few of the major issues faced by higher education today are, in point of fact, 'solvable' in the sense that one solution brings the issue to a permanent and hopefully happy end.

'Problems', if we are exceedingly lucky and our political masters were excessively insightful and sensitive, may be dealt with. Yet they are – alas – rarely solvable on a permanent basis and for all time. At best, the 'solution' that scholarship and its application may come up with may last a generation – say, 30 years. It then tends to reassert itself in a different form and, like as not, trails a different set of consequences in its wake for universities, polytechnics, for the nation's civil servants and very certainly for the three Estates – Academic, Administrative and Student – that make up higher education and higher learning.

Of these 'unsolvable conditions' or 'abiding issues', autonomy is very certainly the most sensitive since, depending on how it is interpreted, it determines the relationship between university, government, the economy and society. It also sets out the responsibilities that institutions and those in them are called upon to assume and thus the way in which the vision of the university is translated into educated citizens – young but increasingly less so as participation in higher education extends to older age groups – into 'knowledge products' without which the future of the so-called 'Knowledge Society' is dark indeed. Autonomy is also an expression of a particular model or vision, which embraces not just the university, but also the society the university ministers to.

That the world is in flux is an exceedingly ancient view, which today sees the financial princes of the planet sharing the millennial pessimism of the Ionian philosopher Heraclites. Heraclites' position as an observer, however, was somewhat more enviable than that of the participants at Davos whose business in the 2009 gathering of that financial species was largely to contemplate in impotence and puzzlement the results of its own handiwork. What the fallout will be for higher education, which has become newly globalized, none can foresee with any degree of confidence. What the bold might suggest, however, is that many of the issues, funding, conditions of academic work, the place of academia in society, the priorities that universities will, once again, be called upon to meet, are not likely to assume the same form as has been the case over the past two decades.

If only for that reason, it is important – and never more so than at this particular juncture – to see what has been achieved. For it is only by having such an account that we know where we are and how far it is within our reach to do 'those things that ought to be done', whatever it is the Prince in his infinite wisdom would have us do to pick up the mess that private greed and public laxity have created. Greed, whatever traders in Wall Street, on the Paris Bourse and similar 'things' in the City would have each other believe, is not good, despite the assertion made almost three centuries ago by the Anglo-Dutch doctor and pamphleteer Bernard de Mandeville.

Private vices may indeed create public benefits, but only when authentic accountability, an effective democracy and the *brigade des moeurs* are notoriously absent, which was very much the case in eighteenth-century England when de Mandeville brought out his scandalous *Fable of the Bees*. And yet, as we all see, even when such elementary forms of economic oversight and moral deterrence are present, private vice and public greed combined still retain a devastating capacity to create recession, layoffs and massive unemployment – in short, one devil of a mess! Had Britain's Stock Exchange and banking system been under the same rigorous oversight as its universities, in all likelihood our troubles would at the very least have been very much less. The same could be said for most of the major banking systems in Western Europe today. Clearly, what is sauce for the goose of finance is not sauce for the gander of learning and teaching, innovation and research.

Whether the clean-up – if ever it takes place – will see sufficient numbers of the one-time 'Golden Boys' standing in the lines of the unemployed to cause our latter-day Libertines to amend their views and their ways is something the rest of us can only hope and pray for. It is one of the few consolations these sorry times guarantee and, being free, is in the bounds of what we can afford – together with loud and ribald laughter.

Over the years, one of the preoccupations that have held my attention has been the development of the Evaluative State and the role it has played as a central construct in higher education. Another, which most long-term students of higher education at one point in their careers have set their hands to, is that protean issue of academic autonomy. Having trained as an historian in the UK at the moment when institutional autonomy was at its apogee, living abroad for the best part of my professional life served, like the Elephant's Child in Kipling's *Just So Stories*, to inflate an 'insatiable curiosity' and especially so when working in university systems that did not, for one reason or another, share that boon to the same degree, still less in the same form.

This 'exploration' of the two issues – institutional autonomy and the Evaluative State – is the fruit of personal good fortune in a very special guise: the invitation, on taking leave of my very good friends and colleagues on my retirement from the Centre for Higher Education Policy Studies (CHEPS) at Twente University in the Netherlands, to come and join Professor Alberto Amaral and his colleagues at the *Centro de Investigação de Políticas do Ensino Superior* (CIPES) in Matosinhos (Portugal) – a suggestion accepted with indecent haste and with boundless gladness. CIPES, like CHEPS, is far more than a research centre. It is a type of 'extended family' where intellectual good fellowship is bonded, not by scholarship football and carpet bowls, but by that most unbreakable of all ties – scholarship, unbounded enthusiasm and gastronomy. These inseparable activities are mutually reinforcing. They are two infallible ways of creating a critical mass! They turn it into a self-feeding and self-stimulating milieu from which none can fail to benefit. I certainly have, and being 'well rounded' in body as in mind is not least amongst the pleasures CIPES confers upon its guests, its members and its denizens.

I consider this 'offering' to be a very small acknowledgement of what I have already received from CIPES, both collectively and individually. Like most works of this nature, it draws on earlier efforts and very particularly on an extension out of a chapter in Alberto Amaral's book *Políticas de Ensino Superior: quarto témas em debate*, published in 2008. Likewise, it is an extension of what is perhaps best described as a 'cadet edition' – less elaborate and without the case studies of France, Spain or Portugal, which appeared under the editorship of Barbara Kehm, Jeroen Huisman and Bjorn Stensaker as *The European Higher Education Area: Perspectives on a Moving Target*, under the imprimatur of Sense Publications of Rotterdam.

This study is offered to CIPES and to friends and colleagues therein – to be one is the same as being the other – whose company I value enormously and hope that it is reflected herein. The errors and infelicities are, of course, no part of this since I assert my exclusive rights to them quite apart from making the formal refusal to share them with anyone!

Part I

A World Set Upside Down

1
Setting the Scene

Introduction

Over the past quarter of a century in Western Europe, immense changes have taken place in the triangular relationship between government, society and higher education. The tasks governments have laid upon higher education today emphasize the obligations it has to 'serve' society's interests and demands, which are primarily construed as economic. Funding, amongst the Prince's most powerful tools in driving policy, has become conditional, subject to both contractual engagement and to close and regular evaluation. Internal governance, for a long time built around the key values of autonomy and collegiality, both of which identified and shaped the internal relationship between higher education's three Constituent Orders – the Academic, the Administrative and the Student Estates – can no longer draw on the stuff of legend and tradition. The Academic Estate, which once proudly traced its origins and its ways of working and teaching back to the medieval guild, now rests on a very different 'referential model': the large business corporation (Neave, 2011a). Last, and most assuredly far from being least, for it was the main driving force behind Europe's orgy of reform, has been the heady and persistent growth in the Student Estate. More than 30 years ago, systems of higher education in Western Europe moved solidly into what the late Martin Trow, one of America's foremost students of higher education policy, termed 'mass higher education'. More than 15 per cent or more of the age group enrolled. Today, these same systems stand on the threshold of 'universal higher education', with upwards of 40 per cent or more of the age group participating (Trow, 1974).

Two cross-cutting themes

In truth, this was a vast upheaval and an unprecedented achievement. This study has perforce to be more modest. It singles out two transversal themes: the rise and place of the Evaluative State and the shifting fate of institutional autonomy. By bringing these two perspectives to bear on the broader developments just noted, a slightly different though complementary account may be had. And there is good reason for this. The period of reform and change that accelerated in Western Europe from the 1980s onwards has, over the past few years, reached crisis point, largely it has to be said as a result of the more enduring and insidious conditions that financial capitalism has inflicted on our societies and as a consequence of the often desperate measures governments have taken to keep crisis at arm's length. The Evaluative State and institutional autonomy are then the twin themes through which we may grasp the implications which arise from the dynamic that development and change imparted to these two constructs and the functions they were expected to undertake during these 25 years. For not only did the meaning that attended them alter, the alteration in meaning served to redraft the external relationship between government and higher education. It also set a new internal 'balance of power' between higher education's three Estates – Academic, Administrative and Student.

1) The Evaluative State

The notion of the Evaluative State has been applied to many systems – Britain (Henkel, 1991, France (Neave, 1988a and 1996a), Germany (Kehm, 2007), Ireland (Clancy, 2007), Italy (Boffo and Moscati, 1998) and further afield, for instance, Brazil (Neave, 2006a). Though the term has currency as a descriptor in the vocabulary of studies in higher education, it has not been systematically developed on a comparative and cross-national basis in one place, though over the years I have chased after this concept across different journals and across different countries from South America to Japan (Neave, 2006b, 2009a). Because it is the key concept – the prime analytical perspective to this account – this chapter will focus on defining it, tracing its origins and the levels at which it operates.

If the origins of the Evaluative State are to be found in the policies, crises and priorities of individual nation-states in Western Europe, this does not mean that the Evaluative State is without its ramifications at the European level. From this it follows that whilst the prime concern of this study remains solidly at the nation-state level, we cannot blithely leave aside initiatives emerging at a level beyond the nation-state and particularly so given the power that the Evaluative State already wields. In short, though this study is resolutely focused on the nation-state, nation-state policy in higher education is, to an increasing degree, influenced by what happens at the European level. As such, it is important to attend to what may be regarded as the 'European dimension' that the Evaluative State has begun to acquire from the turn of the millennium onwards. That we concentrate on the way the players perform does not wholly prevent us from appreciating – if not always admiring – the broader set and backdrop against which they act out their parts.

2) Autonomy

Autonomy – leaving aside for the moment its definitions and operational dimensions, which vary immensely from one country to another – may be considered as the central, historical and operational value that sets the institution of higher education and *a fortiori* the university apart from other establishments of 'training and learning'. The principle of self-determination and freedom of thought has, since the days of Wilhelm von Humboldt, been regarded as the non-negotiable condition for upholding that institution's essential function to provide society with replicable and verifiable scientific and scholarly knowledge (Thorens, 2006: 87–110). For this reason, the interplay between definitions of institutional autonomy and the Evaluative State stands at the heart of this analysis. In this chapter, autonomy will be dealt with in a preliminary fashion by looking first at the internal conditions for operationalizing institutional autonomy. Because it is so central and sensitive an issue, not least because of the changes that 'contractualization' has effectively introduced into the relationship between government, society and higher education, this theme is taken up further in Chapter 2.

Central questions

When the two perspectives of the Evaluative State and autonomy in its various forms are brought together, as they have been with increasing vigour over the past quarter of a century in Western Europe, clearly they are powerful instruments for reform and change. The putting in place of formal, regular and standardized procedures for ascertaining the performance and output productivity of the individual university, polytechnic or higher vocational training institute has gathered weight as a central instrumentality for 'steering' higher education. Seen from a long-term and historical perspective, the Evaluative State bids fair to be more pervasive, more interventionary and more rapid in its consequences for the individual institution of higher education than any of the legal instruments it replaces.

What are the consequences for public policy in higher education? What has changed in the ways in which systems of higher education are 'coordinated' by the rise of the Evaluative State? What impact has the Evaluative State had in changing the operational consequences of autonomy, for universities and for their 'Constituent Orders' – the Academic, Administrative and Student Estates? How has the proliferation under various guises of agencies (mostly national, sometimes regional and more recently at a European level) for overseeing quality assurance, accreditation and evaluation that proceeded throughout the 1990s and beyond in Western Europe reset the ties between government, society and university?

The Evaluative State

1) The dynamic in Western Europe

The spread of the Evaluative State across Western Europe accelerated throughout the course of the 1990s. By the end of that decade, as Schwartz-Hahn and Westerheijden (2004) noted, few indeed were the systems of higher education not endowed with committees and agencies that exercised a regular, close and reiterative scrutiny over the achievements and performance of their institutions of higher education through the use of formal criteria and indicators of performance. Creating self-standing agencies, however, was not the only model. An alternative arrangement saw the functions of quality assessment, institutional accreditation and evaluation assigned to national organizations representing the university or, as a further variation, placing the responsibility for this particular task in the hands of already-extant government agencies whose remit already included overarching coordination for higher learning. As with most activities of humankind, there is always the odd one out. Greece for a long time remained aloof to the general rush to set up agencies of public purpose to assure quality and to tie them in with the public validation and accreditation of diplomas and degrees, courses and programmes that the individual university or polytechnic submitted (Schwartz-Hahn and Westerheijden, 2004).

From a Europe-wide perspective, the rise of the Evaluative State marks an interesting transition in the scope of higher education policy

(Neave, 2009a). At its outset in 1985, the Evaluative State stood very clearly as an example of what may be seen as the 'historic' mode of policy making in the sense that policy dealt with specific issues within the confines of the individual nation-state. Whilst its expansion over the ensuing 15 years remained the individual initiative of governments, the general thrust of the measures introduced around it shared a remarkable number of common features across national systems of higher education and, naturally, an equally marked series of 'locally specific' measures. What may be seen as a *de facto* process of 'voluntary convergence' across individual nation-states took on a new momentum and a new scope. This it did with the signing of the Bologna Declaration in June 1999, an agreement that eventually was to be endorsed by some 45 systems of higher education, including all those that made up the Member States of the EU (Amaral and Neave, 2008; Amaral, Maassen, Neave and Musselin, 2009). Briefly stated, the scope of higher education policy took on a dimension over and above 'voluntary convergence'. In the first place, Bologna injected a *de jure* European dimension to 'voluntary convergence'. In the second place, it added a common model and a common series of objectives – study duration, employability and 'readability' to a shared qualifications structure. Last but not least, it set down a formal schedule for completion by the year 2010 (Haug and Tausch, 2001).

From one point of view, the construction of the Evaluative State may arguably be presented as bringing down the curtain on higher education policy acting within that historic framework the origins of which go back to the mid- to late eighteenth century in Continental Europe and which began with the various reforms that incorporated universities into the service of the nation (Huisman, Maassen and Neave, 2001: 3–75). Amongst them are the Swedish reforms of 1756 (Svensson, 1982) the Josephine Reforms in Austria of the 1780s (Gruber, 1982) as well as the better-known Humboldt Memorandum of 1806 which founded the University of Berlin (Nybom, 2003), together with the decrees that, between 1808 and 1811, put in place the French 'Imperial University' (Charle, 2004).

1) Evaluation beyond the nation-state

The Bologna Process put in place new institutions and procedures in the sphere of higher education policy, new in the shape of meetings every two years at a European level for ministers in charge of higher education, new in the permanency given to participating interests, new in its focusing uniquely upon higher education, new in the sense of re-engineering a multinational higher education system with a continental scope and, last but not least, new in creating a level of decision-making in higher education beyond the nation-state. Whatever one's views on the rhetoric employed to advance it (Neave and Amaral, 2008), Bologna stands as the most complex undertaking higher education has faced since its foundation in eleventh-century Italy.

The unfolding of the Bologna 'Process' gave recognition to new stakeholder groups including governments, higher education organizations and students, but not, until considerably later, the Academic Estate. Though the Bologna Process made scarcely credible gestures towards evaluating its own unfolding (Neave and Amaral, 2008), it is safe to say that creating a 'European dimension' atop the various agencies that made up the Evaluative State at the national level followed a slightly different dynamic, which was slightly more modest and a little aside from the spotlights of Bologna, but no less significant for all that.

3) The Evaluative State and Brussels

In the waltz of the acronyms that imagination has begotten in Brussels, the key bodies that project the interests of higher education onto a European level are known in Commission jargon as the 'E4'. The E4, as its title suggests, brings together four associations, which the Commission holds to be the mouthpiece of higher education at a European level. These are the European Network for Quality Assurance in Higher Education (ENQA), the European University Association (EUA), the European Association for Higher Education (EURASHE), which speaks on behalf of the non-university sector of higher education, and the European Students' Union (ESU). The E4 is, in effect, a coordinative arrangement that at a European level brings together the operational agencies of the Evaluative State working at a national level, as well as providing a channel back to at least two of the three Estates in higher education's Constituent Order: the Academic and the Student Estates.

Within the 'quadruple alliance', the organizational projection of the Evaluative State onto a supranational level emerges in ENQA, a title this organization assumed in 2004 largely due to the momentum generated by the Bologna Process itself (ENQA, 2009a). However, the origins of this network, which is today based in Helsinki, go back to 1994 as part of a pilot project then launched by the European Commission in parallel to the drive towards the Evaluative State at the nation-state level. The remit of ENQA is one of coordination, advice and cross-system information, as well as international reviews of system performance – activities partly funded by the European Commission in the form of projects assigned to ENQA and the subsidization of its conferences.

ENQA has a two-tier membership. It is made up of full members, drawn from some 25 countries and 43 different agencies (ENQA, 2009b), and associate members from 21 states ranging from Armenia to the Vatican *en passant par* Kazakhstan in addition to three European agencies. Currently, three countries have agencies with a 'candidate status', which involves a two-year waiting period before confirmation as a full member (ENQA, 2009c).

ENQA brings together national agencies of public purpose in the area of quality assurance and accreditation. Together with its own particular 'partner associations' of the E4, added to this are Business Europe and Education International, a pan-European teachers' union to which representation of the interests of the Academic Estate was assigned, somewhat tardily, in 2005. ENQA organizes an annual Quality Assurance Forum. It is responsible both for developing and proposing European standards and guidelines in the area of quality assurance and accreditation in higher education. Its task is to sustain, if not to accelerate, the process of convergence by exercising leverage within these two spheres (ENQA, 2009d).

Along with the other three 'partner organizations', ENQA is an active agent in consolidating that underpinning to the European Higher Education Area, propelled by means of 'soft law', a concept that will be examined later in this introductory *tour d'horizon*.

4) EQAR: dealing with millennial dilemmas

More recently, ENQA's strategic weight as an agency of accreditation and recognition has been enhanced significantly by the move on the part of the quadruple alliance to set up a European Quality Agency Register for Higher Education (EQAR). This registration agency, based in Brussels, became operational during the summer of 2008 (EQAR, 2008). Formally speaking, it acts independently from its four founding fathers. EQAR's purpose is to register – and thus accredit – those quality assurance agencies at a national level which, in the opinion of its expert committees, 'substantially comply' with the European Standards and Guidelines for Quality Assurance (EQAR, 2008). It appears to fulfil this delicate task, identified many centuries ago by the Latin poet Juvenal. It acts as the European guardian to the guardian agencies of quality assurance and accreditation operating at the nation-state level. It stands, so it would seem, as an attempt to come up with an answer to the age-old question: '*Quis custodiet ipsos custodes?*'

Since the 'partner organizations' of the E4 are also those that act as the main interlocutors with the European Commission and governments in respect of the Bologna Process, the link between the latter and the Evaluative State is clear and explicit. What remains less clear, however, is the 'direction of penetration' in which both ENQA and EQAR, as its registration agency, drive. The direction of penetration is an issue that, whilst crucial in the relationship between universities and government at the national level, is no less so at the European level. It poses a number of highly germane questions as to the exact nature of ENQA itself. Some idea of ENQA's role, function and positioning may be obtained by posing the following three questions. First, is ENQA to be seen as the culminating point in a network driven from the bottom up? Second, is it to be interpreted as an accumulation of national agencies that seek increased leverage in their particular national stamping ground by invoking 'European standards' to give additional weight to their agendas? Or, as a final possibility, is ENQA a tool of central 'coordination', infiltrated through the ostensible use of 'good practice' in quality assurance, to serve as an instrument to subtly build beyond the primary 'architecture' ushered in by the Bologna Process? These queries are not, however, mutually exclusive. Rather, they may be seen as locating ENQA along the dimensions provided by the answers to the above questions.

The rise of the Evaluative State: the nation-state perspective

1) An historical foray

Though historians never cease to point out that quality has always been an integral part of higher learning, they also have to admit that there have been moments in the history of particular countries and individual universities when quality was a feature less prominent than one had the right to expect. One has only to recall the sorrowful remarks of the eighteenth-century English historian Edmund Gibbon about the quality of the Dons of his day at Oxford[1] or the withering scorn of the poet Byron[2] for Cambridge, his brief Alma Mater, to realize that quality even then could fluctuate amazingly.

The significance of the rise of the modern Evaluative State, however, does not lie in its introducing evaluation as an instrument of policy in higher education. Rather, its significance resides very precisely in the changes it has brought about in the operating mode and in the ends to which evaluation is put. These changes stand in marked contrast to the way in which it had previously been employed to uphold what today would be termed 'quality', in the shape of laying down conditions and standards centrally defined by the appropriate ministry, the fulfilment of which was compulsory if 'certified knowledge' was to be publicly certified and valued on that account.

In its classic configuration, quality assurance in what Clark called 'the Continental European' model of systems coordination (Clark, 1983) was clear and explicit. In certain systems – for instance, those in Belgium, France and Germany – quality assurance took the form of a dualism in the qualifications awarded by public universities. This dualism emerged in the form of legal, national or the *Staatsexamen* diplomas respectively. Each of these three diplomas conferred eligibility for public office upon their holder in contrast to scientific, university or academic qualifications issued by the individual university. The latter qualifications certified the validity of the programme studied. However, they did not qualify those holding them for public employment. Other arrangements were to be seen, for example, in Spain and Italy. There university diplomas were both national and, at the same time, qualified their holders for public office without distinction.

Quality assurance was part of the state's responsibility on the one hand to uphold the principle of meritocracy as the basis of public service and on the other hand to ensure an inflow of those suitably and formally qualified to the services for which the state was directly responsible.

2) Two 'modes' of system evaluation

Under the so-called 'state control' model of systems coordination (van Vught, 1989), evaluation existed. But it existed in what today would be regarded as an embryonic, or even curtailed, form. Broadly speaking, what in present-day jargon would be called 'system evaluation' functioned in two 'modes' – first, the 'maintenance mode' and, second, the 'exploratory mode' (Neave, 1998).

The 'maintenance mode' took the form of formal and legal administrative oversight wielded by the central ministry over such aspects as the official recognition of public – as opposed to 'academic' – degrees in systems where duality of status operated. Often such oversight extended beyond matters of finance to embrace the content of such diplomas, by setting out templates in which content and duration were formally stipulated and set down. Administrative oversight also extended to the confirming into post of senior members of academia, sometimes vested in the Minister of Education or his or her equivalent, sometimes, as was once the case in Sweden, in the Prime Minister's office. These procedures amounted to what is best presented as a routine 'closed cycle' system of administrative verification and accountability that operated between the individual university and the ministry. Its purpose was less to ascertain either performance or output of individual universities as to ascertain that the way the university and its courses were administered was in conformity with and was acting within the formal conditions set down in law or by ministerial decree.

Alongside the 'maintenance mode' of administrative oversight ran a second procedure, which was more searching and more comprehensive in its scope, more time-consuming and, for such reasons, far less common. Essentially, the 'exploratory mode' took the form of special committees of enquiry set up to review a particular issue, to make recommendations for dealing with it or, as an alternative, to review the current state of higher education with a view to introducing wide-ranging reform. Amongst historic examples of 'the exploratory mode' in Britain would be the Prime Minister's Committee on Higher Education, otherwise known as the Robbins Committee of 1963; in Sweden, the Royal Commissions set up to review higher education in 1958, and again in 1968 (Premfors, 1981). In France, the Faure Commission served as a sticking plaster to the uproar that occurred in May in that same year.

What set the 'exploratory' mode apart from the 'maintenance' mode was the former's strategic nature in contrast to the short-term routine of verification that the latter performed. Far more significant, however, recourse to the 'exploratory mode' of system evaluation was the task conferred upon such committees and commissions. Yet, by the same token, the 'exploratory mode' was also a pointer to some of the inadequacies of the 'maintenance mode'.

3) Central assumptions of the two 'modes'

If we look beyond the mere presence of these two types of system evaluation and concentrate rather on what for lack of a better term may be called the 'style' of reform they implied, two things are immediately clear. First, the exploratory mode was often employed to deal with crisis. Second, the exploratory mode dealt with those aspects that had either escaped the control of routine verification or which, by their nature, could not reasonably have been foreseen. Two examples drawn from the 1960s were the consequences of the spiralling social demand for higher education on the one hand and economic prosperity on the other. Yet the central assumption that underpinned the 'maintenance mode' was precisely the stability of the system it administered. By the same token, however, a good case can be argued for seeing the degree of long-term crisis present in any one system in terms of the number of commissions – parliamentary, royal or national – called upon to sit during the course of any one decade.

The model of change implied by both the 'maintenance' and 'exploratory' modes was one of oscillation between a frantic centrally induced overhaul by means of the 'exploratory' mode and periods of digestive quiescence during which the 'maintenance' mode returned to the even tenor of its by then modified ways. Thus, system evaluation in the form it assumed under the 'state control model' of relationship between the university and the government made two crucial assumptions. These were, first, that the 'exploratory mode' of system evaluation was to be called upon only in exceptional circumstances and, second, that reform itself corresponded to a 'stop/go' cadence that worked itself out over a period of anything between 15 and 30 years.

Whether it is justifiable to argue that what changed the classic configuration of system evaluation in the state control model of higher education in Continental Europe was the realization that crisis had replaced stability as a permanent feature in the system is debatable. What appeared self-evident, however, from the outcomes and recommendations that flowed from the 'exploratory' mode was very precisely the need to expand the scope of 'maintenance' by adding further forms of intelligence-gathering so as to obtain a more detailed and dynamic picture of the condition in which higher education found itself as part of the core activities to be undertaken by routine system oversight and verification.

Two radical changes and the Evaluative State

Whilst this requirement did not originate in the present-day Evaluative State, it was nevertheless an identifying feature that accompanied it in the shape of new criteria – performance indicators and other operational instruments, which in their mature state sought to measure throughput, output, finer degrees of purchase over cost and, finally, academic productivity. They were variously aligned around the number of students qualified, publications and contracts won. This phenomenon, perhaps best described as a form of 'statistical sophistication', preceded the current Evaluative State.

Pragmatically, the phenomenon of 'statistical sophistication' is easily tracked. One has only to go through the regularly-published statistical reports put out by the ministry, by rectors' conferences – or their national counterparts – at, say, ten-yearly intervals – to see the steady routine growth in the type, focus and detail of the information gathered as being necessary for 'system maintenance'. This permeative – one is almost tempted to say capillary – phenomenon is the modern Evaluative State amplified. It amplified what was essentially already underway as part of governments' efforts to keep track of higher education's drive towards 'massification'. The development of a more elaborate statistical base, the regular updating of information on the overall size of the higher education system and the addition of such items as the proportion of the age group entering and the social origins of students, viewed within the perspective of expanding the boundaries of the 'maintenance' mode, has its roots in the late 1960s and early 1970s.

But amplification to the 'maintenance' aspect of system evaluation was not the only change that accompanied the rise of the present-day Evaluative State. From the standpoint of sheer chronology, we need to know just when and what was involved in the key events which marked the point at which the state evaluating changed into the Evaluative State. This watershed is relatively clear-cut. The changeover took place when the evaluation of institutional performance moved out from the general 'maintenance function' of the central ministry to become part of what the American policy analyst Martin Trow termed 'agencies of public purpose'. The remit, responsibilities and function of these agencies were wholly concentrated on the single specialized task of evaluation. This aspect, and the national variations in administrative location of this function, will be dealt with in detail in both Chapters 2 and 3. However, the creation of specialized agencies of public purpose was not the only change involved in the transition from the state evaluating to the Evaluative State.

The Evaluative State modifies evaluation

The Evaluative State also brought about two further fundamental modifications to evaluation itself, apart from hiving it off from the central ministry. From the mid-1960s to the mid-1970s, the first drive towards massification saw policy – and thus revision to the 'maintenance mode' – focused on input: how many, who and in which sector of higher education? The onset of a second 'explosion in student numbers' during the early 1980s shifted system evaluation radically to home in on results, performance, output, time taken to graduate, etc. The second change in perspective that the modern Evaluative State put in place was equally radical. It displaced 'the exploratory' mode of system evaluation by bringing what had hitherto been its exclusive task – namely, the process of review, diagnosis and recommendation – into the ambit of the 'maintenance mode'. This is not to say that the 'exploratory' dimension softly and silently vanished away like the wretch who met the Boojum in Lewis Carroll's nonsense poem 'The Hunting of the Snark'. The 'exploratory' mode remains.

Extending the 'maintenance mode' by outsourcing certain tasks to bodies of public purpose that earlier formed part of the 'exploratory mode' may be seen as a process that had two distinct features. On the one hand, there was the need to know what was taking place at an institutional level – that is, to provide a formal and specialized administrative base and as such a 'solution' to the accumulating burden that 'statistical sophistication' represented. On the other hand, a major reorientation of system evaluation around institutional *output* in such a way that, in theory at least, the short-term, reiterative application of evaluation, assessment and review themselves took on a different dimension. This dimension was less a strategic shift in system goals and purposes than a task midway between strategic definition and tactical verification. The emerging scope of system evaluation amounted to an ongoing exercise in 'fine-tuning' at an institutional and thus a system level. To use a sailor's metaphor, evaluation entailed steering by small course corrections. In so doing, the notion of reform as a 'one-off' event gave way to a new perception of 'system change' as an 'ongoing' and continuous process in which the only stability to be had was the prospect of change itself being a permanent condition of higher education.

Thus, the modern edition of the Evaluative State was established to deal with three crucial systemic issues:

- To replace an historic mode of administrative control over higher education with one sufficiently adaptable to being driven by forces external to higher education.
- To draw up criteria and procedures to provide an up-to-date and comprehensive portrait of the state of all sectors and institutions of higher education and to embed it in an institutional form.
- To deal with what may be termed the 'implementation lag', which is nothing less than accelerating the rate of take-up, response and adjustment at an institutional level by the regular and reiterative evaluation of the performance of the individual university.

How these three issues have been broached, the changes they have brought about in the historic relationship between government, society and higher education, and the repercussions they have for institutional autonomy are the subject of this study.

Three snares in the comparative perspective

Though a particular nation may interpret the condition of its higher education system and though the measures it puts in hand to construct the Evaluative State may display similarity in purpose with those of its neighbours, the way it goes about getting these things done is very different indeed. If many of the roads in today's higher education policy lead to Rome, to the Evaluative State or, for that matter, to Bologna, the fact remains that different systems have different starting points. They take different routes. They move at different rates despite much-publicized schedules for completion, which appear explicitly to assume that higher education and building sites are both much of a muchness when it comes to getting the job done on time. That such major goals are rarely achieved on time or are subject to backsliding is not necessarily due to a lack of political will, efficiency, engagement, resources or incompetence – though these may indeed be present. But similar issues bring forth different responses from actors and partners, despite their similarities in terms of condition or status across frontiers. Debate conducted on a similar topic across different lands summons up and has recourse to different historical, not to mention legal, precedents, meaning and symbolism in one political, administrative or academic culture as compared to its neighbour. The same strictures apply to the two issues addressed in this study: institutional autonomy and the Evaluative State.

It is not sufficient – and, still less, wise – simply to lump these differences, nuances and subtleties of different national or academic cultures together under the glib rubric of 'the national context'. To do so serves merely to hide – or, worse still, to regard as of little account – the differences in conditions, perceptions and interests amongst those involved. Such a *reductio ad absurdum* forges a similarity that is merely nominal, though its use may certainly feed the impression – and often the explanation too – into the same straitjacket.

Such voluntary 'restrictionism' – the less charitable would call it deliberate self-imposed myopia – is far from being alien to cross-system studies. Indeed, it is, in part, a function of comparison itself. The more systems are compared, the fewer the dimensions that can be dealt with, save quantitatively. Conversely, the more dimensions we seek to dissect, the fewer the systems we can handle in depth. When we are faced with 27 systems of higher education – as is the case with the EU – and the vast number of internal and external interests and 'cultures' that revolve around them, the higher the level of abstraction required to 'explain' such specific features. However, the common dimension that brings them all together serves precisely to eliminate or pass lightly over both differences and specifics. Quality and nuance go by the board or emerge as a situation described – though more rarely explained – along a series of pre-determined dimensions.

1) Avoiding 'higher educationism'

These difficulties, which are inherent in cross-system analysis, lie at the root of what the British sociologist Roger Dale termed 'higher educationism' (Robertson and Dale, 2009). Dale's main criticism was directed at the tendency in writings on higher education to home in on the 'inner' workings of universities in isolation from the values involved and the implications that followed from these unattended values for society, social mobility and not least educational opportunity.

'Higher educationism' as scholarship in a curtailed form and as an unwitting indulgence in self-censorship also contains other aspects. Prime amongst these is a tendency to view both policy and its implementation in terms of 'procedures' and structures rather than the perspective represented in the classic work by Becher and Kogan, 'process and structures' (Becher and Kogan, 1991), in short, reducing higher education to a series of operational and technical operations divested of, if not separated from, such troublesome matters as authority, power, influence, public values and political ideology, irrespective of whether the situation in which such technical procedures are wielded tends towards hierarchy, subordination, oligarchy or arbitrariness. Disguising the value-laden by the felicitous and apparently neutral technical phrase has been the bugbear of other sociologists in British universities, notably Fuller (2006), just as it has also been identified in certain instances of policy statements emanating from the European Commission (Amaral and Neave, 2008).

2) 'Proceduralism': a venal or mortal sin?

'Proceduralism' as a linguistic and presentational style shades over into a full-blown methodology in the study of higher education. It is not, however, a coincidental development. Rather, it may be seen as the outcome of changes in the strategic position of the Administrative Estate, as it moved over to become the prime shaping force of 'policy as procedure' at an institutional level, in the increasing fascination with 'leadership' generally in higher education and finally as an outcome of the sway exerted by Brussels in the commissioning of enquiries by scholars in higher education.

As regards the first two changes, we may observe an interesting reorientation taking place in the study of higher education in the UK. There, the study of higher education is moving from its classic foci on resources, on the Academic and the Student Estates towards analysing the tasks and responsibilities, qualifications and skills required by the Administrative Estate to carry its functions out, together with what type of responsibility accrues to what level of post (Whitchurch, 2006 and 2009; Smith, Adams and Mount, 2007). By such means, the Administrative Estate becomes a local hero.

The role of Brussels in encouraging 'proceduralism' derives in some measure from the dilemma noted earlier, namely the press to balance coverage against scope and depth. But simply to confine ourselves to this explanation is to engage in the selfsame sin of 'higher educationism'. 'Proceduralism' as a subset of 'higher educationism' fulfils another role in contributing to a very particular form of 'policy mode'. It may even be regarded as scholarship's contribution to what some students of higher education allude to as 'soft law' (Gornitzka, 2005).

3) Proceduralism and 'soft law'

Soft law, otherwise known in the jargon of the European Commission as the 'open method of coordination', has as its prime aim to generate consensus either *in anticipation of* future legislative initiatives or, as an alternative interpretation, *to sustain* a body of opinion favourable to policy-in-the-making when, for various reasons, legislative action *cannot* be envisaged at the present moment, given the views held amongst the public generally or because the mandate of the central agency, which seeks to advance down such a road, falls short of being able to enforce it by formal, legal means (Amaral and Neave, 2008).

'Proceduralism' in effect acts as the analytical handmaiden to 'soft law'. It is so by dint of the fact that it is far easier to tack a consensus together and thus claim a pleasing convergence around the identification and charting of pragmatic operational procedures – good practice, shared provision and common administrative techniques – than it is to 'harmonize' or 'create a common architecture' to accommodate differing and often deeply held values, visions and the priorities to which they give rise. The former remain the secret garden of the 'technician' or specialist. Values and visions, however, especially when they engage national identity or issues held to be inseparable from it, can be dealt with only through public debate and through full formal negotiation at a political level.

Procedures and techniques, once they have been identified as already in place or are held to be shared and thus accepted because they are already shared, may in turn provide a pragmatic and therefore non-controversial basis on which to proceed further. On such a pragmatic basis of acceptance, new priorities, principles and further practice held to be desirable may subsequently be grafted as a second 'bonding layer' across different sectors of higher education or across different national systems. The technical aspect can therefore serve to provide an initial legitimacy for what are subsequently more controversial initiatives. Advancing by recourse to the apparently technical, 'practical' and anodyne is, if the truth be told, the essence of that process sometimes alluded to as 'policy creep' (Pollack, 1994, 2000) which 'soft law' seems designed to encourage and advance.

'Policy creep' is the way of moving forward by small, quasi-imperceptible increments which eventually mature into the policy equivalent of a *fait accompli*, at which point those faced with the situation have either to accept it or to put themselves to the additional inconvenience of expressly undoing such a surreptitious advance. Proceduralism as an analytical perspective serves as a vehicle to bring about the equivalent in the policy arena of the concept of 'indirect strategy' in military affairs. However, whether such a feline approach amounts to what software experts would call a 'work round' for bypassing transparency and accountability or even due process in public policy making remains a very moot point indeed.

Autonomy and its changing face

Having set out the formative trends that shaped the Evaluative State, we now turn briefly to developments that have borne down on autonomy, the second analytic dimension in this study. This dimension will be taken up more fully in Chapter 2.

The issue of autonomy, whether academic or institutional, is the constant and abiding value and preoccupation of academia, especially so when it also attracts the attention of politicians, their advisers, policy makers and university presidents. In the course of the past 20 years much has changed in terms of the way in which the issue has been posed and debated. *Grosso modo*, the debate can be divided along two lines: first, the defence of the historic construct of academic – or personal, or alternatively positional, autonomy; and, second, the gradual modification of this historic model under pressure from the reforms that proceeded throughout the course of the late 1980s and the 1990s.

Amongst the more germane in re-contouring and thus re-stating both the substance and the extent of autonomy were closer public control over higher education expenditure, the press for greater institutional accountability, the quest for a more adaptable and flexible relationship between higher education, government and society (Neave and van Vught, 1994), the rise of the Evaluative State (Little and Henkel, 1999: Neave, 2006a; Neave, 2007; 2009a) and the general shift of policy from being driven by social demand to being urged on by demands exerted primarily by 'market forces' (Dill, Jongbloed, Amaral and Teixeira, 2004).

In defence of autonomy as a *droit acquis*

A very real example of academic autonomy defended as a historical construct took place in 1988 with the signing at Bologna (Italy) by the universities who were members of the then European Rectors' Conference (*Conférence des Recteurs Européens*: CRE)[3] of the *Magna Charta Universitatum*. The term *Magna Charta* is heavy with symbolism. The title alone evoked that other Great Charter, which in the England of 1215 marked a first step away from the monarch's more outrageous abuses of the occasional decencies that upheld feudalism's social order. At the same time, the document also commemorated the 900th anniversary of the founding of Europe's first university, the University of Bologna. The *Charta* was endorsed by the universities in Western Europe both as a re-statement and as a reassertion of the traditional values and rights that had been attached to higher learning and very particularly to the freedoms to teach and to learn (Thorens, 2006).

The Bologna Charter was not a mere happy coincidence. On the contrary, it was deliberately and expressly conceived as a riposte to what university leadership then saw as a fundamental threat to the historic boundaries of academic freedom posed by changes in the steering of higher education systems in the mutating relationship between government, higher education and society at its broadest level.

The changing context of institutional autonomy

More than 20 years later, the terms used in the debate over the issue of autonomy today are indeed different. The difference is clearly to be seen in the shift from autonomy interpreted *qua* personal or positional freedom to its present definition in terms of *institutional* autonomy. Such a shift in perspective has come about largely as a consequence of changes that in the meantime were introduced into the higher education systems of Western Europe at other levels, some national and others regional, and in other spheres of government and national administration, notably funding, quality assessment, institutional evaluation and, more recently, accreditation procedures (Schwartz-Hahn and Westerheijden, 2004). Thus, a very good case can be made for seeing the present preoccupation with institutional autonomy as a species of 'end game' – the final definitional step that takes place only because the boundaries within which institutional autonomy operates have already been re-set in an indirect manner by the reforms preceding it.

Today, autonomy is subject to scrutiny on its own account and more particularly at an institutional level, that is to say, as it applies to the inner workings of institutions, to the distribution of power and authority which current *educanto* wraps up in the notion of leadership[4], its distribution and location across different organs, levels of responsibility and, with it, the organizational re-assignment of responsibility to different postings or appointments within the institution. It is possible to entertain at least two perspectives on this subject: first, the evolution and general context in which the issue of institutional autonomy arose, which is a dynamic account over time, in short, a subset of the recent and contemporary history of the university up to the present day; and, second, an operational analysis of the changes that brought it about.

Current concern and debate are naturally products of both of the above perspectives. Over the past half-decade or so, *institutional* autonomy has become the object of active legislation in the Austrian, Dutch, Danish, French, German and Spanish systems and is a matter of prime concern in Portugal (Amaral, 2008) and Sweden (Bladh, 2007). Legislation represents the first official move towards operational reform. It sets out to re-designate and re-distribute functions, powers and authority and to assign them in an organized form to new units, bodies and committees. An alternative approach involves the law changing the remit, composition and oversight of long-established organisational entities – senate, faculty, president or rector. These provide the framework within which the activities and responsibilities of the three Estates of higher education's Constituent Order are set down.

Three focal systems

Considerations such as these have borne down heavily on the choice of which 'focal systems' may serve to trace the detailed unfolding of the Evaluative State. In higher education policy, as in much else in a world held to be 'globalizing', the Anglo-Saxon perspective – that is, the views, implicit values, rationale and vision grounded predominantly in the USA, the UK and Australia – occupies the referential high ground. To a large extent, it dominates both the conceptual framework and the technical terminology in which reform in higher education is both thought about and justified. Another feature is the constant attempt to associate and to align national policies around both models and norms by countries that have little if any common reference with Anglo-Saxon political and administrative cultures. The quest to legitimate national policy by tracing the occasional feature that bears some resemblance to New Public Management is another. The Evaluative State as a framing concept is not necessarily incompatible with New Public Management. Indeed, depending on the circumstances and context, there are certainly degrees of proximity between the two. It could be argued that New Public Management acts a subset – a means to operationalize – the Evaluative State.[5]

In choosing the concept of the Evaluative State as the '*angle d'approche*' to the issue of institutional autonomy, this study takes a normative stance less influenced by established convention. This, of course, is to swim against the tide and deliberately so. The choice of higher education systems to illustrate the interplay between the Evaluative State and the push towards institutional autonomy follows this same rationale. To be sure, the three chosen are far from being immune to the Anglo-Saxon vision of reform or to the norms that lie beneath it. Even so, they are culturally and politically distant from what may be seen as Anglo-Saxon attitudes. Indeed, they have been chosen precisely for this reason.

The detailed scrutiny of the dynamic within the Evaluative State and the interplay between the Evaluative State and institutional autonomy will examine these issues as they have emerged within France – a country where, as Clark (1994) observed more than a decade and a half ago: 'In France, everything is different.' The two other systems are Spain and Portugal. Including Spain is justified on the grounds that higher education in Spain is an example of a recently federated, multi-agency model of the Evaluative State. As was pointed out earlier, this arrangement is a significant variation to the predominant pattern. Portugal is included primarily on the grounds that, like France, it is currently engaged in extending both the scope of the Evaluative State and embedding institutional autonomy into its system of higher education.

Institutional autonomy and the Evaluative State

Before focusing on these three systems of higher education, however, Chapters 2–4 examine the broad background against which the two issues of institutional autonomy and the Evaluative State took shape over the past two decades. This is done by examining some of the basic instruments – legal in the main – that have 'coordinated' higher education. They also dig deeper into the assumptions implicit in what is sometimes alluded to as the 'state control' model of coordinating higher education in Western Europe (Neave and van Vught, 1991). Some of the more general points raised in the present chapter are followed up in a number of different national settings. The background to the emerging Evaluative State and the changes accompanying it in institutional governance are explored by looking at three pioneering models. These highlight the initial variations across different systems in constructing the Evaluative State. These are the French, the Dutch and the British models. They provide a broad backdrop which pinpoints key issues that are to be taken up in detail in Part II.

Part II focuses on France and Spain, while Part III undertakes an indepth study of Portugal. Portugal was chosen for several reasons. The simplest would merely echo the reply that the mountain-climber George Mallory gave when asked why he wanted to climb Mount Everest: 'Because it is there.' There is a second reason: sheer personal curiosity fired by time I spent in Portugal. The third reason is perhaps the most telling of the three: there are no studies in English that examine the unfolding of Portuguese higher education policy over the past two decades from the perspective of the Evaluative State, though recent scholarship has produced a parallel account (Neave and Amaral, 2011).

Part IV brings together conclusions from the three detailed country case studies. Finally, it examines certain key issues that appear to be in the offing. Given what has been learnt about the dynamic of the Evaluative State across the three systems, what are likely to be the challenges it faces at a time when crisis, like change itself, seems never-ending?

In Part IV the attention turns to some key issues that the Evaluative State is very likely to face in the near future and particularly issues that involve defining both institutional criteria and the institutional mission for which institutional autonomy may be said to be a necessary condition. These latter aspects raise acute and delicate questions. In the drive towards increasingly diverse systems of 'tertiary education', is institutional autonomy to be assigned across-the-board to all or is it to be 'rationed' between universities depending on their particular tasks, status, demonstrated performance or sustained achievement? Are different degrees of institutional autonomy to be granted to institutions of higher education in the light of their differing purposes and different missions? To this may be added the possible consequences of the current financial crisis with which most states in Western Europe are currently grappling and concerning which no economist worth his or her salt has as yet entirely ruled out the spectre of a 'match replay'. A number of scenarios are examined, including whether a new and very different relationship will not emerge from the interplay between the Evaluative State and institutional autonomy as a result of the current financial disarray, confusion and in certain quarters the determination to continue with their very special version of 'business as usual', which the Book of Proverbs[6] lambasted with rather less gentleness.

2
Autonomy and the Changing Contract between the State and Higher Education

The Prince and his pleasure

University autonomy is not only the university's central value, which in its classic form enshrined and guaranteed academia its two basic freedoms: freedom to teach (*Lehrfreiheit*) and the freedom to learn (*Lernfreiheit*); it is also the Ark of the Covenant in the relationship between the state and higher education, irrespective of the differences either in its scope, its application or what is involved in the particular arrangement found in one system of higher education as against another. Such variations, as we shall see in the course of this chapter, are very substantial. To a significant degree, they reflect the vagaries and specificities of a nation's cultural, historical and political history.

University autonomy, from a purely legal or even philosophical perspective, is a contract between the Prince – that is, the state – and the university. The nature of this contact is no less variegated. Two basic forms stand forth. In the first, the contract is *actual*. In its actual form, the contract is to be seen in the predominant use of formal legal codification that both determines and, from time to time, revises details in this relationship in mainland European systems. The second model sees the contract as *historical* or *customary*. Such was once the case in the UK.[1] Leaving aside the motives that inspire – or impel – the Prince to act, it follows that the contract, be it actual or customary, expresses the will – whether benign or malign is a matter of personal opinion – of the Prince. University autonomy, conceived in its generic form, is then in a very real sense the Prince's pleasure. It is what it pleases or is convenient to the Prince to grant, negotiate or, for that matter, to revise or to overhaul root and branch.

25

Why has the Prince seen fit to modify his pleasure? What were the reasons for him to have second thoughts? Or, to move beyond the allegory, what is the current importance of institutional autonomy for the changes in the contract between the state and higher education, and, by extension, for putting the relationship between state and society on a new footing? What were the challenges faced by the Prince that drove him to act? What were the apparent obstacles in university autonomy that justified its revision? What was the 'solution' the Evaluative State held out?

In policy, just as in leadership and strategy, the ability to anticipate and to be borne out by subsequent developments is given only to a few. As the American humorist Mark Twain pointed out more than a century ago, prophesying is a dangerous business (Twain, 1889). It is well then to bear a number of *caveats* in mind. Amongst the very first of these is the tendency to 'over-project', that is, to under-estimate the time necessary for new developments or practices to embed themselves into the institutional landscape.

An excellent illustration of such over-projection in the contemporary landscape of higher education can be seen in that central exercise of implanting a standardized study structure across Europe's nation-state higher education systems – the Bologna Process. To the official mind, the process was scheduled for completion by 2010. However, recent studies from the EUA, one of Bologna's prime sponsors (Purser and Crozier, 2007; European Commission, 2007), suggest that its final embedding into institutional routine still has a long way to go. To a considerable degree, 'over-projection' is caused by the over-confidence of the political leadership, which tends to rely on the legal, legislative and outward aspects of reform as evidence of progress rather than attending to the more delicate and protracted task of take-up and complete assimilation within the routine of individual universities (Neave and Amaral, 2008).

Getting a grip on implementation

Yet, the very process of embedding legislative reform into the individual university and, more particularly, whether the importance attached to it is to be real or symbolic are matters of prime significance in themselves. As numerous case studies of implementing reform in higher education have shown on both sides of the Atlantic (Pressman and Wildavsky, 1984; Cerych and Sabatier, 1986), implementation rarely if ever follows the tidy path of linear progression, the so-called 'engineering model', which earlier planners so often counted upon and, as a result, were so often grievously disappointed (Kallen *et al.*, 1984).

As its name suggests, the 'engineering model' holds progress to be rational, logical, controllable, linear and sequential. Its origins may be traced back to the military sphere, more particularly to logistics and operational research, subsequently applied to civilian industrial production and to science and technology policy during the 1970s. The engineering model is primarily concerned with developing management and control systems to gain further purchase over quality, to speed up output whilst making both more efficient and/or cost-effective. Whilst the Evaluative State may in part be seen as an outgrowth from the engineering model, even in countries which, like Portugal, applied it to science and technology, the engineering model did not remain in vogue for very long: a mere eight years in Portugal's case (Heitor and Horta, 2011).

In higher education, carrying policy down into the institutional fabric tends to be a reiterative process, untidy, vacillating and interspersed with negotiation, interpretation and re-negotiation as it filters downwards (Stensaker, 2004; Weiss, 1977). How far the strengthening of leadership and management in the higher education systems of Western Europe during these past two decades does not itself reflect an element of frustration on the part of authorities, anxious to press forward with the *tarantella* of reforms successfully enacted but brought up short by the reality of institutional caution, must for the moment remain a matter for future scholarly attention.

The linguistic ambiguity of autonomy

The debate about the boundaries and substantive elements in university autonomy suffers to a considerable degree from linguistic ambiguity. As we noted earlier in this chapter, the concept of university autonomy is both contextually and politically defined (Neave and van Vught, 1994a and 1994b). How it is defined, and thus the ways in which it is operationalized, reflects the very particular historical, political and economic forces that have shaped the individual system, even though the value of university autonomy defines the status of the institution to which it applies. At the same time, university autonomy stands as the central universalism of an institution whose identity is indissolubly tied to the universal recognition of the importance of teaching, learning and 'knowledge production' at advanced levels. If the notion of university autonomy transcends frontiers, then the political theories, social constructs and the mission of the universities that attend it, the operational features that accompany it by and large do not (Huisman, Maassen and Neave, 2001).

Two key dimensions...

Even when account is taken of both the historical and contextual differences in the way in which university autonomy has acquired operational meaning, the term itself suffers from an essential imprecision. In effect, university autonomy embraces two very different constructs in the relationship between university, government and society. There is 'academic' autonomy and there is 'institutional autonomy'. The first alludes to what is sometimes termed 'the pedagogical act',[2] essentially the freedom to teach and to learn and the freedom of those engaged in these acts. This is sometimes presented as 'personal' or 'positional' autonomy. However, the recognition of 'personal' or 'positional' autonomy in no way implies the recognition of institutional autonomy. Nor, for that matter, is it axiomatic today that institutional autonomy necessarily underpins positional or personal autonomy. As we shall see later, evidence from systems as contextually different as England (Henkel, 2007), Sweden (Bladh, 2007) and France[3] suggests that the very latitude granted to the institutional level involves re-defining *de facto* the limits of academic autonomy within the individual university. It does not always follow, however, that extending institutional autonomy automatically entails extending 'personal' or 'positional' autonomy.

a) Institutional autonomy

Legislative intent is very different from institutional take-up,[4] either in respect of the time this latter exercise requires to work its way through the individual university or in respect of what has been achieved at any given moment. In short, if legislation enfolds intent, it does not always guarantee capacity. Today, the ability to guarantee capacity is itself a major issue in the general *problematique* of institutional autonomy inasmuch as capacity, from the standpoint of institutions, tends to be identified in terms of resources allocated over and above those currently assigned if new priorities are to be taken up and developed. By contrast, many of the initiatives currently associated with extending institutional autonomy are *not* a guarantee of resources assigned. Rather, they exert pressure upon the institution *itself* to find, acquire and develop on its own this capacity so as to better secure the resources necessary to carry forward the reform the legislator has in mind. Today, institutional autonomy is seen in a rather different light by the legislator than it is by the Academic Estate. From the standpoint of the legislator, institutional autonomy is seen as putting in place the conditions of self-management and institutional self-governance, the identification and building up of precisely that institutional capacity which ought to allow the institution to secure those resources as a consequence of embedding the new patterns of leadership and responsibility within the institutional fabric.

b) The new interpretation of institutional autonomy

At the heart of the contemporary interpretation of institutional autonomy lies a syllogistic and circular argument. It places upon the institution the burden of acquiring additional resources – or changing its current profile of activities, programmes, courses, responsibilities and services in such a way that will enable it to secure the means to do precisely that. From this perspective, the extension of institutional self-management and the reinforcement of the leadership function stand as a magnificent example of what is known in the jargon of the policy analyst as a 'means/ends' reversal. Clearly, as they had been constituted until the late 1980s and early 1990s, neither management nor leadership appeared to those in authority at the national level to command sufficient capacity to raise the resources that public authority had shown itself to be reluctant to set aside for the task of reform. Accordingly, the explicit purpose of institutional autonomy has itself undergone mutation. No longer is it regarded as a condition that is good on its own account, though that does not prevent many in academia from arguing that it is. Rather, institutional autonomy has itself become instrumentalized as a presentational subset in the broader issue involving the transfer and enlargement of latitude in decision-making down to the institutional level. The purpose of this policy is to endow individual institutes of higher education with a re-distribution of power and authority, with new procedures and mechanisms for self-exertion to meet public expectations – but to do so as a result of their own efforts.

This in itself is a watershed in the relationship between government, university and society. Capacity generation no longer resides, as once it did in Europe, wholly and exclusively in the nation's public budget for higher education. Rather, it is increasingly the outcome to be secured *by* the individual institution through individual measures of good husbandry, identified and enacted *within* the individual institution. From this standpoint, it is not at all exaggerated to see the commitment of the *pays politique* (Neave, 2002a) to institutional autonomy as a way to hand off responsibility for generating the capacity for reform to the individual institution at the very moment when the *pays politique* itself implicitly recognizes its reluctance – if not always its sheer inability – to fulfil that very same function at the system level.

Paradoxes in the legislative perspective

Nor is the legislative perspective, as a means of understanding what is happening in higher education, without its risks either. The greatest risk lies, paradoxically, in the very coherence and apparent tidiness that legislative enactment conveys. It provides a vision – a condition – that the legislator, acting in the name of government and society (and its interests), holds to be desirable and necessary for higher education to assimilate. Such ostensible clarity, however, finds itself bedevilled by two very different conditions that attach to the legislative act. Legislation is employed in two very different modes.

The first mode sets out the framework, terms and conditions that define how reform is to be carried out, its purposes and its rationale. In such circumstances, legislation is the initiatory act, the electric shock to which the appropriate level or institutional type is formally required to respond. Viewed from the standpoint of the individual university, the first mode sees the institution behaving 'reactively'. Legislation serves as an instrument of overhauling or coordinating in a 'top-down' manner.

The second mode, by contrast, has the institution assuming a 'proactive' stance to which the law responds by acknowledging and conferring retroactively the legal basis for the particular practice that has developed pragmatically and widely across a particular institutional type or across the higher education system generally. Such 'grounded practice' is given official standing by dint of being enacted by legislation. Such practices or procedures have evolved pragmatically inside the higher education system. They exist *de facto*. Leaving aside the rationale for their being accorded legal recognition, that is, an existence *de jure*, the law nevertheless takes cognizance – it reacts to the initiative originating within the fabric of higher education.

Put bluntly, the basic dilemma legislation confronts derives neither wholly nor exclusively from the massification of the university, though this is certainly a contributory factor. Rather, the basic dilemma arises from the belief, as widely held amongst political and administrative elites as it is amongst more sober-minded students of higher education, that the pace of institutional responsiveness needs to accelerate and, indeed, ought to *continue* to accelerate further the closer the university is brought into the 'innovation system'.

This interpretation sheds a somewhat different light upon both the legislative perspective on the one hand and the rise of the Evaluative State as a prior condition for the reinforcement of institutional autonomy on the other.

The shortcomings of legal homogeneity

Coordination and control through legal instruments and legislative means have long been the main channels through which the systems of higher education in Western Europe have been shaped and adapted (Clark, 1983; de Groof, Neave and Svec, 1998). But the use of legislative instruments, framework laws, legislative acts and their more detailed forms of the ministerial decree or circular are no longer adequate *on their own* to adjust higher education's response to rapid changes in the perceived needs either of society, the economy or industry. 'Steering' higher education systems by a wholly legislative instrumentality was viable so long as higher education's basic mission was predictable and could count on social stability on the one hand, whilst being assured of long-term stability in terms of the ways in which the higher education system was financed and operated on the other. However, 'coordinating' higher education by legislative fiat cannot give an adequate account of the status and condition either of the higher education system in general or of the particular types, segments or individual universities within it at any given moment.

The clarity of the legislative vision in higher education rests on one major assumption: that the stipulations set out in legislation are taken up and operate in a relatively uniform manner within the different sectors or segments to which they apply. Thus, the tidiness of the legislative vision both presumes and thus paints a picture of higher education which, whilst not false, tends to over-estimate the degree of coherence present in any one system. Likewise, it tends to assume that individual universities – or other types of establishment that make up a nation's provision – each command a similar capacity for adaptation.

Coordinating higher education on the basis of legal homogeneity presumes a high degree of *homogeneity* in the capacity of individual universities to translate legislative intent into institutional practice. These assumptions lie at the heart of 'legal homogeneity', which served as the fundamental instrument in determining and shaping the provision of higher education within the nation-state from the moment higher education was brought into the oversight of government (Neave and van Vught, 1994a and 1994b; Huisman, Maassen and Neave, 2001). However, this is not to say that legal homogeneity is able to provide a satisfactory vision of this system at any given moment. True, legislation in its 'reactive mode' may serve to remedy or give recognition to developments within broad segments or sub-types of institution. But it is rarely adequate to *anticipate* such developments. In effect, this means that only when matters have reached crisis proportions does notice tend to be taken of them.

Re-writing the contract

'Steering' and coordinating higher education by legal and legislative instrumentality *alone* become highly problematic once the forces of diversity, change and expectations within both society and the economy are viewed as a continual, sustained but not necessarily predictable process from which higher education cannot remain aloof. Under such conditions, the question of 'feedback' and its insertion as part of a more elaborate, sensitive and sophisticated component in the policy cycle comes to the fore. The issue of 'feedback' may certainly be precipitated by problems of public expenditure, by a spectacular growth in student numbers entering higher education and by the attendant problems of how to deal with a Student Estate that is more diverse in terms of its ability, ambition, career plans and sheer learning capacity. But these are catalysing elements, just as they also serve largely to justify subsequent initiatives. They are not in themselves the basic cause.

Rather, the central issue is, at one and the same time, more subtle, more indirect and very certainly more radical in its implications. It emerges in the belief that the purpose which higher education in Western Europe met over the best part of the two preceding centuries – primarily that of maintaining social and political stability – can no longer be sustained. Instead of being the recipient of public support and acting as a distributive agent of 'the common wealth', the university is now called upon to play a deliberate and direct part in actively generating 'the common wealth'. In short, the tacit 'contract' between university and state that lasted for the best part of both the nineteenth and twentieth centuries in Western Europe is being rewritten. And the new 'contract' dissolves what some observers have termed the 'Humboldtian Concordat' between the state and universities in Europe (Neave, 2008a; Nybom, 2007).

Institutional autonomy as conceptual shorthand

Viewed against this backdrop, the press to extend 'institutional autonomy' represents a form of conceptual shorthand – the equivalent in higher education policy to the operational counterpart of 'de-regulation' in the inimitable terminology of economic policy. The loosening ties between the state and universities find reflection in the recent burgeoning of self-designated types of university: entrepreneurial (Clark, 1998 and 2004), service (Tjedvoll, 1998), responsive, European or even, as the supreme oxymoron, the 'learning university' (Neave, 2004c: 154–5).

The new 'contract', intended to secure the rapid and continual adjustment of society and its talents to the demands, all too often unpredictable except in the short term (Nybom, 2007), of a post-industrial 'knowledge economy' is in effect the polar opposite of the so-called Humboldtian Concordat. The Humboldtian Concordat rested on the principle of distance between university and society as a means of ensuring academic or positional autonomy. The new nexus, however, endorses the contrary principle – that of proximity and close involvement with external interests – a notion that stands at the heart of what is variously termed 'the third task' of the university (Brulin, 2006; Marton, 2007) as an 'add on' to teaching/learning and research. A parallel interpretation views this nexus as the university adjusting to the 'stakeholder society' (Enders and Fulton, 2002).

The Humboldtian Concordat stood on its head

Re-defining the university's responsibility in terms of proximity and of serving new external constituencies are not the only fundamental reversals of the Humboldtian Concordat, for this entente also rested on the concept of a single, national community. Over the past two decades, the idea of the university serving the national community in Western Europe has fragmented in two directions: the rise of sub-national regionalism on the one hand and the shaping of higher education in terms of multi-system continent-wide provision in the construction of the European Union on the other. Clearly, the current interpretation of institutional autonomy in varying degrees re-shapes the place the university ought to occupy in these cross-cutting agendas. Furthermore, since the debate over institutional autonomy focuses on the capacities and the optimal structures that the university will need to command to acquit itself well in the light of expectations publicly laid upon it, it is self-evident that institutional autonomy engages issues that go far beyond the institutional level alone.

In truth, we do ourselves no service if we examine the transition from academic freedom to institutional autonomy simply by limiting our attention to shifts in power and responsibility within the university. Rather, we have to pay attention to the wider context within which institutional autonomy is set. If institutional autonomy is the 'end game' in the current policy cycle, we have in all logic and conscience to pay a little heed to such matters as the re-definition of the powers of central government over higher education, to their devolution to other administrative levels and to 'de-regulation'. Important though each component is, when taken together, they pose an equally significant modification to that other principle – legal homogeneity. Legal homogeneity, it was suggested, was the dominant construct in the historical mode of coordinating higher education in Western Europe. The search for an instrumentality over and above the purely legal, able regularly to monitor the current condition and status of both the system and the individual establishments within it, had two consequences. The first involved shifting the focus away from legal homogeneity. The second did not involve replacing legal homogeneity so much as introducing a second instrumentality, which supplemented it. The 'second instrumentality' took the form of an extremely sensitive addition to the armoury of policy-making. This was evaluative homogeneity. Evaluative homogeneity sets the overall context, which in turn shapes institutional autonomy.

Prior developments

Scholarship has laid a number of terms upon the mechanisms and approaches involved in welding higher education to the economy and to market-driven change: 'remote steering' (van Vught, 1989; van Vught and Maassen, 1988) 'de-regulation' at the system level or 'self-steering' at the institutional level. Whatever the conceptual map alluded to, it is clear in Western Europe that the process of 'system adaptation' passed through two stages. These involved, first, the development of strategies of adaptation focused on the system level and, second, bringing reform directly to bear on the institutional level in the more recent push towards defining institutional autonomy. If, from an analytical standpoint, it is reasonable to separate these two developments, in reality, the line is far from hard and fast. Change applied at the system level is rarely limited in its repercussions to that level. It has 'knock-on' effects, which, however indirect, have their impact upon the individual institution. In other words, whilst institutional autonomy is currently subject to revision by direct legislation, it has also been modulated or re-shaped as a result of earlier reform, the primary purpose of which is not, initially, focused upon institutional autonomy as such. Succinctly stated, the experience of higher education in Western Europe during these past two decades shows that pragmatically, institutional autonomy has been under revision far longer than the legislation, which today has institutional autonomy in its sights. For this reason, one cannot examine institutional autonomy simply within the legislative frame, which the Prince announces as dealing with that issue alone. We have, in short, to take account of prior developments.

3
The Evaluative State: A Formative Concept and an Overview

Introduction

With a hefty dose of hindsight, one of the most important of the prior developments, which we can now see as a 'pre-conditioner' to overhauling the contract between the Prince and his university subjects, is the advent of the Evaluative State (Little and Henkel, 1999; Neave, 1998a; Clancy, 2007; Henkel, 2007; Kehm, 2007; Neave, 2009a). Effectively, it is within many of the dimensions which contribute to the rise of the Evaluative State that the basic rationale and justification for re-engineering institutional autonomy are first to be found. Viewed within the broader context of institutional autonomy, the Evaluative State stands as a prior and transitional stage in which many of the issues that subsequently figure as key elements in reforming the institutional level are first rehearsed.

The Evaluative State is important in its own right for at least two reasons. First, within the Evaluative State, many of the answers to the problems posed by legal homogeneity – its rigidity and inability to rapidly and effectively 'steer' higher education towards the new goals, purposes and objectives the 'knowledge economy' demanded – were first tackled. Second, because the advent of the Evaluative State re-cast the central element in reconstructing higher education in Western Europe. This metamorphosis changed autonomy. No longer was it conceived as a broad-ranging value. Nor, in some instances, was it held any longer to be a privilege conferred upon universities as a *prior* condition to their fulfilling their long-term task in society (Thorens, 2006).[1] Rather, autonomy became an operational, multi-faceted, renewable and therefore largely conditional *contract*. As we have seen in Chapter 2, the relationship between the Prince and the university had always been contractual to varying degrees of implicitness. The transition from the first definition of autonomy, which hitherto permeated the systems of higher education in Western Europe – that of *personal* and *positional* autonomy – saw autonomy moved on towards a formally more expanded interpretation as *institutional* autonomy. Institutional autonomy, however, is not necessarily either wholly or completely coterminous with its earlier version. This operational transmutation took place as part of constructing the Evaluative State.

The Evaluative State: the quest for a more adaptable and flexible system

In contrast to most meta-constructs in higher education, the Evaluative State did not spring like Athena fully-grown from the thigh of an administrative Zeus. Rather, it was the outcome of an evolutionary though rapid process, the origins of which have to be teased out carefully and retrospectively. Nor did it emerge as a self-conscious and deliberate strategy of constructing from the first what later emerged as the Evaluative State (Musselin, 2004). Still less was it viewed as such by its architects when scholarly attention turned to it.

... and its origins

1) French

The origins of the Evaluative State go back to the mid- to late 1980s. They were first seen in France, the Netherlands and the UK, although in each case the purpose behind these first glimmerings differed considerably. In France, for example, the purpose behind establishing the *Comité National d'Evaluation* in 1984 was less to detect a lack of efficiency amongst individual universities (Staropoli, 1987). Rather, the *Comité*'s mandate sought, on the one hand, to stimulate institutional initiative by using the process of institutional evaluation to disseminate real examples of successful practice, examples that would hopefully be followed by other universities; on the other hand, its aim was to speed up the pace of change at the institutional level by showing what was already in progress elsewhere in France's system of higher education (Neave, 1996a).

The French initiative provides us with an interesting variant for establishing a regular feedback mechanism. It recognized implicitly one of the major blockages that a high degree of legal homogeneity, plus the need for formal authorization from the central ministry, imposed on French universities, which, unlike either their British or Dutch counterparts, were not then under pressure from budgetary constraints (*Comité National d'Evaluation*, 1989; Staropoli, 1987). In effect, the feedback system *à la française* was primarily to strengthen system capacity for change within the existing closed mode of accountability between the universities and the ministry by trying to prod the former into bolder action.

2) Dutch

This was not, however, the prime concern for the Dutch. Already towards the end of the 1980s, the Dutch Ministry of Education, Science and Culture set out to develop a more radical and far-reaching alternative 'steering system' to the classic and detailed 'state control' model that had hitherto been dominant. Unlike the French strategy, the Dutch strategy did not seek simply to update the procedures of 'legal homogeneity' – its objectives were broader and more ambitious. The question the Ministry had to address was how could a system of coordination be set up which would, at one and the same time, ensure clarity in the strategy to be adopted at the system level, encourage a more rapid take-up at the institutional level and, last but very far from least, reduce the time-consuming procedures of clearance and authorization? In short, how could the minutiae of central government control be reduced? Initially, the problem was tackled by applying what was called a 'cybernetic' approach to the relationship between government and universities (van Vught and Maassen, 1988: 64–75).

Such a 'self-correcting' system offered several advantages. It placed the burden of adjustment on the individual institution. At the same time, it opened up the possibility for the central administration to concentrate on identifying and analysing potential *strategic* priorities rather than being absorbed with exercising an oversight that was both close and detailed. The concept later evolved into the notion of 'remote steering' (van Vught, 1989). Remote steering re-shaped the function of the central administration. It replaced detailed 'state oversight' with a more loosely coupled arrangement in which the main task of national administration became 'facilitatory' – that is, to lay down new procedures and conditions conducive to rapid and appropriate adjustment at the institutional level (Neave and van Vught, 1994a). Unlike the French approach, the Dutch model called for a simultaneous overhaul of the central administration and of the capacity to adapt at the institutional level, as well as putting in place a system of feedback and monitoring, based on academic performance and output indicators entrusted to the Dutch Association of Universities (Jenniskens, 1997).

Different in scope though the French and Dutch reforms were, both shared the belief that central to providing the higher education system with an inbuilt capacity to adapt rapidly to change was the demand for a greater margin of initiative at the institutional level. This was to be ensured *entre autres* by updating management and revising the structures of governance. To be sure, at the outset of reform in the early 1990s, this agenda was not formally presented in terms of extending institutional autonomy, though revisions to internal management and governance may certainly be interpreted in this light.

3) British

The situation was very different, however, in the UK. Paradoxically, the British university system had long been identified – and most certainly so in the minds of its denizens – as having certain unique operational features which, ironically, possessed a degree of kinship with the vision entertained by the Dutch, though not, it must be said, by the French. Indeed, the British university system possessed the feature towards which the Dutch were groping. It was largely self-regulating, driven forward by the initiatives of individual universities and therefore progressed in what is best described as an organic manner. In contrast to both French and Dutch universities, British universities were not legislatively driven. Most noteworthy of all, they were endowed with an extremely high degree of institutional autonomy, legally guaranteed by the terms of each university's founding charter and upheld by a very particular relationship between the central government and the individual university. This relationship is often illustrated with reference to the setting up in 1919 of the University Grants Committee – an intermediary agency which negotiated the overall national university budget directly with the Treasury (Britain's equivalent of the Ministry of Finance) on behalf of all universities (Eustace, 1998). This entente reflected the classic interpretation of the 'proper' relationship between government and university, which owed much to nineteenth-century English liberalism (Rothblatt, 1997) and particularly to the then-prevalent view that in university affairs, the intervention of the state was best kept at arm's length, if not further.

Thus, under such a tacit agreement, appointment to positions of leadership (Neave, 1991), academic recruitment, promotion, the granting of tenure, the holding of – and sometimes the canvassing for – endowment capital, the selection of individual students, the determination of curricular content and the methods used to evaluate student performance, including the awarding of degrees, were all very real operational instances of the UK's universities governing their own affairs as well as the substantive nature of their autonomy.

Other differences followed from the UK's entente between the government and the universities. Not least was the view that institutional autonomy was itself the prior condition that guaranteed academic autonomy. To the British academic, without the first, the second was precarious at best. This is a very different interpretation of the ties between academic autonomy and institutional autonomy. In effect, the latter defined the former. By contrast, the Humboldtian Concordat looked to the state[2] to uphold academic or positional autonomy. In France the notion of the Jacobin university looked to the state to sustain the same principle by preventing the incursion of occult or particular interests into the affairs of academe.[3] The British, with not untypical originality, looked to institutional autonomy laid down in the terms of the individual university charters to protect the university and learning from the state itself (Neave, 2008).

Institutional autonomy was then the central and basic principal that permeated British universities. It set them apart from their European counterparts. This particular relationship found its clearest expression in the fact that until the late 1980s in Britain, system-wide legislation – the rock on which the principle of legal lomogeneity rested (Neave and van Vught, 1994b) – was unknown. Rather, the legal basis of each university, its structure, pattern of governance and administrative procedures were enshrined in an individual parliamentary act – the individual university's charter, which was specifically tailored to the purpose and mission the founding fathers laid upon a particular university. Such founding legislation laid down the individual university's responsibilities, structure, inner workings, regulations and procedures. Powers of oversight and verification that in Europe formed part of the university's responsibility to the collectivity were in Britain vested in the individual university and were exercised in keeping with the terms of the founding charter – or its modification.

The Evaluative State: national variations on a strategic theme

1) French

The rise of the Evaluative State naturally introduced subtle variations to national priorities. In France, for instance, the basic principle of 'contractualization' – that is, moving away from central planning and instead 'steering' higher education by negotiations between the individual university and the central ministry over the objectives to be attained for the coming five years (Chevaillier, 2004) – in no way altered the status of the university as a public service. Still less did it modify the universities' commitment to meeting social demands (Neave, 2004a). If the press for more efficient resource usage, improvement in quality and competition were present, the latter applied to a very different sphere. Rather than pitting one university against another for resources, the initial French version of the Evaluative State was grounded in the rousing rhetoric of competition abroad and national cooperation and solidarity at home (Chevaillier, 2004; Neave, 2004b).

2) Dutch

By contrast, the Dutch operationalization of the driving principles of modernization, marketization and institutional efficiency, whilst enthusiastically applied on the home front, was very definitely seen as an 'exportable' model, both within Europe and further afield. This latter point, though a relatively minor aspect at the time, is nevertheless interesting, if only for the fact that it placed the Dutch edition of the Evaluative State in a position that appealed to national consensus and solidarity (de Boer, Enders and Leisyte, 2009: 44). The Dutch form of solidarity drove in a direction diametrically opposed to its French counterpart. Solidarity at home and the rapid take-up of the Evaluative State on the domestic front were not just the prior conditions for the viability of the 'Dutch model'. They were also the conditions for its credibility abroad. More to the point, they provided a clear demonstration that the shaping and modernization of Europe's higher education systems did not necessarily have to draw on the experience of the major and historic 'referential systems'[4] of France, Germany and the UK. That the 'smaller nations' of Europe had their part to play and indeed had the capacity to modernize far more rapidly than their 'bigger brothers' was a theme milked for all it was worth. Indeed, much was made of it during the run-up to the Dutch Presidency of the then European Communities from July to December 1991, though the outcome was not what the Netherlands had hoped for (van Keulen and Rood, 2003: 71–3).

Nor, for that matter, was the notion of competition between universities at home subject to the same disapproval in the Netherlands as it was in France. Why this was the case is by no means a simple question. It could be argued that as a land which had relied on foreign trade throughout virtually the whole of its existence, competition could be seen as deeply rooted in Dutch culture, politics and *mores*. Thus, competition enjoyed a far greater legitimacy than it did in France.

Far more important from the standpoint of its universities, the Dutch edition of the Evaluative State could very certainly be seen as strengthening the institutional initiative whilst conferring an evident and thus pleasing degree of trust on academia, though the Prince's pleasure tended to sour as the decade passed (de Boer, 2003). Two aspects of the Evaluative State recommended it to the Dutch Academic Estate. In the first place, evaluation itself was entrusted to the Dutch universities. It was offloaded in their official representative body, the Dutch Association of Universities (*Vereeniging van de Samenwerkende Nederlands Universiteiten*: VSNU). Here was a very real gesture of rolling back the frontiers of the state. In addition, which if anything served to underline the agreement of the government for academia to be the master of its own house, was the no less remarkable rolling *back* of the Student Estate. In the name of managerialism, the principle of tripartite representation on university boards, which the Student Estate had won during the uproar of the Time of Troubles from 1972 to 1978, was steadily worn away (de Boer, 2007: 35).

Above all, the shaping of the Evaluative State in the Netherlands is noteworthy for the attention paid to the 'international' or 'European' dimension. If anything, this dimension has, over the years, assumed a central place in Dutch higher education policy. Nor is it entirely surprising that both the 'European' and the 'international' should figure largely in the profile of the Dutch variant of the Evaluative State. Thus, the years from 2002 onwards (CHEPS, 2007) saw the Dutch Evaluative State evolve from being a unitary model towards being a multi-agency model. Such a dynamic began with the establishment of the *Nederlands Vlaamse Accreditatieorganisatie* (NVAO: Accreditation Agency for the Netherlands and Flanders). It grew with the mutation of the VSNU into the Quality Agency for Netherlands Universities (QANU). The year 2004 saw the establishment of a separate quality assurance agency, the Netherlands Quality Agency (NQA), for the polytechnic or professional non-university sector (*Hoger Beroeps Onderwijs*).

Dutch 'exceptionalism'. Whilst all three Dutch agencies rely on the classic procedure of external review and internal self-assessment, two features set the Dutch version of the Evaluative State apart. The first is its outreach and the second is its institutional scope. Unlike other variations within the Evaluative State, the Dutch model goes beyond national frontiers. In effect, it is grounded less in a *national* than in a *linguistic* dimension. Thus, the NVAO, significantly the first step in the further strengthening of the Dutch Evaluative State, was created as a result of an agreement signed in 2003 between the Netherlands and Flanders for the accreditation of all study programmes – those in place as well as new programmes seeking accreditation (NVAO, 2009). The second specific feature is the remit of NQA. It is not unusual to have a separate agency to deal with the non-university sector. Portugal, as we shall see later, set up a separate branch in its short-lived multi-level agency CNAVES to deal with the polytechnic sector.[5] The originality of the NQA, however, lay in the fact that its remit did not cover the non-university sector alone. It also covered the continuous improvement of the quality of education in secondary schools, schools of senior secondary vocational education, higher professional education establishments (*hogeschoolen*), universities and in-company training courses (NQA, 2009).

In short, the Dutch application of the Evaluative State was not confined to higher education. On the contrary, it flowed *backwards* into the upper secondary school sector and it flowed *outwards* to the area of company training, a feature that was less prominent by far elsewhere.

3) British

British higher education policy foreshadowed a third variant in both strategy and purpose, namely modernization *through* marketization. Given the strength of institutional autonomy in British universities, imposing the canons of neoliberalism – competition for resources (both financial and human), the strengthening of procedures of public accountability and the regular verification of institutional performance – it is not surprising at all that the British strategy developed in a direction diametrically opposed to trends in mainland Europe. Fuelled by a rhetoric that extolled the 'rolling back the frontiers of the state' so as to better open up the university world to the driving forces of the market, the British administration found itself engaged in precisely the opposite exercise, that is, the laying down of a regulatory layer that was if anything more invasive and very certainly more deeply penetrating into the higher education system than the centrally driven, legally codified administrative 'style' found in many of its European counterparts.

Leaving aside the fact that a framework law had no precedent in British higher education, its technical specificity lies in the provision for the government to add further conditions – to fill in what are perceived retrospectively to be gaps – in the law's initial promulgation. These 'reserve' powers in fact give the government an additional margin of manoeuvre to close whatever regulatory gaps may subsequently emerge. First employed in France to settle the 1968 student riots and in West Germany to a similar purpose in 1976, framework laws in higher education stand manifestly as legislative devices of exception and as such act as a pointer to the perceived depth of crisis that the government of the day thinks it faces.

Thus, in the UK, the emerging Evaluative State drove higher education from being grounded in a form of organic development towards a 'regulated' *system*, with an increasing and accelerating emphasis on active government steering, exerted through specially created 'agencies of public purpose' (Henkel, 2007). The newly forged intermediary bodies effectively reversed what may be termed 'the direction of penetration', long sustained by the University Grants Committee.[6] From being held at arm's length, the Prince now embraced the world of learning with a steely claw.

The proliferation of agencies of public purpose in the UK's higher education system boosted the numbers of oversight bodies to a degree rarely found elsewhere. The new layer of oversight and verification provided a direct channel for injecting the will of the government into the university world. System-wide re-engineering called forth system-wide legislation in the shape of the Education Reform Act 1988, the Further and Higher Education Act 1992 and the Higher Education Act 2004. The first was unprecedented. In effect, it was the first Framework Act (*Loi d'Orientation, Rahmengesetz*) ever to be applied to the British higher education system. The second legislative round, the reform of 1992, created a unified system by granting university status to former polytechnics. Whilst it fragmented by regionalizing the funding systems for higher education, it also laid out a corporate model of institutional governance, standardized in terms of its role, size and composition across all institutions, the status of which had been raised to a university level (Williams, 2004). The third round – the Higher Education Act 2004 – ushered in a further flurry of national standardization, together with the introduction of differential tuition fees. In addition, it laid out system-wide conditions for determining the amount individual universities could charge their students (DfES, 2004).

Three remarkable truths...

The British strategy unveiled three remarkable truths. First, it showed that the long-established construct of institutional autonomy was in fact conditional on a 'self-denying ordinance' on the part of the Prince. That is, whilst the government certainly possessed the means to set conditions around institutional autonomy, it had chosen hitherto not to exercise this power. By choosing to act, the Prince demonstrated, as if demonstration were needed, that the distinction between institutional autonomy as an inalienable right and academic freedom as a theoretically revocable privilege could, in practice and faced with the determination of the Prince and his servants, be rendered rather less distinct than many had once believed.

Second, the British strategy sought to modify the very feature around which other systems were building their strategy of modernization, namely self-adjustment and self-correction at the institutional level. The fundamental concept of 'organic development' which historically lay at the heart of the British university system was seen by the government as not sufficiently adaptable or, to make a slightly more nuanced point, was not *sufficiently adaptable within the timeframe* envisaged by the authorities.

Third, in the absence of a 'market' mechanism in higher education, the British central administration found itself in the passably delicate obligation of having to put itself forward as a hopefully temporary *erstaz*. Having the government act as a 'pseudo market', which to all intents and purposes is the same thing as regulation, save that it is referenced to and justified by allusions to market rhetoric, injected into British higher education an unprecedented degree of 'juridification'.[7] Whilst in no way comparable to the degree of legal homogeneity that historically had 'steered' higher education in Western Europe, the British drive toward juridification – a term usually presented by British scholars as 'regulation' or alternatively as 'New Public Management' (Pollitt, 1995) – was plain for all to see and most certainly so in a system which had long evolved without it. As one long-term student of British higher education observed: 'government in the UK employs the rhetoric of the market in connection with higher education, but since [the] government controls the price universities can place on their services and the amount and variety of services they can sell, universities operate not in a market but in something like a command economy' (Trow, 1996).

The Evaluative State: different perceptions

With the British construction of the Evaluative State as an instrument of feedback, based on institutional output rather than the time-honoured practice of coordination by input measures, British universities faced a situation that was markedly different from their European fellows. Whereas the latter, by and large, were engaged in laying down the institutional basis, procedures and criteria for assessing institutional performance, they were also engaged in extending the range of institutional initiatives in such dimensions as staff appointment, curricular development and enhanced self-management, which had long been an established practice in British universities. In Western Europe, shifting the balance between legal homogeneity and the Evaluative State seen in the delegation of responsibility previously exercised within the framework of legal homogeneity by central administration down to the institutional level sought to strengthen institutional latitude. Arguably, it proved acceptable in this respect. In Britain, by contrast, the construction of the Evaluative State entailed two distinct tasks: the strengthening of an overall regulatory framework represented by system-wide legislation; and, at the same time, the linking of the regulatory framework to a powerful network of evaluative and verificatory agencies, which in the case of the four Higher Education Funding Councils, linked funding to performance.

. . . and their consequences

There is, however, a different perspective that may serve to draw an even starker contrast between the rise of the Evaluative State in Britain on the one hand and in mainland Europe on the other. Western Europe, in the classic relationship with government, subscribed to an arrangement involving 'dual lines of accountability'. In its classic form, this model of accountability is sometimes described as a 'bicephalous model of administrative control' (Lane, 1982). It bore a considerable similarity to the medieval concept of 'ascending and descending hierarchies' (Ullman, 1961).

Prior to the advent of the Evaluative State, this bicephalous arrangement was the key element underpinning legal homogeneity. It linked university and ministry (Lane, 1982; de Boer, 2003). Such an arrangement took the shape of a *descending* administrative hierarchy emanating from ministry to university and terminating in the person of the Secretary General in French universities, the *Regiringscommissaris* in their Flemish counterparts, the *Kanzler* in Germany or the Administrative Director in Sweden. These appointees were civil servant administrators. They exercised legal oversight within individual universities on behalf of the ministry. In parallel ran an *ascending* academic hierarchy that culminated in the person of the *Président d'Université* or the rector who, to varying degrees of magnificence, represented the Academic Estate.

By extending the boundaries of institutional self-management, one of the major consequences of the Evaluative State has been, formally at least, to weaken the descending administrative hierarchy, whilst strengthening the *administrative* responsibility attributed to the head of the ascending academic hierarchy. Not untypical of this was the Dutch Law for Modernising University Governance of March

1997 (*Modernisering Universitaire Bestuursorganisatie*) (de Boer, 2003). It strengthened institutional self-management, opened up new ties with local interests and concentrated executive authority, hitherto dispersed across senates and boards of curators, into a three-member executive board. For the first time in their history, Dutch universities found themselves endowed with a monocephalic administrative structure (de Boer, 2003).

In mainland Europe, the Evaluative State shortened and concentrated the descending *administrative* hierarchy at the institutional level. By contrast, the active intervention of the British authorities effectively *brought into being* a form of dual hierarchy at the very moment when this arrangement was being actively abandoned in mainland Europe. If anything, the British version of the descending administrative hierarchy, which assumed rapid shape during the early to mid-1990s, was more redoubtable by far than its earlier European equivalents. The British version of the Evaluative State was redoubtable precisely because it was constructed around agencies of public purpose, which wielded retrospective oversight for the regular assessment, evaluation and verification of institutional achievement. Furthermore, the British version of the *descending* administrative hierarchy was all the more powerful for incorporating a sophisticated and searching instrumentality. Finally, the descending hierarchy *à la britannique* was powerful precisely because it formed an evaluative mechanism linking institutional funding to institutional performance.

4
The Significance of Evaluative Homogeneity

Introduction

The creation of a technically sophisticated and deeply penetrative system for evaluating performance and quality, which comprises the essence of the Evaluative State, re-defined the procedures involved in accountability. The Evaluative State thus offset the more evident rigidities that *legal* homogeneity perpetuated. This it does by bringing evaluation to bear on the *individual* university rather than on whole sectors or institutional types, which had long been legal homogeneity's operational focus (Teichler, 2007). What has not changed, however, is the principle of homogeneity. Agreed, one may observe a shift in the point at which the new principle of *evaluative homogeneity* was bought to bear as also in the procedures through which it is expressed and operationalized. Effectively, the essential identifying feature of the Evaluative State lies in re-focusing an oversight previously exercised *a priori* and through legislative means by an oversight expressed through evaluation and assessment exercised *a posteriori* by means of an evaluative instrumentality in addition to legislative fiat (Neave, 1998a).

Thus, the Evaluative State, as a counterbalance to *legal* homogeneity, brought with it what is best described as *evaluative* homogeneity, that is, the setting of standardized criteria for minimum levels of performance and quality applied to the individual university (Neave, 2009a). Nor did it necessarily share all the basic assumptions behind *legal* homogeneity. *Evaluative* homogeneity did not, for instance, assume institutional capacity to change and adapt to be homogeneous across different types of institutions. On the contrary, far from taking institutional adjustment for granted, the purpose of the Evaluative State was very specifically to identify *incapacity* and to put pressure on the peccant by disseminating such information publicly, a technique sometimes alluded to as 'naming and shaming'. The latter is one of the less readily admitted purposes of league tables and rankings.

Evaluative homogeneity

The Evaluative State fulfilled two principal functions. It acted first as a powerful instrument for the formal assessment of higher education; second, it did so through the operationalization and application of standardized procedures and uniform rules in the areas of quality assessment, accreditation, institutional performance and output (Bleiklie, 2007). Once the twin principles of transparency and public accountability are factored into evaluative homogeneity, the Evaluative State becomes both central and indispensable to society's understanding of how its higher education system and, within the system, individual universities perform, achieve and fare, for better or for worse! As its name implies, the Evaluative State brings together a basic instrumentality, which systematically, in a standardized format regularly updated, makes information on higher education publicly available. Such information on institutional output, performance and achievement shapes society's readiness to fund individual establishments and influences the choice students make between different institutions and courses. It provides feedback for leadership to determine institutional strategies and priorities by making it possible to compare output and performance with other institutions of a similar condition or to identify those whose achievements are worth emulating.

The Evaluative State today is the central construct in the relationship between the university and society. In effect, it ascertains how far the former has met the priorities the latter wishes to be reflected in the nation's provision for higher learning. It also represents the termination with extreme prejudice of what was presented earlier as the historic 'concordat' between higher education and society in Western Europe, for whilst the earlier concordat was grounded in the state's acting as protector of the university, the Evaluative State re-states the role of the state primarily as the protector of *society's* interests – economic, social and developmental – vis-à-vis the university. To make no finer point, having resigned its historic role as the 'guardian of learning' the (Evaluative) State now acts as the 'overseer of higher education for the Market' (Neave, 2008a: 45–70).

Evaluative homogeneity: its potential – for better...

However, the transition from *legal* homogeneity to *evaluative* homogeneity as the prime driver in coordinating higher education is not without its ambiguities. It is not surprising then that interpretations as to its viability, potential and the exact ways in which it may shape higher education are by no means clear-cut. On the one side stands the argument that evaluative homogeneity is logical and necessary. It provides a counterweight to institutional diversity and overlap in programmatic provision, modes of study – on-site or distant – and means of diffusion (Kaiser and Huisman, 2003: 135–45). By operating through standardized criteria, dimensions and procedures, focused on higher education's output, coherence and order are upheld at the very moment when the national community is in a process of fragmentation, when regional interests assume greater importance in shaping institutional priorities. It plays a central part in confirming or denying institutional claims to status. At a time when institutional identity, under the pressure of both markets and competition, has, to an increasing extent, become the product of institutional self-advertisement and 'mere puffery' rather than the long accumulation of a reputation built up over the years, evaluative homogeneity provides an immediate and corrective sobriety.

Viewed from this perspective, evaluative homogeneity simply updates the basic feature that has long been a characteristic of higher education in Western Europe, namely that it is a regulated system. Agreed, some have argued that the backwash of 'de-regulation' – a relative concept in itself – has brought regulation to new and unprecedented levels of conformity and constraint (Daxner, 2006; Amaral and Magalhães, 2007). Evaluative homogeneity and its operational instrumentality uphold a central and additional objective, namely that market forces now replace social demand as higher education's prime policy driver. In no way has the fragmentation of the national community in effect diminished regulation. On the contrary, regionalization – and especially when both evaluation and funding are 'repatriated' to the regional level – ensures regulation that is better targeted and hopefully better aligned with regional concerns as a result of a better grasp of institutional performance and achievement.

...and for worse

Evaluative homogeneity brings clarity at a time when institutional diversity is all the more evident precisely because the historic administrative framework of higher education, if not dissolving, is at very least subject to increasing overlap (Huisman and Kaiser, 2003).

Yet, one cannot avoid the knotty problem of the impact evaluative homogeneity may have upon system development itself. One of the purposes of institutional evaluation is, in theory at least, to speed up the institutional response to externally determined priorities. By the same token, it is also believed to speed up institutional self-differentiation over and above the explicit public differentiation between institutions that ranking lists and league tables bring out. These latter developments are not coincidental. They are integral to the neoliberal vision of higher education as being at the service of the economy and society.

Stratification, differentiation and evaluative homogeneity

The price of clarity is not negligible, however. Indeed, for many students of higher education, one of the outgrowths of systematic evaluation has been to precipitate the dual process of institutional stratification and differentiation.

Stratification and differentiation are not exclusively the work of evaluative homogeneity alone. They are also the result of the individual university taking measures to consolidate its position in league tables or to improve it. In other words, within the broad sectors of higher education – whether officially designated as legally part of the university or the non-university sector – sub-groupings emerge, whose individual performance and achievement shape their ranking and standing as perceived by, and as presented to, the public. Stratification and differentiation, though sometimes taken for granted in such decentralized systems as the UK and the USA, have always existed *de facto* in Western European systems. And whilst officially the Commission of the European Union has set its face against formal recognition being given to a European equivalent of the American Carnegie Classification of Universities, this is far from the last word on the matter (van Vught, 2009). In the domain of higher education policy, there is a distressing tendency in Brussels to bring back through the tradesman's entrance what was thrown out with enthusiasm and vigour through the front door!

Legal homogeneity, as was pointed out earlier, did not take either differentiation or stratification into account, save in terms of broad sectors whose component establishments were held to be on a footing of legal equality. The status of individual universities was thus defined by their inclusion in a particular legally and administratively defined sector. Standing and identity were then collectively defined by 'institutional types'. Belgium provides a particularly nice example. There, higher education, like Caesar's Gaul, is divided into three segments – university, long-course higher education outside the university (*Hoger Onderwijs buiten universiteit: HOBU*) and short-course higher education outside the university (Verhoeven and Devos, 2002).

The mutation of legal homogeneity into evaluative homogeneity dissolves both stratification and differentiation as the means of distinguishing *different types* of establishment on the basis of their collective standing that follows from being part of a given sector. Rather, evaluative homogeneity *individualizes* institutional status. In contrast to legal homogeneity, for which legal stratification and differentiation served as devices for assigning *permanent* status and identity to universities, evaluative homogeneity employs stratification and differentiation as *provisional* and dynamic driving forces. Irrespective of whether they bring reward or penalty, fame or ignominy in their wake, stratification and differentiation occupy a central and strategic function as opposed to previously serving as a descriptive registration. Through this new mechanism, institutional status is explicitly linked through, and made dependent upon, institutional services and performance. In turn, criteria employed to assess performance determine the standing, reputation and recognized excellence that the individual university commands – or lacks!

Autonomy and the Evaluative State

The putting in place of macro-steering systems, analysed here in terms of the quest to increase efficiency, performance and output on the one hand, and on the other an equally determined search by governments for a focused and reiterative mechanism to rapidly transplant national strategy into institutional execution, is clearly central to the change which re-defines academic autonomy from being personal or positional and re-constructs it in terms of institutional autonomy. Though some scholars have argued that institutional autonomy and personal autonomy are the heads and tails of the same coin (Bleiklie and Kogan, 2007), this view pertained, at least historically, only in the Anglo-Saxon systems of higher education. The prevalent pattern in Western Europe, by contrast, extolled positional autonomy, but never conceded that universities were autonomous institutions (Hirsch and Weber, 2001). Regardless of whether one agrees with the accuracy of the term 'institutional autonomy'[1] to describe the complex process of offloading responsibility on the one hand and placing additional conditions upon the individual university on the other, it remains an empirical fact that each mode represents a very different pattern in the distribution of internal power.

1) Positional autonomy

The principle of positional autonomy enshrined a very ancient pattern of governance, which persisted across many centuries, namely the responsibility for internal governance shared amongst senior scholars in the academic guild (de Groof, Neave and Svec, 1998). Today, this is translated as 'collegiality'. However, today's institutional autonomy obeys a very different rationale. By and large, it derives from corporate business practice. The change from one to the other reflects another equally marked change in the purpose of higher learning and culture. This purpose has moved from the contemplative and the spiritual to the applied and the expeditive.

2) Institutional autonomy

Institutional autonomy can naturally be justified on much the same grounds as its earlier expression, that is, as ensuring the conditions necessary for and conducive to sustained, creative and original thought which, when maintained at a consistently high level over time, leads to excellence. Its contemporary construction has to do with the management of the university as a publicly responsible institution[2] and more particularly with creating the optimum administrative structures that permit its leadership to develop and carry through strategic decisions. These decisions enable the institution to discharge the responsibilities and tasks which major external interests and stakeholders have laid upon it and to do so with speed and within cost. To meet the requirements of the expeditive culture, power, rather than being collegial and thus dispersed, is concentrated around institutional leadership. In other words, the principles of good husbandry and accountability to major stakeholders – of which the government is held to be one – assume a structural form. More to the point, institutional autonomy is both an operational task and the individualization of a once shared and collective responsibility.

What is an autonomous institution?

The growing range of responsibilities placed on individual institutions begs the following question: what precisely are the essential functions a university must control if it is to exercise institutional autonomy as an authentic rather than as a symbolic condition?

Already in 1994, the German sociologist Rudolph Stichweh set down a number of key areas, which he believed were necessary if institutional autonomy was to have substance. These were the university's right and competence:

- to decide independently the areas which would engage its commitment;

- to endorse specific value systems and to define capital, career systems and incentives;
- to decide independently on the basic institutional principles and forms of institutional governance;
- to control the criteria of access both for students and academic staff;
- to define its strategic tasks and to set institutional goals;
- to determine both the formal and informal links to be developed with other sectors of society; and
- to assume full responsibility for the decisions taken and to be fully accountable for them (Stichweh, 1994, cited in Nybom, 2007).

One may question the appropriateness of these dimensions. Nevertheless, they are interesting and not merely from an historical standpoint, though that too has its importance. As a theoretical typology of institutional autonomy that appeared relatively early on in the reforming decade of the 1990s, Stichweh's template builds out from the same basic proposition as positional autonomy. In other words, the internal self-governance of academia by academia is enlarged from, and extended beyond, the fundamental freedoms of teaching and learning to embrace and include all activities undertaken within the purview of the individual university. Strategic planning, the setting of institutional goals and the nature of the ties between the university and external community are, under such a scheme, internally decided by the Academic Estate, with the Administrative Estate serving as executants of them.

Institutional autonomy, as Stichweh presented it, is grounded in an internal dynamic that is firmly set in the principle of academic self-government, although it is tempered by recognizing the necessity of being accountable to government and society. In his construct, institutional autonomy is driven by the internal disciplinary and epistemic evolution within the university. In summary, it is an interpretation remarkably close to its one-time British counterpart[3] and very particularly with respect to the selection of students and the nomination and appointment of staff, both of which, in the German context of the day, were immensely indelicate, not to say heretical propositions.

Institutional autonomy re-shaped ...

Stichweh's theses are interesting precisely because they allow us to identify – and thereby contrast – more closely the features of institutional autonomy as they emerged within the rise of the Evaluative State and, in addition, to set those features against changes in the distribution of power and authority within the institution itself. In effect, the overall framework within which recent legislation is set stands in direct contrast to Stichweh's vision. Whereas Stichweh regarded accountability as flowing from the nature of internal academic self-government, its contemporary counterpart places accountability at the centre of the university's external obligations. In retrospect, we may see the repositioning of accountability and the obligation *to submit* to the assessment of performance, achievement, financial efficiency and good husbandry as a natural concomitant of an equally fundamental feature of institutional autonomy in the knowledge economy. This fundamental feature involves the reversal of the relationship between the university and external society, the replacement, as was pointed out above,[4] of distance by proximity and involvement – in effect, the projection into the university of external society reaching in.

Such a radical re-definition brings equally radical consequences to the internal patterns of decision-making. With the university agenda being externally driven, the key issue is not whether the university may exercise choice between various demands of external interests; it is rather how it should organize itself in light of the demands placed upon it. The translation of these demands into the institutional tissue is, in effect, the central purpose of that other silent social revolution that has emerged within the groves of academia over the course of the past two decades, namely the rise to prominence of, and the weight placed upon, leadership. Internal organization is thus externally driven.

The upshot, as Bleiklie and Kogan pointed out in a recent review of trends in the organization and governance of universities in Western Europe, is to create powerful managerial infrastructures. These infrastructures run in parallel to (if they do not supplant) academic structures built around deans, heads of departments and the professoriate, once the personification and apotheosis of positional autonomy (Bleiklie and Kogan, 2007). It remains unclear, for the moment, whether institutional autonomy in its new construct acts as a constraint upon, or is relatively neutral vis-à-vis, academic autonomy in its positional guise. Evidence from Sweden suggests that its impact is relatively marginal. The Swedish experience proposes that more important by far is the fact that both institutional and academic autonomy appear to be increasingly dependent on external actors (Bladh, 2007).

...by dependency and conditionality

Yet, it is not simply dependency alone that distinguishes the contemporary version of institutional autonomy from its positional predecessor.

One may equally well argue that positional autonomy was no less dependent on the government in order to uphold the Humboldtian Concordat than it was on the state budget. Nor, for that matter, is dependency any the less when it is transferred from the Prince to the guild of merchants, from public revenues to private contracts, eked out by payment for commissions and services.

Of much more importance than dependency is conditionality. This is because conditionality implies instability, though it is rarely recognized as such, whether it takes the form of contractualization or the need to continually renegotiate with external interests, both of which provide the basic justification for the contemporary version of institutional autonomy. For just as the boundaries between institutional autonomy are subject to continual negotiation in keeping with the expeditive ethic, which demands that higher education keep abreast of continual and largely unpredictable change through negotiations between the government, the market and academic institutions (Henkel, 2007), so too are the conditions that determine whether the individual institution is able – quite literally – to afford even the remnants of positional autonomy within it. Both are subject to the same constraints. Henkel's proposition that neither institutional nor academic autonomy today are fixed in stone and for all time cannot be gainsaid, either for the UK or, for that matter, those systems of higher education currently committed to building up the knowledge society's equivalent of institutional autonomy. But to see academic autonomy in terms of boundaries contested between the state, the market and academic institutions merely confirms – though in a different vocabulary – the basic unpredictability to which academic autonomy is now hostage. For if academic autonomy is not entirely out of the control of academia, by the same reasoning, neither is it wholly within the powers of academia. Put slightly differently, this diagnostic is tantamount to admitting autonomy's oscillating and unpredictable quality.

This view is partly shared by Bleiklie and Kogan. They argue that the Academic Estate with its accompanying collegial 'style' of decision-making has become integrated into the Administrative Estate less as decision makers than as the executors of institutional policy. In becoming so, collegiality is replaced by top-down line management. The ending of collegiality, they argue, transfers the basis of legitimacy from the Academic to the Administrative Estate (Bleiklie and Kogan, 2007). Thus, inverting the relationship between the Academic Estate and the Administrative Estate is one of the more significant developments in the mutation of autonomy from being a broad-ranging value and organizational ethic to becoming a species of intellectual shorthand for the strengthening of managerial hierarchy as the principal means to ensure demonstrated efficiency and expedition under the rubric of institutional autonomy.

... by re-defining leadership

One of the more puzzling but less questioned aspects in 're-engineering' the universities of Europe is precisely why an institution so specific and exceptional in both its public and private lives (Trow, 1975) should lend itself to being invested with a notion of governance and administration, the origins and application of which took virtually no account of the context in which it was imposed. As students of higher education have not ceased to point out, there is very little that can be counted as common between a university and a business, though an accommodating halfway house has sometimes been advanced under the notion of 'academic capitalism' (Leslie and Slaughter, 1997).

1) The UK

No domain better illustrates the virtues of institutional autonomy as a device for organic change than the changes that took place in British institutional leadership from the mid-1980s onwards. Vice-chancellorial appointment was not subject to national legislation but rather to the individual founding charter. Thus, modifying the role and its responsibilities did not require national legislation. Change may be – and is – introduced by the individual university. The major change in the responsibilities of vice-chancellor to chief executive officer re-defined the status of leadership from being first in the Academic Estate. The chief executive officer, however, derives legitimacy as head of the Administrative Estate, not as first amongst equals in the Academic Estate.

These are not the only aspects to have changed over the past 20 years in Britain. Changes in the methods and criteria for recruitment to positions of institutional leadership have been equally marked. Though the UK has a long way still to go before individuals can make a lifetime career as a 'professional' president – a practice well established in the USA (Kerr and Gade, 1986) – significant developments are to be noted here too. One is the extension of recruitment to beyond the UK and indeed beyond academia. Some of the UK's more globally sensitive universities now 'headhunt' for well-known manager/scholars with an outstanding track record. Nor is recruitment to university leadership limited to the scholarly world. Civil servants and figures from business are also to be seen in the ranks of leaders, though academic credentials, if desirable, are not always sufficient on their own. The balance between managerial acumen and a proven track record for institutional development may be a pointer both to the weakening of academia's power to organize its own institution and to academia's re-assignment as 'managed professionals' rather than scholar/managers (Rhoades, 1998).

2) The Netherlands

The replacement of representational status by executive management powers, if evident in the UK, is equally visible elsewhere. Typical of this is the Dutch Law of 27 February 1997 on Modernising University Governance (*Modernisering Universitaire Bestuursorganisatie*). Here the governance structure overhauled the basic duality mentioned earlier whilst re-defining the descending administrative hierarchy. The governing board is smaller in number. The administrative hierarchy has evolved with the president as the direct and explicit representative of external interests. The rector, still formally elected from amongst the senior professoriate, has seen his or her executive powers for the internal management of the university strengthened. However, the rector reports to the president. The president represents civil society. He or she replaces the classic descending chain of oversight that bound the ministry to the university. He or she serves in a strategic role as intermediary between civil society and the university. Today the rector is responsible for the execution of the strategy determined in the governing board. He or she acts as intermediary between the board and the constituent interests *within* the university (de Boer, 2003).

3) Denmark

These are not the only variations to the strengthened leitmotif of leadership. Since this issue will be developed in greater detail in the three case studies in Parts II and III (France being one of them), we will venture a little further afield for further evidence.

The Danish University Act of 2003 stands as a further variation on the general theme of reforming governance. The managerial aspect, which is a central characteristic in the present-day version of institutional autonomy, is clear. Executive management is vested in a board not greatly dissimilar to the American Board of Trustees. Whilst the Dutch version has outside interests speaking through the person of the president, membership of the Danish University Board has an external majority of members of whom the chairman is one.

Envoi

When the Evaluative State is examined in terms of the way in which it re-works the contract between the government, society and higher education, one feature stands out, which is what the sociologists of language would call a 'shift in discourse'. This, the testy might argue, is far less significant than the re-distribution of authority within the individual university or the growing weight of the instrumentality that the Prince via the Evaluative State has brought to bear on higher education. But shifts in discourse are important. They shape the frame within which policy is debated, presented and, if successful, made permanent.

If the truth were out, the rise and impact of the Evaluative State was not confined solely to the business of metrics, benchmarking, evaluative procedures and indicators of performance, even if these were its most visible manifestations. Its impact also came from an agenda advanced under the flag of strengthening institutional autonomy. Indeed, the very terms used to hawk around one of the purposes of the Evaluative State – to strengthen institutional accountability and raise output – sits with very little ease when examined from the standpoint of autonomy as a 'traditional' or even pseudo-historic framework. True, to describe the re-distribution of internal power and authority in terms of 'strengthening institutional autonomy' was not without its conveniences or its advantages. Not least amongst them was the impression that public policy sought to convey to the university world: namely, that at long last, the Prince was engaged on a policy that itself could be seen as a form of continuity across the decades, if not the centuries. Precisely by claiming to re-establish the *institutional* dimension to autonomy and self-determination, which in Western Europe had largely disappeared in the course of the nineteenth century as the university was incorporated as an axial – and public – institution into the nation-state (Huisman, Maassen and Neave, 2001; Neave, 2008a and 2009c), the measures this presentational rhetoric created in its wake could be seen as correcting the lack of generosity – or trust – of the Prince's forefathers.

Holding out the bait of granting institutional autonomy was almost Sicilian in its subtlety. As presented, it was indeed an offer the university could not refuse. By wrapping up the consequences of the Evaluative State in terms of enhanced self-government and leadership as a thing of effective power, a new agenda could be floated in a language that the university could not easily counter without being seen to go against its own central value and ethics. Thus, the sheer radicalism entailed in the shifts and concentration of power around figures of manifest leadership were neatly disguised – 'packaged' would not be an inappropriate term – by presenting so substantial a displacement of authority and the transfer of responsibility from the Academic to the Administrative Estate as a generous and desirable move to restore to academia a long-lost freedom. The discourse, which served to camouflage the means, accordingly justified the ends.

Part II

Re-engineering Two Higher Education Systems

5
France: The Asterix Syndrome and the Exceptional Case

Introduction

On 10 August 2007, a new stage in the development of the Evaluative State was reached in France with the promulgation of Law 2007-1199. Officially entitled the 'Law bearing on organizing the new university' (*loi portant organisation de la nouvelle université*), it was deftly wafted onto the statute book at the very moment when the minds of the nation, academia, administration, students and parents were given over largely to sun, sea, sand and surf, if not sex! Although presented as the brainchild of the Minister of Higher Education and Research, Valérie Pécresse, it was clear nevertheless that overhauling the 'freedoms of the university'[1] was already under active consideration during the latter days of the Presidency of Jacques Chirac (Neave, 2008a).

There was excellent reason for such discreet timing. The Fifth Republic has for a good many years lived with the volatility of the Student Estate. At various rousing moments, the Student Estate had brought the career of the Republic's founding father, General Charles de Gaulle, to a shuddering halt, caused the head of at least one Secretary of State for Higher Education and Research, Alain Devacquet, to bounce down the corridors of power in December 1986 and, in 1997, provided the detonator to a series of nation-wide stoppages which put paid to the right-wing government of Alain Juppé, then Prime Minister and today Minister of Foreign Affairs.

Yet the French case merits closer attention on other grounds as well. France places the development of the Evaluative State in a system of higher education that is in many respects unique, though not without its influence on the Mediterranean nations in Western Europe. French exceptionalism was recently described by no less a figure than the President of the National Agency for the Evaluation of Research and Higher Education (*Agence d'Evaluation de la Recherche et de l'Enseignement Supérieur*: AERES) as France's 'Asterix Syndrome'[2] (Dhainaut, 2008). French exceptionalism is very wide-ranging in higher education. All too often, its many characteristics cause great puzzlement if not outright exasperation in those who view it from the outside or those whose careers have been shaped by the assumptions and practices of the Anglo-Saxon systems such as those in the UK and the USA. Exceptionalism reaches deep into the organization, structure and status of French higher education. It reflects a very particular social and political model, which even today stands largely in opposition to the neoliberal current that has, to varying degrees, sought to shape higher education in Western Europe over the past two decades.

Structural and administrative uniqueness

1) The Grandes Ecoles

Structurally, higher education in France is unique in that the university sector *stricto sensu* does not carry the elite status it enjoys elsewhere. Rather, the elite sector in French higher education is to be found in the 226 *Grandes Ecoles*. The *Grandes Ecoles* are far smaller in student numbers, highly specialized and ferociously selective. Unlike the 86 universities, which fall under the general authority of the Ministry of Higher Education and Research, the *Grandes Ecoles* are closely associated with the particular ministry for which their graduates are often destined – the Ministry of Defence, Agriculture or Education (Durand-Prinborgne, 1992: 217–18). Amongst the most prominent are the *Ecole Polytechnique,* founded in 1795 to provide the basis for weapons technology and technical training in engineering and ballistics for the armies of the French Revolution (M. Neave, 2009), the *Ecole Normale Supérieure,* founded in 1808 to provide a teaching elite for the nation's schools in the shape of the *corps enseignant* and the *corps universitaire,* and, finally, the *Ecole Nationale d'Administration,* created in 1946 to renew and modernize the training of high-level cadres for the nation's civil service. The essential and central identifying feature of these establishments is their symbiotic relationship with *state* service at the highest level.

As the heartland of the French version of formal meritocracy, the *Grandes Ecoles* provide what may best be described as 'practice-based' training in such widely differing areas as government, engineering, defence, aeronautics and agronomics. They differ from universities by dint of their formal status as *Ecoles d'application,* that is, they provide grounded and specialist training to those who are already graduates or, alternatively, provide specialized in-service training to civil servants who already hold positions. Amongst this latter category are such prestigious establishments as the *Ecole Nationale des Ponts et Chaussées*, the *Ecole Nationale Supérieure des Télécommunications*, the *Ecole Nationale Supérieure de l'Aéronatique et de l'Espace* – commonly alluded to as 'Sup' Aero' – or the *Ecole Nationale de la Statistique et de l'Administration Économique*.

2) The 'non-state' sector of French elite higher education

Whilst the *Grandes Ecoles* in general and *the Ecoles d'application* to an even greater extent are intimately bound up with the commitment of this sector of higher education to state service,[3] a sub-sector exists within it whose prime *raison d'être* fulfils a parallel function directed towards the private sector. However, its historic origins are very different. 'Non-state'-sector *Grandes Ecoles* grew up outside and apart from both state-sector *Grandes Ecoles* and from public universities. They were founded largely under the aegis of local Chambers of Commerce and Industry. The apex of this sub-system is to be found in the *Ecole des Hautes Etudes Commerciales* (HEC), which is today generally held to be one of Europe's leading business schools. Founded in 1881 by the Paris Chamber of Commerce and Industry, with its diplomas being recognized by the state nine years later, the HEC has over the years gradually assimilated certain of the key features that underpinned the enviable status of its state-sector counterparts – competitive entry examinations (*concours*) in 1920, together with a highly restricted student output.[4]

HEC stands at the pinnacle of this non-state, specialized sub-sector of French higher education,[5] the base of which plunges deep into a heterogeneous range of establishments with varying degrees of selection and ambition, often alluded to as 'petites *Grandes Ecoles*' (sic): *écoles de commerce* and *écoles supérieures de vente*. Some recruit directly after the *Baccalauréat*, others after two years post-*Baccalauréat* study in the *Classes Préparatoires aux Grandes Ecoles*.[6]

The extent of the division between what may be qualified as the 'closed sector' of French higher education and what is formally and legally an 'open access' university – open, that is, to all holders of the upper secondary school-leaving certificate, the *Baccalauréat* – is fundamental to understanding the tensions and thus the political response that so differentiated an arrangement has engendered. Those who seek to tackle the issues that the French university *stricto sensu* both faces and, at the same time, creates cannot do so adequately if they focus wholly and deliberately on the university alone. To do so is tantamount to playing Hamlet without the Prince. Nor, for that matter, is it possible to have a balanced understanding of what is involved in university governance, its modification or the way in which such issues are perceived in the world of the French university if the *Grandes Ecoles* are dismissed on the otherwise specious grounds of their being either anomalous, deviant or both when viewed within the canons of other systems of higher education.

3) *Segmentation* à la française

French higher education rests on a segmented model which, whilst having a minority 'non-state' dimension that certain Anglo-Saxon scholars stubbornly equate with 'private' higher education (Geiger, 1986), also involves a *tripartite* institutional stratification built around *Grandes Ecoles*, universities and university institutes of technology.[7] This configuration stands out from the more habitual binary pattern found elsewhere, for instance, in Germany, the Netherlands and Portugal, where the line is drawn between universities on the one hand and 'short cycle' non-university establishments on the other (Markiewicz-Lagneau and Gruson, 1983). The *Grandes Ecoles*, whether state or non-state sector, are not alone in forming a 'closed' sub-sector of French higher education. University institutes of technology, France's counterpart to the Dutch *Hoger Beroeps Onderwijs* (HBOs or polytechnics) or to the German *Fachhochschule*n, also fall within the 'closed' sector inasmuch as admission to them is also selective. What sets the elite element of the closed sector apart is a selective barrier above and beyond that which usually exists in upper secondary education. This 'double layer of protection' operates after the *Baccalauréat*, the upper-secondary school leaving certificate. It winnows out all those *not* accepted for entry to the *classes préparatoires*. The second hurdle is the competitive entry examination to the *Grandes Ecoles* for those who triumphed over the first pitfall.

The essential feature of the French elite sector is its ability *wholly* to control the quality of student inflow both in respect of the level of attainment demanded and of the number of places available. However, such filtering is only *partially* available to the university. It also takes a different form. Whilst the 'two protective barriers' of organizational stratification and selection at the secondary level serve to protect the *Grandes Ecoles*, their absence in the case of universities transmits the full weight of student demand onward and upward. Certainly, the university is not devoid of mechanisms of selection to control student 'through flows', but formally they cover only a limited number of fields. They operate only at the end of the first year for such programmes as medicine, pharmacy, dentistry and engineering (Journal Officiel France, Arrêté du 22 avril 2002) just as they do for admission to three-year programmes within *Instituts Universitaires Professionnels*. Nevertheless, the bulk of selection within the university emerges in a negative form – that of student *self-selection* through high dropout rates, switching programmes or starting anew. Thus, the *Grandes Ecoles* rest on an *a priori* system of selection, whereas for the most part the universities, because access is legally guaranteed to all those holding the *Baccalaruréat*, are forced to rely on an *a posteriori* mode of selection, regardless of whether this latter mode is the consequence of formal assessment or of an informal process sometimes alluded to in American higher education as 'cooling out' (Clark, 1960). In short, the *Grandes Ecoles* demand brilliance to *enter*. The university, however, demands brilliance to *graduate*.

This Manichean construct, divided between higher education dispensing an extremely rigorous technical training and a no less rigorous political socialization preparatory to state service and a university given over to the public service of providing mass higher education to the nation's citizens, masks the fact that by far the greater effort of French higher education policy over the past four decades has been taken up with attempting to solve problems of authority, purpose, study and curricular structure generated by the sustained growth of the Student Estate in the universities, not the *Grandes Ecoles*. The greater part of the legislative effort at 'system adjustment' in the shape of the various Guideline Laws of 1968, subsequently updated in 1984 and again in 1989, aimed at settling the internal balance of power between the Academic Estate, the Student Estate and the administrative services. By the same token, such efforts have tended to mask two basic facts that were themselves generators of the very tensions the Guideline Laws sought to deal with: first, that of all the Western European systems of higher education, France was the first to pass beyond the threshold of mass higher education, commonly held to be reached when the participation rate goes beyond 15 per cent of the relevant age group (Trow, 1974) – this it did in 1972; and, second, that the effervescence of France's Student Estate rarely if ever penetrated into the *Grandes Ecoles*, which, by and large, remained oases of privilege and enjoyed an unwonted tranquillity which gratitude for such privilege tends to create.

Shaping of the French Evaluative State

It is against this backdrop that France took the decision in 1984 to put in place the first stage in the development of what later was to be described as the Evaluative State. The creation of the *Comité National d'Evaluation* (Journal Officiel France, 1984 and 1985) in that year was not simply a European 'first' in this area. The circumstances that attended its birth were also of particular note. The conditions surrounding the 1984 Higher Education Guideline Law (Journal Officiel France, 1984), often known as the Savary Law after Alain Savary, the then Minister of Education who piloted it through the National Assembly, were very different from those in the UK. Whilst the latter was in the midst of a thousand cuts from Mrs Thatcher, France was under the aegis of a left-wing coalition. And whilst French higher education policy shared with the UK the swelling of the Student Estate, in contrast to the UK, France rode on an expanding higher education budget.

The significance of the Savary Law was not, however, confined to providing the legal framework within which the Evaluative State took shape in higher education. Rather, in retrospect, its long-term importance lay in its re-statement of some of the fundamental practices and beliefs that underlie the French notion of public service itself. Yet this particular point is not simply a matter confined to France alone. It also has its external ramifications and very particularly so when the siren song of neoliberalism and its operational expression 'New Public Management' emerged as the central driving forces in higher education reform in Western Europe. In short, the Savary Law of 1984 and its successor of 1989, introduced by Lionel Jospin, who would later go on to be Prime Minister from 1998 to 2002, placed the development of French higher education on a very different trajectory from its neighbours and one, moreover, that was explicitly and overtly hostile to the scriptures of neoliberalism.

The 1984 Guideline Law as an instrument of change

As an instrument for change, Law No. 84-52 of 26 January 1984 recognized the priority of bringing higher education, and very particularly the universities, into closer proximity with the demands of the economy. This it did both symbolically and concretely, first by changing the terminology that since 1968 had described the base units of teaching and research which were re-designated as *Unités de Formation et de Recherche* – Units of Training and Research (UFR) in place of the earlier *Unités d'Enseignement et de Recherche* – Units of Teaching and Research (UER). Second, it opened up the first tentative steps towards greater administrative coordination across the two major segments of French higher education – the *Grandes Ecoles* and the universities – by strengthening the ties at the inter-ministerial level between the various ministries with responsibility (*Ministères de tutelle*) for higher education establishments by setting up an inter-ministerial commission. The commission's remit involved joint cross-sectoral forecasting in such areas as employment prospects and qualification requirements for both the public and private sectors of the national economy (Journal Officiel France, 1984: Article 10). It is within this specific policy line that the French version of the Evaluative State was to take shape. Third, the 1984 Guideline Law opened up a further line of development that was to assume particular weight in the Guideline Law of 1989, namely spatial planning (*amenagement du territoire*) and regional development. Both were to be bolstered by establishing a high-level exchange between universities and regional authorities (Journal Officiel France, 1984: Article 6).

The Evaluative State: modest, not 'ultra-liberal'

This latter 'policy strand' figured as a central dimension that was to evolve and in the mid-term to shape the French Evaluative State around a system of 'partnerships' and multi-annual contracts on the one hand between the state and the regions, and on the other hand between the state and the universities. This agenda acted as the major vehicle that carried forward an incremental but no less crucial change in the relationship between higher education and the state (Chevaillier, 2001 and 2002). In short, what some scholars are pleased to see as France's counterpart to New Public Management (Pollitt, 1995; Chevaillier, 2001 and 2002), whilst present, nevertheless retained certain essential features that set it radically apart from its Anglo-Saxon counterpart. Certainly, as the Evaluative State took shape in France from 1987 onwards, the balance between the central state and the regions shifted. But it shifted without the ideological overtones of neoliberalism. Nor, for that matter, did the key measures involved go so far as to stand the basic relationship between the state and the market on its head by 'rolling back the frontiers' of the former so as to better make the latter the juggernaut of unbridled change. In short, the initial version of the French Evaluative State deliberately and vociferously eschewed any explicit commitment to what French discourse branded as 'ultra-liberalism'. The 'frontiers of the state' were not to be rolled back. In the words of Michel Crozier, one of France's leading organizational sociologists, reform ought to be rather 'more modest' (Crozier, 1987).

Such modesty emerged in a two-pronged strategy: on the one hand, to provide a degree of encouragement to academia to be more 'proactive' in the conduct of university affairs at the level of the individual university, particularly in the development of new courses to meet the increasing diversity of abilities and ambitions amongst the Student Estate; and on the other hand, to engage the 'partnership' of the regions in financing and developing appropriate curricular provision (Neave, 1996a: 74–6). In effect, the strategy introduced by the first phase in the development of the Evaluative State *à la française* saw the multiplication of what later came to be viewed as 'stakeholders' (Enders and Fulton, 2002) together with a degree of de-centralization in extending administrative responsibility for the nation's system of higher education. Here was a commendably pragmatic policy, aimed primarily at making public service more efficient and better able to cope with the rising numbers of the Student Estate. No less important, it did not challenge that abiding consensus in French society, which construed the university as a public service and, with singular perversity, as an expression of 'social cohesion'. Still less did it set out to undermine the status of the Academic Estate as public servants or revise its legal identity as an official service of the state enshrined in its legal designation as the '*corps universitaire*' (Kessler, 1986).

The 1984 Guideline Law as an instrument of consolidation

However, in its role as an instrument of modest change, the Savary Law was counterbalanced by two other thrusts, each of which reflected its engagement with the principles of 'collegial democracy' and its reassertion of the university as a prime instrument underpinning the concept of public service. By creating the notion of a 'university community', the Guideline Law of 1984 consolidated the principle of 'democratic management' just as it laid out the attendant principle that institutional management was shaped by the representatives of academic, administrative and technical staff, by students and by 'external personalities' (Journal Officiel France, 1984: Articles 27–8). Institutional management was most firmly cast as both collegial and collective across higher education's three Estates (Academic, Administrative and Student).[8]

The Savary Law remained adamant in maintaining the role of higher education as a public service 'independent of any hindrance [*emprise*] whether political, economic, religious or ideological' (Journal Officiel France, 1984: Article 3).

The French construct of 'public service'

The French notion of public service is intimately associated with the role that the state fulfils vis-à-vis its citizens and, with it, the underwriting of a particular construct which is directly related to a value which the French academician Max Gallo identified as widely shared amongst his fellow countrymen, namely 'an extreme sensitivity (*susceptibilité*) to formal inequality' (Gallo, 2009).

Single-cause explanations must by definition be suspect. Even so, Gallo's insight provides a useful point of entry for interpreting the general thrust of the Savary Law as well as that particular mentality or political mindset that has long flowed as a strong current beneath the surface of French higher education policy and which is implicit in the French construction of the Evaluative State. Indeed, it is arguably precisely the present-day attempts by the regime of Mr Sarkozy to break with this mental collectivism, which its opponents belittle as a form of 'corporate self-interest', that have stoked up once again the unceasing war of attrition between government and the universities, to which the spheres of justice and hospitals appear recently to have added their weight (Leparmentier, 2009).

As Gallo himself acknowledged, extreme sensitivity to formal inequality has a long history in France, going back to well before the Revolution of 1789 (Gallo, 2008). It may be debated how far the actions of the state create inequality, legitimize privilege or, indeed, whether the state itself is inimical to the freedom of the individual or acts as a restraint on his or her talent for being entrepreneurial or innovative, cultivated, criminal or capitalist (Savidan, 2007). The fact remains that the assumptions currently surrounding the role of the state in the UK and the USA, for example, stand at the polar opposite position to those that surround it in France. And, in effect, Gallo's insight gives us a useful handle to explain so marked a difference.

The French concept of public service is far wider – and, for that matter, far older – than the contemporary Anglo-American definition of delivering what the customer (or client) has paid for and expects. Whilst these elements are certainly present today, they are not seen in France as being at the heart of the matter. The reconstruction of the university's affairs around the economic imperative, in which the Student Estate is cast no longer as citizens so much as consumers – the heart of Anglo-Saxon 'ultra-liberalism' applied to teaching and learning – remains a matter of the utmost delicacy. Both the French and Anglo-Saxon systems are hotly disputed and both firmly remain inseparable from the political arena. Students as customers and, indeed, knowledge itself as a 'saleable commodity' are both profoundly antithetical when proposed as an *ersatz* for a far broader, more complex and permeative value system that enjoys the full weight of popular legitimacy, the roots of which are deeply political, social and historical. However, the surreptitious infiltration of individual features of neoliberalism rather than its general doctrine has today placed the older construct under considerable stress.

If the truth were out, public service – the *res publica* – by its very nature has long stood as the essential expression of French Republicanism, of its predominant values and, last but not least, of its particular identity that originally rested on a centralized unitary state. In symbolic terms, the Republic upholds liberty and equality under a political order once qualified as 'one and indivisible'. This latter concept is both an administrative and a geographic rationale that in turn defines and upholds these two primordial principles. Public service and public institutions define, operationalize and uphold the rule of law and the equality of citizens under that law. Public service embodies that other basic principle which has persisted since the Revolution of 1789, namely public careers open to talent, the foremost expression of meritocracy. In short, public service is an expression of what is often alluded to as 'Republican rigour'.

Republican rigour stands as the obverse to Gallo's comment about his countrymen's extreme sensitivity to formal inequality. One of the central obligations laid upon public service is precisely to ensure the *absence* of formal inequality. This central value receives its clearest expression in what was earlier referred to as the principle of 'legal homogeneity'. Applied to higher education in France, 'legal homogeneity' is simply the projection of the broader principle of enforcing formal conditions of procedural equality into the institutional context and circumstances surrounding higher education in its capacity as one of the public services that function as 'value allocating bodies' (Easton, 1965) to underpin national cohesion, institutional stability and identity.

Legal homogeneity and Republican rigour

Though 'legal homogeneity' has already been explored as an operational concept, together with the place that it occupies in the relationship between the government, society and higher education, it nevertheless remains true that this general construct is shaped by specific national circumstances and above all in France by the weight of political culture, by the place of the university in the polity and, last but not least, by the *droits acquis* that have accumulated around the higher education system.

The basic assumption that pervades French Republicanism – and, for that matter, those nations which drew heavily on it[9] – is that cohesion and order are ensured by uniform and rational processes codified in law and extended into society. Uniformity of institutional status – legally, all universities were held to be on an equal footing, a symbol and an earnest of both institutional and national cohesion – by uniformity in the formal conditions of access. Thus, for instance, holders of the *Baccalauréat* have a formal right to a place at university. The same principle of national uniformity extended to the diplomas that certified the successful completion of a programme of study. Whilst individual universities issued their own awards, these were neither the most significant nor, from the perspective of the Student Estate, were they held to be of great value. On the contrary, value lay not in the degrees awarded by individual universities; rather, it lay in the diplomas the university issued on behalf of the state – in the so-called 'national diplomas' that are still today the direct expression of the state's public underwriting of their validity and 'quality', though less than they were, as being the path to jobs in the public sector.

The rise of the Evaluative State in France

The first phase: 1985–2000

The drive towards the Evaluative State in France in no way presented the market as an alternative to either the state or to the recognized values that focused on the consensual construct of public service. It endorsed the notions neither of privatization nor of competition as prime instruments in the domestic overhaul of the university as a key institution in the social fabric. Certainly, lip service was paid to both competition and to market forces, but more as a potion reserved in the first instance for external application alone – that is, for improving the standing of the French higher education system vis-à-vis its European partners rather than as an instrumentality of whip and knout, wielded on the home front to enforce a new and radical relationship between government, society and university (Neave, 2009a: 551–68).

Why, in moving towards the Evaluative State, were the French authorities so reticent in summoning up 'the market' to justify reform? Clearly, there is no single answer, though the strategic modesty of the first phase in constructing the Evaluative State in France could derive some consolation on tactical grounds alone. Student unrest in the winter of discontent in 1986, spurred on by proposals to extend selective entry to higher education, put paid to the reforms associated with the unfortunate Alain Devacquet. Student unrest thus added – although retrospectively – tactical wisdom to strategic modesty.

However, of far more significance, the symbolism of 'the market' as an agent of ideological mobilization, the credo central to both Reagonomics and Thatcherism, did not command either the same legitimacy or wield the same ideological weight in France as it did in those lands where possessive individualism had enduring roots. The French construct of public service placed a very different role and purpose on the central state. It was not, as in nineteenth-century American and British liberal theory, a lesser evil, to be kept as far as possible at arm's length and most certainly so in cultural and educational matters. On the contrary, it was the active expression of the general will and entrusted with implementing this will, thereby giving it shape, both legal and institutional. Thus, one of the key functions that the national administration fulfilled was 'to establish a level playing field' in the formal conditions of access, inscription and the certifying of knowledge acquired by delineating content and thus quality through formally stipulated 'national standards' (Staropoli, 1987) set down and upheld through detailed legislative oversight. If modesty entailed freeing up some of these 'curricular guidelines' (*maquettes nationales*) (Guin, 1990), it by no means absolved the state of its secular mission to reduce the formal advantages of privilege, whether social, residential or fiduciary, that often served to falsify the twin imperatives at the heart of French Republicanism, namely meritocracy and equality. These key values, for instance, underwrote the formal conditions of access to educational services which were held formally to be of a similar quality for a similar range of abilities (Savidan, 2007). By the same token, the role of the state in the domain of national cohesion was very precisely to limit as far as possible the arbitrary and individual advantage the market was seen as fostering, both as a partial and as a particular interest as opposed to the General Interest.

Shaping the Comité National d'Evaluation

Drawn up at the same time as the re-statement of 'democratic collegiality' as the basic principle in the internal governance of the universities of the Republic, the *Comité National d'Evaluation* (CNE) introduced a strategy into French higher education that was both exploratory and hortatory – hortatory in that its purpose was to encourage greater initiative and boldness in decision-making by the three collegially-based Estates and more particularly to urge them towards self-generated reform at the institutional level. The CNE's strategy was also exploratory in the sense that if such initiatives were to truly flourish as a new dimension in the Republic's higher education policy, the individual university needed to know what others in the *Grandes Ecoles*, universities and *Instituts Universitaires de Technologie* had undertaken, were undertaking or intended to undertake. In short, the task of the Evaluative State was publicly to bring out regular and official statements on the condition of higher education in France. Evaluation was thus to be an integral part of public knowledge. By so doing, it also provided hitherto unknown – or unrecognized – concrete examples, options and practices of what was possible and indeed what was pragmatically feasible under currently existing legislative frameworks. By letting everyone know what others were doing and had already achieved, the CNE sought to encourage reform from beneath and to 'depoliticize' institutional decision making itself. This latter practice, a less attractive feature of French academia, which had grown up largely as a perverse effect of the institutional three Estates seeking to minimize conflict between them, tended to hand the poisoned chalice of difficult decisions onward and upward to Paris as the ultimate legal authority – an interesting variation *à la française* upon the more general notion of the 'overloaded state'.

Initially, the CNE's mandate was not limited to prodding the French universities toward 'bottom-up' policy initiatives alone. If it were to enjoy the confidence of both the Academic and Student Estates, the CNE had to be seen to represent a very different relationship from the usual hierarchical ties between the universities and the central national administration. In short, if evaluation was to benefit from 'a positive attitude' on the part of those evaluated, those evaluating had without peradventure to show their independence from both state and political parties (Neave, 1996a). In this respect, the independent status of the CNE was underwritten by two provisos that served to guarantee its status of honest broker. First, it did not report to the minister responsible for higher education. On the contrary, it reported publicly and directly on a two-yearly cycle to the President of the Republic, the ultimate guarantor of the Committee's autonomy and of its independence from the normal lines of administrative oversight. A second earnest of its independence lay in the composition of its Administrative Board (*Conseil d'Administration*), half of whose 26 members hailed from the worlds of universities and scholarship. The remainder were drawn from what is best described as 'watchdog' agencies or constitutional bodies which themselves exercised the power of monitoring, oversight and coordination at various interfaces between the state, law, finance and relations between the state, employers and employees. These were respectively the *Conseil d'Etat*, the *Cour des Comptes* (Audit Court, Office of the Comptroller General) and the Economic and Social Council (Neave, 1996a: 74–6).

During its first phase, the Evaluative State *qua* the CNE focused on reviewing individual higher education establishments. Thus, between 1985 and 2000, all universities *stricto sensu* underwent review in addition to some 30 *Grandes Ecoles*. Over and above evaluating individual higher education institutions, the Committee undertook 'theme-based' assessments to provide a snapshot of the state of various disciplines from a cross-institutional perspective. It also undertook the occasional foray into 'transversal topics', for example, the evolving relationship between higher education and the regions (Documentation française, 2009b). The latter was not just a crucial element in higher education policy; it also reflected a broader strategy, which extended beyond the world of academia to embrace the evaluation of urban planning, regional planning (*amenagement du territoire*) and research as part of a general bid to ensure better control over public expenditure, above all during the period 1989–92 (Documentation française, 2009a).

Millennial goals and changes: the watershed

The very strength on which the Evaluative State sought to capitalize – reform based on the goodwill of academia itself – was viable just so long as the changes that academia was asked to back could be seen by academia as either extending the degree of initiative granted to it, as a loosening of hitherto close and detailed ministerial oversight or, last but not least, as a continuation of the established conditions (*droits acquis*) regulating the three Estates. Thus, the introduction in 1992 of the procedure known as 'contractualization' – the negotiation of both the budget required and the objectives an individual university set itself over a four-year period – could certainly be seen as opening up a greater margin for 'collegial governance' to shape policy in the light of the establishment's particular strengths and circumstances. To this extent, contractualization could certainly be seen as a major step forward in the delegation of power away from the centre and as strengthening the decision-making capacity of the Academic Estate. Contractualization can, however, be put to other uses.

Prior to 2000, contractualization, though a marker point in the evolution of the French model of the Evaluative State, unfolded as a process parallel to but separate from the exercise of evaluating the individual university or higher education institution. Indeed, the 'hortatory strategy' that marked the early days of the CNE was largely dependent on keeping both exercises running on parallel tracks.

Such *delicatesse* came to an abrupt halt in 2000, when the specific *evaluative* cycle was locked into the general cycle built around negotiating the terms of the university's four-year 'contract' with public authorities. The linking together of the evaluative cycle with negotiating the terms of the individual university's contract fundamentally changed both the purpose and the status of institutional evaluation, as well as the strategy that lay behind it. The strategy of persuasion and consensus, designed to encourage boldness and initiative from beneath, withered before a more overtly directive stance by government and more particularly by the Ministry of Higher Education. Evaluation effectively took on new dimensions. In doing so, it assumed a new form of leverage. The results that evaluation obtained were henceforth to serve not just the universities; they were also to provide an 'input' for use by 'partners' – the central ministry and regional authorities – when negotiating the terms of the university's four-year contract. The transition of the evaluative 'style' in the policy cycle from hortatory to negotiatory heralded other changes quite apart from the explicit but indirect ties between funding and the setting out of intended objectives of performance which negotiating the individual contract entailed.

There are, not unnaturally, a number of interpretations of this particular development: the reassertion of that long-established *dirigiste* style of higher education policy making in France (Premfors, 1981); the determination of the government to set a new framework around the drive to encourage institutional initiative; and, last but very far from least, the belief, which was growing in certain quarters, that if 'bottom-up' readjustment had its place, it was not sufficient on its own to fall in with either the degree of change required or the pace at which that change ought to take place. In short, whilst agreement on maintaining the 'modesty' of the state persisted, the scope of the reforms needed was indeed very far from being 'modest'.

The second phase: 2000–9

Thus, the first decade of the twenty-first century marked a second phase in the evolution of the Evaluative State in France. This saw, on the one hand, the strengthening of the evaluative arm of the state and, on the other hand, the pressure to hasten the 'offloading' of responsibilities to the institutional level (Documentation française, 2009b). Both priorities were presented within and justified by an extremely cautious rhetoric which combined 'efficiency' and rationalization. Initially, little mention was made in the justifications presented both to the public and to the university world of 'market forces' as such. Other, less emotionally charged and more acceptable watchwords were hawked around. Thus, the urgency of higher education reform was brought home, first, as the natural and inevitable prior condition if France was to retain its place in the greater task of European integration and, second, as part of the necessity to instil firmly in the Republic's institutions of higher learning that 'entrepreneurial spirit' which globalization and competition appeared to demand (Dhainaut, 2008).

Despite a sustained emphasis on 'efficiency', good husbandry in resources together with calls for more detailed and more extensive transparency in higher education, this apparent continuity served to camouflage some very fundamental changes indeed. Not the least amongst them was a basic re-definition of French Republicanism's central credo, namely the notion of what constituted the General Interest and the particular institutional forms that upheld it. According to the classical interpretation of this notion, which prevailed and was consolidated by the Third Republic from 1876 onwards, neither 'the market' nor for that matter 'industry' – still less the 'private sector' – was conceived as part of the General Interest. Rather, they figured amongst the 'particular' or 'occult' interests. Occult interests were deemed illegitimate where they were not overtly opposed to Republican rigour, perpetuating their own 'particular' interests in contrast to those of the nation. Indeed, the very essence of the 'mission of public service', as was argued earlier, was to protect the individual citizen from the excesses of self-interest exercised by such non-accountable groups and interests – a self-interest often interpreted as attempting to restore or uphold the return of privilege. Privilege by definition was illegitimate as well as antithetical to the formal equality that stood as foremost amongst the Republic's key historic and identifying values.

Whilst certainly radical in the assumptions they made both about the role of the state and its part in upholding social cohesion and economic viability, the scriptures of neoliberalism appeared – and remain in the French setting – if anything even more radically extreme. Neoliberalism appeared extreme and unacceptable on that account, precisely because of its basic incompatibility with the Republican concept of public service and no less so with the institutions, not least higher education, the function of which was inextricably embedded and bound up with public service.

Reversing the 'public policy ethic'

The period from 2000 onwards saw the re-casting of the private sector of the economy as a central element of the General Interest, as opposed to the association that it had long dragged behind it of being a 'particular' interest. With this 'reversal in the public policy ethic' went an equally marked departure in the role of politics in determining which agenda was to figure as part of the General Interest. The process was neither straightforward nor ideologically coherent. As elsewhere, notably in the UK (Neave, 1988b: 273–83; Williams, 2004), the forcible conversion of the 'policy ethic' began as a series of pragmatic measures which, as they were operationalized and implemented, could retrospectively come to be identified as neoliberalism's form of 'policy creep'. Under successive right-wing governments, its momentum steadily built up in French higher education from 2002 onwards. Thus, 'the drift towards ultra-liberalism' in France saw the thrust of politics focused on the implementation and re-definition in operational terms of key agencies to enforce the economic agenda – now presented as the 'supreme being' in the nation's General Interest.

Here was an astounding reversal in the basic assumption that had governed the relationship between economic progress and social cohesion, a relationship that has characterized French higher education policy since the end of the Second World War. In effect, the public service/welfare state model turned on the belief that social stability and cohesion were themselves the prime determinants of economic advance. By holding on to the conviction that economic development conditioned social stability, neoliberalism stood this relationship on its head (Neave, 2007).

Infiltrating the central values of ultra-liberalism – competition coupled with closer managerial oversight and both harnessed to institutional performance – also reversed that assumption which characterized the first phase in the development of the French Evaluative State: namely, that competition was primarily for external use between higher education systems rather than for shaping policy within them, the latter being an interpretation furiously rejected by the French Left. Importing competition as an operational principle was in itself an interesting tactic, marked as it was by widespread official recourse to the rhetoric of 'gearing up to the Bologna Process' as a justification to gain leverage on domestic reforms rather than being primarily concerned with advancing international cooperation (Musselin, 2009).

6
Strengthening the Evaluative State: Strategy, Values and Rhetoric

Introduction

Despite the role that France played in pioneering the Evaluative State, it is evident that the French government faced a dilemma not very different from one that the UK had confronted a decade earlier. If higher education was to be 'freed' from the heavy hand of the state to benefit from the joys of competition between individual higher education establishments, a rather different approach was needed. It was not enough merely to make encouraging noises and gestures, and very particularly so given the growling hostility of two of the three Estates in the university world – the Academic and the Student Estates – to the notion of 'market forces' as the great liberator. However, it is one of the more remarkable paradoxes that neoliberalism, a doctrine wedded to rolling back the frontiers of the state, could advance only by rolling them forward. This bizarre example of policy's equivalent of cognitive dissonance is sometimes alluded to as 'Amaral's Paradox' (Amaral and Magalhães, 2007; Neave, 2008b). It was as much in evidence with the sharp smack of government in Thatcherist Britain as it was in the higher education policy pursued under the presidencies of Messieurs Chirac and Sarkozy.

The second phase in the development of the French model of the Evaluative State injecting neoliberalism into higher education took place at two levels – within central government itself and within the individual university. The two thrusts of policy were closely related as much in terms of the overall strategy they introduced as in their timing. Their formal expression emerged in the decree of 20 March 2007. This decree was rapidly followed five months later by Law 2007-1199 of 10 August 2007. The former saw the CNE ingested into a new and broader ranging administrative agency now designated as the Agency for the Evaluation of Research and Higher Education. (*Agence d'Evaluation de la recherche et de l'enseignement supérieur*: AERES). As its title made plain, the Agency was to serve as the spearhead for overhauling both higher education and research. However, the greater weight of legislative effort bore down on the institutional level through the provisions in the 'Law bearing on Organizing the New University'.

Re-peopling the corridors of power

In its operational scope, the Agency differed markedly from its predecessor. Membership of its Governing Council (*Conseil d'Administration*) was slightly shaved – instead of 26 notable personages, the Agency contented itself with 25. Where significant change was to be seen, however, was in the interests and constituencies they represented, and in the balance between them. Nine 'qualified personalities', recognized for their scholarly achievement in France, the EU or enjoying international renown, bolstered the ranks of the *Prominente*. At least three of their numbers were drawn from the *private* research sector (Légifrance, 2009a). Higher education establishments were assigned seven representatives, chosen not just from academia but also from the technical services (*ingénieurs*) of higher education institutions, with a third constituency consisting of 'experts' who hailed from various evaluative bodies 'recognized as competent'. Also included were one senator and one deputy. Such a membership profile differed radically from that of the now defunct *Comité National d'Evaluation*, as it did in the political intention that its creation demonstrated.

Changes in membership heralded, officially and formally, a redoubling of the proactive strategy initially introduced five years previously. Once again, the driving force of reform focused around the agencies of central government. Also significant was the very real reduction in the numbers representing what may be described as the 'university presence', diluted on the one hand by the unprecedented and explicit inclusion of private sector research interests and on the other by the splitting of the university constituency among academic staff and senior members of university technical and support services. Far from being an independent body *au-dessus de la mêlée*, by dint of the make-up of its Governing Council, AERES took on all the trappings of a coordinating agency, acting within an *a posteriori* framework and with the clear remit of driving reform onward and downward, thereby strengthening evaluation yet further as a directive instrument. Thus, the purpose of evaluation shifted. No longer was it confined to assessing institutional performance alone. Its scope now involved the Agency in singling out areas for improvement and making recommendations for the government and national administration to act upon (Dhainaut, 2008).

New strategy, new priorities: the mission of AERES

What the shortcomings in French higher education were and what strategy was to be employed to deal with them, together with the precise role AERES was to play in both, were set out with admirable clarity in 2008 by its incoming President, Jean-François Dhainhaut, President of Paris Descartes University and a medical doctor. Dhainhaut's interpretation of AERES' mission corresponded fully with the notion of the 'modest state', for whilst the Good God and Moses once sought to civilize the behaviour of the Children of Israel via a ten-point programme, Dr Dhainhaut limited AERES to a mere five! Boiled down to their essentials, these were:

1) the grafting of quality management onto individual universities and their service bodies;
2) the introduction at the institutional level of individual bonus payments over and above the national academic salary scale;
3) a particular focus on doctoral schools – the French equivalent of the American Graduate School – as a means of building up research capacity, innovation and attracting the support of external partners;
4) encouraging closer collaboration across the university/*Grande Ecole* divide and most especially the setting up of cross-sector research units;
5) enhancing the value and relevance to industry and to the world of business (*le monde économique*) of university-based qualifications, particularly at the doctoral level (Dhainaut, 2008).

The five points were, it was claimed, the outcome of AERES' assessing some 65 higher education establishments undertaken from May 2007 (Dhainaut, 2008) – an undertaking of quite remarkable intensity. What was no less remarkable was the shift in focus that AERES brought about. Rather than concentrating primarily on overall institutional performance, the first diploma level included, AERES placed the major priority on the research and research training systems, ostensibly on the grounds that these two functions more than anything else accounted for the desolate position of French higher education in international league tables and rankings (Dhainaut, 2008).

Arguments of convenience and opportunity

This argument was somewhat ingenuous. It took at face value France's unfortunate rankings in various international league tables, principally those published by Shanghai Jiao Tong University (PRC), by the *Times Higher Education Supplement* and their counterparts bruited abroad by Leiden University (Dhainhaut, 2008). However, as no member of the research fraternity in France could fail to be aware, research in France has, since its organization around the *Centre National de la Recherche Scientifique* (CNRS) in 1939 (*Comité National d'Evaluation*, 1987: Neave, 1993), developed along very different lines from the predominant model found in Anglo-American or German universities. Whilst research units and individuals, financed and regularly evaluated by the CNRS, were often physically located in universities, their organization and the career paths were separate financially, structurally and administratively from those of their university host. CNRS research staff, unlike their Anglo-American counterparts, were full-time researchers, an arrangement not dissimilar to the one-time Soviet model of research grouped around various national academies (Rabkin, 1992). In short, the assumptions made by international league tables about the place of research reflected an organizational reality that had no bearing whatsoever in France. Indeed, these league tables took not the slightest account of these very substantial differences, the most evident of which was that the elite-sector *Grandes Ecoles*, despite certain notable exceptions, tended by and large to remain outside the 'research connection'.

In effect, the CNRS acted as an umbrella organization for the management and oversight of publicly financed research in France. It stood as the crowning height of an exceeding complex pattern of interlinked 'sectoral' research agencies,[1] amongst which were the *Institut de la Santé et de la Recherche Médicale* (INSERM), the *Organisation de Recherche Scientifique pour les Territoires d'Outre-Mer* (ORSTOM), the *Commission à l'Energie Atomique* and the *Institut National de Recherche Agronomique*. To these, the Fifth Republic added the *Centre National d'Etudes Spatiales* and the *Centre National pour l'Exploitation des Océans* (CNExO), together with the *Central National de Recherche en Informatique et Automatique* (Neave, 1993: 170). Though it was limited to the world of research, there are good grounds for arguing that the CNRS constituted an embryonic form of the Evaluative State which was older and strategically more weighty by far in the direct influence it wielded over research and research policy, and above all over what has come to be known as 'research management'.

Strengthening the Evaluative State

The issue that the creation of AERES posed for the CNRS was delicate to the highest degree. As the spearhead of reform through evaluation, was AERES to take over part of the responsibility for evaluating research as a key dimension not just in institutional performance but also in assessing how far the objectives a university had agreed upon when negotiating the four-year contract with its 'partners' – national or regional – had been fulfilled? Or, as an alternative possibility and one that had existed *de facto* since the founding of the *Comité National d'Evaluation*, was AERES to share this responsibility with the CNRS? Nor did the issue stop there, for if responsibility was indeed to be shared, which of the two agencies was in effect to be 'the senior partner'?

What was clear from perusing the five-point programme assigned to AERES was the overwhelming priority attached to re-shaping the place of research in the tissue of French higher education rather than continuing with the organizational separation into two clearly delineated spheres. Equally marked was the determination of the government to bind research more firmly into the twin cultures of quality and management, whilst shifting its base more firmly into higher education.

These were crucial issues. Stated dramatically, could the intent to strengthen the Evaluative State yet further be taken seriously if research evaluation remained subject to another, parallel authority? These were not the only conundrums to emerge. Equally pressing was the need rapidly to act, a need apparently justified on the one hand by the perceived absence of 'excellence' in the international ratings of French higher education and on the other by the no less pressing need to align the 'products' of the research *training* system around the requirements of business and industry. In France the research *training* system is predominantly the responsibility of the university *stricto sensu*, though certain individual *Grandes Ecoles* have developed this function (Neave, 1993). Seen from such perspectives as these, reforming research and handing its evaluation over to AERES was not simply a pointer to the radicalism of the policy envisaged; it also called for very substantial revision in the status of the CNRS itself. With the task of evaluating research stripped from the CNRS and vested entirely in AERES, the CNRS had henceforth to content itself with a mandate that was much reduced. By confining the CNRS to the 'strategic piloting of research' (CNRS, 2009), no longer did it serve as the nation's major and indispensable forum for the negotiating, advancement, financing and assessment of public research, something that it had done for more than six decades.

The abasement of the CNRS, hotly contested though it was (Mazet, 2009), provided a substantial point of leverage for a broader reform agenda that was no less radical in the changes it contemplated at the institutional level.

Research evaluation: reform's Trojan horse

That the research function possessed such leverage was not simply because of the critical role it was held to play in adjusting the university to the demands of the 'knowledge society'. No less significant, the research domain, whatever the role the polity assigns to higher education, is the one area where both individual and institutional competition, merit and their outcomes in the form of excellence and repute have their being. It is here, as the American sociologist Burton R. Clark pointed out more than a quarter of a century ago, that 'the gold coin of excellence is minted' (Clark, 1983). By focusing the reinforcement of the Evaluative State – the main thrust of policy during the second phase in its development – on research and on the research training system as prime areas for action, AERES' strategy outflanked, even if it did not entirely persuade, the counter-arguments put forward by the defenders of the 'public service' ethic. For none of the supporters of the university as a public service could possibly deny the place of competition in identifying ability, talent or merit in the assignment of resources for scholarly inquiry and research. No less important, now that the basic principle of competition was acknowledged as a condition inseparable from efficiency in research in one crucial domain, that same principle could be extended as the fundamental justification to be applied to others.

In the bid to infiltrate the tenets of neoliberalism via the Evaluative State into the higher education system of France, gaining purchase over the evaluation of research fulfilled a role not greatly dissimilar to that of the Trojan horse. It flung the gates to the groves of academia wide open. Once opened, other functions could be subordinated to the same rationale. By putting an end to what had effectively been a dual system of evaluation, split between the CNE and the CNRS, not only was the power of the Evaluative State reinforced through conferring a monopoly status on AERES; the powers of 'steering policy' *a posteriori* through the evaluative process, coupled with the recommendations AERES might make, were themselves reinforced by that same token.

The transfer of research evaluation from the CNRS to AERES was a signal and strategic victory for the forces of neoliberalism over the supporters of the public service model of French higher education. Into the breach thus opened, other measures rushed swiftly, prime amongst them Law 2007-1199 of 10 August 2007, which set out the framework for France's 'new university', which followed less than four months after AERES became operational (AERES, 2009).

Continuity and change

The titles the legislator confers upon his works are never to be taken lightly. For this reason, it is rarely wise to dismiss the significance of the exact wording that describes them. That the purpose of the Law of 10 August 2007 was to create a '*new* university' carried with it a high degree of political symbolism, just as it entailed consequences for French higher education that were both concrete and radical. The political symbolism fell in with the much-publicized programme of the newly-elected President Nicolas Sarkozy, namely to 'make a break' (*politique de rupture*) with established political convention. As far as higher education was concerned, the 'break' entailed accelerating the pace at which neoliberal policies were injected into the country's institutions, not least universities. Yet, as one of Mr Sarkozy's presidential predecessors, Valery Giscard d'Estaing, once pointed out, in the midst of change there are always elements of continuity.

Continuity was evident in three areas in particular. These were the maintenance of the basic three-part division in the structure of French higher education, the further elaboration of the procedures involved in 'steering by contractualization' and, finally, the use of the same line of logic to justify the 'autonomy' granted to universities that had served to confound the obduracy of both the Academic and Student Estates over the issue of research and the place of competition as the central value, which the 'new university' was called upon to ingest.

1) Continuity

Despite the lamentations of AERES' president over the 'Asterix Syndrome'[2] and notably the abyss between *Grandes Ecoles* and universities, the prospect of formally merging the two sectors was never directly entertained as a policy option. Why this should be so is not easy to determine. A number of explanations are possible to account for so curious a continuity in so radical a reform. The first is that merging *Grandes*

Ecoles and universities had long been a much-flogged hobbyhorse of the Left. As such, it was unacceptable to a right-wing government for that very reason. A second explanation is the possible bad blood such a move would very certainly have caused amongst the various ministries, other than the Ministry of Education, and particularly in those ministries that exercised responsibility over individual *Grandes Ecoles*. A third explanation is an extension of the second – in other words, the possible effervescence and lobbying that the graduates of the *Grandes Ecoles* would very certainly have undertaken in defence of their particular alma mater. Since graduates of the *Grandes Ecoles* occupied the highest echelons in state service – quite apart from being ensconced in equally powerful posts in the private sector – clearly caution suggested that it was better to let sleeping civil servants (or board members) lie. The risk of uproar inside the corridors of power coinciding with predictable outrage in the university world was a scenario too horrific to be contemplated. The solution, as we have seen, was indirect. It took the form – at least on paper and through expressed intent – of strengthening research collaboration between the two sectors: universities and *Grandes Ecoles*. This too was a policy of continuity, since the previous 20 years had seen the timid and gradual extension of research and some research training into the *Grandes Ecoles*. This latter option was specifically taken up in the Programme Law of 8 April 2006 (Légifrance, 2009b).

The second element of continuity was different. It built upon, and pushed further, the initiatives already undertaken at the start of the decade, initiatives which brought together the two cycles of evaluation and 'contractualization'.[3] The University Reform Law of 2007 added a further dimension to this mechanism of 'steering' through evaluation and contractualization. This it did as part of the overhaul of governance in French universities and very particularly by conferring upon the university president very real powers for negotiating and implementing the university contract with public authorities both national and regional (Montlaur-Creux, 2007).

Whilst changes in the role, power and status of the university president in France will be analysed later, it is important to place them in a setting wider than simply the shifts in formal status and responsibility that the reform of 2007 assigned at the institutional level to the university president. This is not to play down the importance of the changes that the legislation brought about; rather, it is to place such measures in a slightly different perspective. This perspective may also provide a further example of the way in which procedures and lines of control, developed as part of the reinforced Evaluative State, are extended down to the institutional level. By establishing continuity across different dimensions involved in policy making across different levels from the central national administration to the individual university, we obtain further insight into the dynamics of the Evaluative State itself.

Viewed from this broader perspective, legislation in the summer of 2007 added a third dimension to the mechanisms already in place that had knitted together the evaluatory and negotiatory cycles. To this it added what may be termed an *'electoral* cycle'.

Knitting together evaluative, negotiatory and electoral cycles. The Law on the 'new university' stipulated that the duration of the presidential mandate was also to be directly and explicitly aligned on the two other evaluatory and negotiatory cycles. Not only was the presidential mandate made deliberately to coincide with the timeframe of the university contract – that is, four years, though the president could seek one further mandate. The timing of presidential elections and the signing of the *Contract d'établissement* were closely and explicitly linked together (Montlaur-Creux, 2007). Effectively, the link between all three cycles – evaluative, negotiatory and electoral – established what is best understood as a procedural 'chain of command' of the most unambiguous sort. Under this new arrangement, the 'steering mechanism' began in the evaluation procedures at the level of the central agency (AERES), passed into the negotiatory cycle with funding 'partners' and terminated in ultimate and formal responsibility at the level of the individual university, firmly vested in the remit and responsibilities of the university president.

A third element of continuity emerged in the logic of the arguments that the government employed to justify the granting of institutional autonomy. The argument that competition and merit were integral to university research created a powerful precedent and an implacable logic to justify restructuring the CNRS and boosting the weight of AERES. By a similar logic, the extension of the Evaluative State into the intimate workings of France's universities rested on an analogous mode of reasoning. If 'quality culture' was justified in the name of efficiency and 'relevance', then embedding more weighty and expeditious management structures together with assigning new responsibilities to the individual university – responsibilities that extended to budgetary, personnel recruitment and careers as well as the management of buildings and property (Montlaur-Creux, 2007) – were presented and justified as the means to extend (some historians might argue to 'restore') the equally fundamental value of *institutional* autonomy to French higher education. Since autonomy, learning and scholarship are held to be interdependent – and desirable on that account – surely the Academic Estate had good cause to rejoice that the recognized principle of positional autonomy was now made to embrace institutional autonomy as well?

The Prince's cunning and academia's dilemma. By coupling reform with institutional autonomy, the Prince sought to make an offer none of his academic subjects could possibly refuse. Furthermore, if any of his university subjects were to be so ungrateful as to scorn his pleasure, they could be held up to public opprobrium for refusing to accept the very value and essential condition that was universally recognized and historically inseparable from the advancement of learning in their own house. After all, the advancement of learning, training and research was academia's prime public responsibility and charge. Within the logic that accompanied the launching of the 'new university', for the Academic and Student Estates to seek to impose their very own version of autonomy within the autonomy that the Prince proffered was not merely fractious, it was an evident nonsense.

Thus, rejection of details in the overall 'reform package' could be presented to the public as a refusal to acknowledge the essential principle – institutional autonomy – that the Prince claimed he sought to enact. By rejecting the promise of institutional autonomy, the Academic Estate would thus appear guilty of defending 'restrictive practices'. Worse still, it could be portrayed as battling to perpetuate its own particular interests and privileges. By refusing the offer that the Prince held out, both the Academic Estate and the Student Estate in France ran the very real risk of being seen to play fast and loose with the General Interest of the nation in order to better maintain their own particular established privileges. By their own action, both Estates would thus appear to actively undermine the very notion of public service they so ardently defended.

2) Change

One of the more fascinating features of policy negotiation in contemporary Europe is the recourse that policy makers have to historical constructs to legitimize programmes whose content represents a radical break from established practice by dressing them up in pleasing historical 'tinsel'. Major schemes for student mobility and transfrontier research collaboration are bundled together to invoke the glorious figures of the past – the Erasmus, Leonardo, Socrates and Marie Curie projects being much caressed. Thus, the masters of change manufacture their very own version of continuity by suggesting that what is involved is not radical so much as a belated recognition of earlier practice that is now presented as historically inevitable, of pressing actuality and grounded in unimpeachable precedent. Nothing innovative should ever be presented as taking place for the first time.

Though it is not admitted anywhere, presenting France's reform programme for the 'new university' as a bid to strengthen institutional autonomy could not easily disguise the radical nature of the measures envisaged. As the central academic ethic, institutional autonomy as opposed to positional autonomy had little place in either the Napoleonic university or its successors. Indeed, if one were to seek the last time such institutional independence figured in the French university system, one would have to go back to the *Ancien Régime* prior to 1789 (Weisz, 1983). The historian would have to admit that university autonomy *qua* institutional autonomy was effectively abolished – as was the university itself – by the Le Chapelier Law of 1791. The French Revolution put paid to guilds and corporations as well, on the grounds that they and the universities all represented institutions of inherited and unmerited privilege (Verger, 1986; Charle, 2004).

If institutional autonomy had little part to play in the French concept of higher education as a public service, it was precisely that concept of public service itself which determined the fundamental conditions of positional autonomy by according civil servant status to established and recognized members of the *'corps universitaire'* (Chevaillier, 2001). This essential difference in no small degree accounts for the ferocious resistance shown by the Academic Estate to the revision of the 'public policy ethic' that neoliberalism entailed.[4]

The place of academia in the polity

The formal and legal status of the individual academic as a 'servant of the state' (*fonctionnaire*) is often presented as the French counterpart to the Anglo-Saxon concept of 'tenure' (Neave and Rhoades, 1987). Whilst useful as a descriptive shorthand, the term 'tenure' is not a happy fit. It has the inconvenience of passing rather too lightly over the remaining features that the condition of being a 'servant of the state' carries with it. Yet, such features deserve rather more attention for two reasons. Without exploring the conditions that come with civil servant status, it is difficult in the extreme for non-French scholars to grasp precisely why the 'new university' reforms of August 2007 stoked up such fires of discontent and protest within the Academic and Student Estates. Changes that the 'Law bearing on organizing the new university' made to the formal status of the Academic Estate were an important pointer to the radical nature of the reform. They also provide a clear illustration of the fact that reinforcing the Evaluative State in France was truly a break from established conventions and recognized rights (*droits acquis*) that had been in place in French higher education for a very long time indeed.

7

Discord Dissected: The 'New University' and some of its Discontents

Introduction

When weighing up the impact of legislation, it is useful to distinguish between the immediate thrust of the legislator's intent on the one hand and on the other the significance of the measures enacted for those who see themselves 'having reform done to them'. Accordingly, this examination of the Law of 10 August 2007 and the ways in which the French model of the Evaluative State was re-shaped as a result will be split into two parts. The first part focuses on the formal provisions contained in this Law. The second part pays particular attention to the implications that arise for the future shape of higher education in France as perceived by two of the three Estates in higher education's Constituent Order – the Academic and Student Estates.

Part 1: Madame Pécresse's programme

The Law of 10 August 2007 incorporated certain generic features that also accompanied reform elsewhere in Western Europe. Amongst the more obvious was the strengthening of the power, authority and responsibility thrust upon the university president. The role of the president in French universities as expressed by the legislator had less to do with representing his or her peers so much as acting as a 'team leader' – *animateur d'équipe, porteur de projets* – qualities which, whilst broadening the basis of presidential legitimacy, possessed overtones more redolent of the 'Club Med' than of a university! As with Dutch legislation of 1997,[1] which also set out to modernize the universities through overhauling internal governance, so too in France ten years on. The formal responsibilities discharged by the university president moved rapidly beyond the largely honorary, ornamental and representational, which echoed the limits of presidential servitude and grandeur hedged around by 'collegial' or 'participant' democracy.[2]

In the 'new university', by contrast, the powers of the president were central, operational and situated at the intersection of both the academic and administrative chains of command (Montlaur-Creux, 2007). Though nowhere explicitly stated as such, it is evident that the Law on University Reform saw presidential power deriving largely from the responsibility that the president exercised as guardian and executive overseer of the university's strategy. The individual university's strategy was formally set out in the four-year *Contrat d'établissement*. As has been noted earlier, strategy was heavily anchored in the previously defined overall procedures, set down and exercised by AERES as the heart of the strengthened Evaluative State.

Re-peopling the corridors of power: Act Two

Increased presidential powers went hand in hand with very substantial changes in the composition and re-drawing of constituency boundaries within the individual university's structure of governance. This initiative may be seen as replicating at the institutional level the broad shift along the same dimensions that accompanied the setting up of AERES, although with one notable difference. Whilst AERES kept the numerical strength of its Governing Council almost constant, the corresponding body at the level of the individual university – the *Conseil d'Administration* – was reduced by Madame Pécresse's law from 60 to between 20 and 30. The reduction in overall membership went together with an equally marked rise in the number of 'external personalities' on the Council. Outside 'notables' now occupied between seven and eight places.

From a comparative perspective, these measures may be seen as French higher education policy falling in with patterns well established elsewhere. From this standpoint, it could be argued that Madame Pécresse simply translated into the French setting a policy model not far removed from the British reforms of 1992. The elevation of British polytechnics to 'new university' status also involved cutting the numbers of governing board members back heavily, as well as injecting a 'corporate' style of governance into the 'new universities' of the UK (Shattock, 2003).

Re-defining the ties between universities and their immediate economic and political environment together with a shift in balance between those constituencies that were formally recognized echoed initiatives in other systems of higher education. This has already been touched upon in the case of the Netherlands (de Boer, 2007; de Boer, Enders and Leisyte, 2009). The same process was equally evident in Norway (Stensaker, 2004) and, as we shall see later, also in Portugal (Amaral and Carvalho, 2008).

The place of external interests

However, in France, rather more telling was the way in which external interests effectively reinforced the scope of presidential influence, discretion and authority inside the institution. Extending presidential influence was particularly evident in the way that 'external personalities' were taken on to the Governing Council. Members representing the 'external interest', which, depending on the overall size of the Governing Council, might account for between 27 and 29 per cent of its total membership, were nominated by the president and subject to the approval of the Council. Mischievous though it might be to see 'outsiders' as the president's liegemen – or women – at the very least they were certainly beholden to presidential beneficence. A further clue to the 'presidentialization' of university governance ushered in by Madame Pécresse and her Law was evident in the changes to the make-up of the academic constituency.

The Law of August 2007 provided the academic constituency with 8–14 places on the Governing Council, which meant that representation of the Academic Estate enjoyed a somewhat fluctuating status. Again, depending on the overall size of the Governing Council, the Academic Estate commanded between 40 and 47 per cent of the votes. However, the academic interest was split. Only half of its members were drawn from full chair-holders.

Shifts in the presidential power base

Thus, the presidential power base shifted away from what Clark termed 'the academic oligarchy', senior chair-holders, '*mandarins*' or '*baroni*' (Clark, 1977 and 1983). Whether the role of kingmaker has now slipped into the hands of the president's nominees remains unclear, though it certainly merits further empirical scrutiny. That the French university president has the possibility of becoming literally a 'self-made man' is not the only change the law accomplished.

While less radical than similar reforms in Dutch or Danish universities, both of which elevated an external personality to the chairmanship of the Governing Board, French legislation nevertheless broke clearly with the long-standing practice of choosing university presidents from amongst full-time academic staff of the university where the vacancy occurred. The eligibility to be a candidate for the office of president was also modified. In the 'new French university' it was extended to part-time or associate academic staff and, no less significant, to those who may be 'invited' – though by whom remained subject to a certain creative silence – to consider the servitude and grandeur of presidential status. Thus, the terms of eligibility were no longer the exclusive right of the Academic Estate in the individual university where the mandate of the President had reached its term. Rather, an element of 'co-optation' was introduced into the process of 'identifying' presidential candidates. To this, further restrictions were placed on those eligible to vote in presidential elections. In place of the previous system of direct election, university presidents were to be chosen by an electoral college limited to members of the *Conseil d'Administration* who were themselves subject to election. Henceforth, presidents were appointed on the basis of a simple majority of the votes cast.

This was an improvement on previous practice. Under earlier legislation, in order for a presidential candidate to be duly elected, it was required that the number of votes cast by each constituency should reach or go beyond a formally stated minimum percentage (Montlaur-Creux, 2007). A failure to reach this threshold invalidated the election.

Concentrating executive power

Calling in the 'new world' of external interests to adjust the balance in the 'old world' of university governance was not the only aspect to be solidly modified by France's Law on the 'New University'. The composition of, and electoral procedures in, the *Conseil d'Administration* as the key decision-making body went hand in hand with an equally marked revision in the relationship between that body and the two other internal decision-making organs – respectively, the Academic Council (*Conseil scientifique*: CS) and the Council for Teaching and Internal Affairs (*Conseil d'Etablissement et de la Vie Universitaire*: CEVU). On the basis of the formal remit assigned to the latter two Councils, the application of managerialism to the 'new university' both concentrated executive responsibility and restricted it. Of the three main bodies of internal governance, the Governing Council (*Conseil d'Administration*) alone has the power to make decisions. Neither the Academic Council nor the Council for Teaching and Internal Affairs has this responsibility. Rather, they have to be content with submitting recommendations and proposals to the Governing Council to act on – or not. Significantly, only the president is a member of all three bodies, a further illustration as clear as ever one might wish of the 'presidentialization' of university governance in France as it is of the clear operational subordination of academia, teaching and internal affairs to the executive.

New operational and strategic responsibilities

In addition to parcelling up power and responsibility between the different internal governing bodies of the 'new' French university system, further operational tasks were laid upon the individual establishment. These involved shaping the university's disciplinary profile on the one hand and on the other endowing institutional leadership with the legal power for organizing teaching and research units (*Unités de Formation et de Recherche*) – the functional equivalent in the French university to the division into faculties or schools elsewhere. Decisions to create or close, to amalgamate or regroup teaching and research units were brought into the specific oversight of the Governing Council. They represented at one and the same time a key element in increasing the margin of manoeuvre the legislator sought to confer upon the individual university whilst strengthening both its capacity to adapt – and rapidly so – to changing external demands, be they national, regional or both.

Delegating these responsibilities imposed on the university leadership the *obligation* – as opposed to the gentle *encouragement* that marked earlier policies – to act decisively and boldly. Handing down such operational leverage was intended to give university leadership purchase over those functions that would be indispensable if it was to have a firm strategic decision-making capacity. Overhauling the operational responsibilities of the 'new university' had other purposes as well. The first was to deal with the notorious reticence of the Academic Estate to take the initiative, a reticence that had long bedevilled its behaviour at the institutional level.[3] The second was to complete the policy cycle that involved putting in place the new 'chain of command' that flowed from strengthening the Evaluative State and which, at the institutional level, was closely bound up with defining and negotiating the university's strategic plan (*contrat d'établissement*).

Embedding strategic capacity at the institutional level may appear perfectly natural and for that reason thoroughly uncontroversial to observers from university systems where political and academic cultures both subscribe to the separation of powers in the sphere of learning, as indeed it is for those systems that had long incorporated the principle of cultural autonomy at the regional level (Richter, 1992). In systems such as these, the fact that the university determined the conditions of employment and the conditions of teaching and research, as well as setting out the career tracks for technical and clerical appointments, is taken for granted, as is the fact that the individual university also exercises responsibility for academic recruitment, appointment and advancement. Responsibilities such as these are held to be nothing less than sure signs of the presence, strength and widely agreed characteristics that underline the reality of institutional autonomy that is present and recognized in a given system of higher education.

Part 2: the French Evaluative State – a contested vision

Viewed from this perspective which, if not avowedly Anglo-Saxon, is very certainly alien in France, the argument the Prince advanced on his own behalf – namely that he was engaged in bestowing a generous measure of institutional autonomy upon his university subjects – could not easily be denied. But denied it was, with loud cries, vehement slogans and much protesting by students and lecturers, professors and researchers, up and down the major thoroughfares of the nation's capital from the Place de la République to the Place de la Bastille and back again. However, such intemperance cannot be dismissed as simply another demonstration of Gallic hotheadedness and perversely persistent exceptionalism. On the contrary, it raises one question. Precisely why did both the Academic and Student Estates in France rise up against measures that elsewhere provided for the very conditions which ensured that their counterparts (in the UK and the USA, for example) possessed the self-same freedoms that students and academics in France sought furiously to cast aside?

Even those charitably disposed towards the 'new university' could not deny the short shrift given by legislation to the two basic principles that had governed French higher education since May 1968 – participant democracy and collegiality in the conduct of the internal affairs of the individual university. The 'presidentialization' of institutional governance, compared with previous provision, the degree of marginalization of the Academic Estate and very certainly the Student Estate from the executive sphere of decision making, could be interpreted as a form of *'cordon sanitaire et decisionnel'* designed to keep the Academic Council and the Council for Teaching and Internal Affairs away from decisions of an executive nature. Interpreted in such a way, these bold steps did not meet with cries of acclaim from either Estate. On the contrary, presidential power appeared so concentrated that, to some observers, it seemed to herald nothing less than the return of 'feudalism' to the groves of academia (Jourde, 2008).

Faulty rhetoric

Nor was the rhetoric employed by the Prince's servants received with much respect either. Supporters of the reform argued that strengthening presidential power was simply the means to introduce into French higher education that same form of governance on which the worldwide reputation and standing of the great American Research Universities had been built. It was an argument that owed more to convenience than to scholarly precision.

Powerful though the president of the American Research University undoubtedly is (Kerr and Gade, 1986), he or she has also to negotiate with two other centres of power, both of which are significant bodies. In the University of California system, for instance, these are the Board of Trustees, which wields considerable influence in shaping institutional strategy and overall priorities, and the Academic Senate, which holds similar sway over academic affairs (Kerr, 2003). As those familiar with American models of governance pointed out, arrangements in the French Law on University Reform of 2007 bore a connection that was at best tenuous with the original that it was claimed had inspired them (Berger, 2007). Powerful though the president might be in American Research Universities, presidential power was not gained at the price of abolishing the Senate, merging it with the Board of Trustees and partially gagging the remaining organs of governance (Neave, 2011b). Despite the government's claims to be following a tried, tested and successful example, Anglo-Saxon institutional autonomy remains very different in its organization and distribution of power and authority from the profile developed for French universities, despite the Prince's bluster that it was his dearest wish to have it installed in the universities of France.

Powers transferred: the anatomy of discontent

Riding roughshod over the principles of participant democracy and confiscating collegiality were not the only sources of grief. More important to the Academic Estate was the conviction that the price to be paid for institutional autonomy was too high by far. It was too high precisely because the Academic Estate believed it alone was being asked to bear the brunt of extended *institutional* autonomy by being forced to sacrifice those long-established conventions that in its eyes were the essence of *positional* autonomy.

How this situation came about may be taken as yet another illustration of French exceptionalism. In essence, the bone of contention related to the transfer of certain key and operational responsibilities, which the Law on the 'New University' moved from central government to the institutional level. These were the recruitment, appointment, promotion and career advancement of academic staff, the introduction of performance-related bonus payments over and above national pay scales, and the laying down and, where necessary, modification to the individual academic's conditions of employment. These were the prime instruments of leverage that allow leadership to engage in 'micro-steering', 'fine-tuning' and adjustment within the institution without which strategic management tends to remain a desolatingly nominal farce.

The French Academic Estate was not alone in facing what is all too often the literal 'cutting edge' of neoliberal policies in higher education. Their colleagues in the UK, for example, had seen the principle of tenure substantially modified by the Education Act of 1988. Performance-based budgeting and the principle of performance-driven payments had long been embedded in the landscape of British higher education. Their Dutch colleagues had seen the break-up of national pay scales and the transfer of salary negotiations down to the level of the individual university as much as a decade earlier (de Weert and van Vucht-Tijssen, 1999).

To argue that others had bowed before measures not dissimilar to those faced by the French Academic Estate may provide some consolation. However, they do not provide an explanation. Nor do they completely explain the face-off between the universities and the government, which ate up the best part of the 2008/2009 academic year, which assumed all the features of higher education's version of the Battle of Verdun, a bloody engagement of attrition in 1916 between two entrenched opponents. That the French Academic Estate sought to preserve the recognized rights (*droits acquis*) which it associated with positional autonomy shows clearly that if explanation is to be sought, it lies not in the destination so much as in the distance to be travelled to reach it.

What those who 'do reforms' often see as necessary instruments for 'micro-steering' a university are perceived very differently by those who 'have reforms done to them'. By that same token, the very same procedures, because they bear upon the Academic Estate, shape its identity, its self-perceived standing and, most assuredly in France, its place in the polity. Though there are a few characteristics that make the French Academic Estate comparable to the status of a 'profession', which is how it is defined in the Anglo-Saxon world (Perkin, 1969), this is far from being the complete picture (Neave and Rhoades, 1987; Chevaillier, 2001). As has been noted earlier, the legal status of French academics designated them as members of a collective body serving the interests of the nation, a responsibility that is inseparable from their formal status as civil servants.[4]

Exotic practices

Such a status was underlined by a number of practices and conventions that strike the outside observer as exotic indeed. The first of these, though arguably a pointer to it being a 'profession' rather than an Estate, was French academia's capacity to determine who its members shall be. Significantly, the Law of August 2007 left this untouched. Creating a 'pool' of what in British terminology would be called 'recognized teachers' – those qualified and eligible for appointment – remained a *national* responsibility, vested in the *Conseil National des Universités*. What changed – and also brought with it an uncomfortable shift in self-perception – was the practice of nomination into post by the central authority. For many decades, this task had been performed by the now-defunct *Conseil National de l'Enseignement Scientifique et de la Recherche* (CNESER) or its predecessors.[5] However, in the 'new universities', the power to recruit individuals was handed over to individual universities to strengthen institutional autonomy, which they did by designating formal responsibility and oversight for these tasks to the president (Montlaur-Creux, 2007).

Precisely why handing over this function to the university president should cause a '*levée en masse*' amongst the Academic Estate would be incomprehensible if account were not taken of the concrete as well as symbolic connotations that had accumulated around this procedure. Being assigned into post by central authority formed part of the obligations of those with civil servant status – that is, to be at the disposal of the Republic and to be assigned by central authority to where public need was greatest. Nor was the change involved in the symbolism of personal status as serving the nation, as opposed to being an employee of the university, easily swallowed, let alone shrugged off. Still less were the issues at stake simply confined to changes in the French Academic Estate's material condition. Arguments also turned on the place of the Academic Estate in the Republic.

The *de facto* unravelling of civil servant status and its replacement with the demoted status of 'employee' fuelled arguments that went well beyond the simple defence of academia's 'corporate' interests. Agreed, issues such as 'merit pay' could certainly be seen in such a light. The government and its supporters were not slow in counter-attacking along these lines. Furthermore, they argued that such innovations were crucial in stimulating an 'entrepreneurial attitude' within academia, just as the delegation of such powers would bring an end to the 'even tenor' of supposed bureaucratic indifference and procrastination.

The particular identity of French academia

As a *'corps de l'Etat'*,[6] the Academic Estate identified itself with reference to and – to boot – saw itself as a bulwark upholding key values that were central to the Republic. It was then not entirely surprising that resistance to the transfer of decisions involving recruitment, appointments, conditions of service and advancement drew heavily on two arguments. It infringed on the notion of formal procedural equality. It traded off public, standardized, national and recognized procedures and criteria in order to better replace legally established practice with arbitrary decisions taken by a limited number of individuals whose personal inclinations, bias or favouritism could never be excluded. In conclusion, *institutional* autonomy could advance only to the detriment of *positional* autonomy – a process all too evident in the fundamental change to academia's legal status in the 'new university': no longer the trusty servant of the Republic, but rather the hired hand of the university president.

Institutional autonomy, as the legislator set out in the Law on the New French University, was unacceptable to the Academic Estate. The new status it outlined appeared to those 'having reform done to them' as an enforced, sudden, accelerated and evident decline in the French equivalent of Donnish Dominion. Nor was this the only bone of contention. It was by no means clear whether the real purpose beneath institutional autonomy, as set out in the Law of August 2007, was not itself simply a means to concentrate presidential power – a concentration all too evident in other spheres of national life!

Envoi

The unfolding of the Evaluative State in France is central to our understanding on the one hand of the wider background against which it developed and on the other of the particular and specific circumstances it sought to shape in one system. France is important for two excellent reasons. It was the first country in Western Europe to set up a system-wide independent agency that regularly monitored the current condition and performance of higher education. Yet – something that this chapter has constantly sought to bear in mind – higher education in France is very different in structure, in status, in its relationship with the government and in the political theories which have both created and therefore serve to explain these differences. These social and political constructs act as points of reference to the dialogue between polity and university and are sometimes used to maintain and to perpetuate such differences. Still, as sociologists know full well, there is much to be learned from deviant cases – Asterix included!

Almost a quarter of a century has passed since France took the first step in establishing the Evaluative State. The intervening period has seen this construct assume an increasing centrality in higher education policy and with it a parallel increase in the leverage that evaluation provided to public policy in general. More than in other systems, higher education in France is inseparably and overtly part of the national political process. As this chapter has noted, French higher education is intimately bound into this process by a very particular interpretation of higher education as an integral element in public service. The French public service ethic is a central, widely held and very potent, not to say emotive, doctrine, which commands immense power for both physical and political mobilization. For this very reason, it may sometimes act as a popular veto over public policy.

Amongst the characteristics that set the French Evaluative State apart from others in Western Europe is, first, that it was in place well before the onset of neoliberalism. Indeed, even after that credo began to shape higher education policy elsewhere, the Evaluative State, reflecting the views of the French nation, remained largely impervious to neoliberalism's wiles. Second, at its outset, the French Evaluative State was conceived largely as a handmaiden to the polity and above all to the Academic Estate. Punitive it was not (Neave, 1996a); rather, its mission was to provide a 'positive leverage' for the policies in place.

The situation changed in 2000. The years following saw the Evaluative State regressing to a more regulatory and interventionary role. By doing so, it took on a very different mission, more akin to its counterparts elsewhere: namely, as an agency to monitor and through monitoring to identify shortcomings in the immediate functioning of universities. Evaluation became diagnostic with the explicit purpose of suggesting remedies, which could subsequently form the basis for national policy. With the foundation of AERES in 2006, evaluation ceased being a direct handmaiden to the university world. It was re-appropriated by central administration. It acquired the procedures, powers and trappings of an agency of public purpose. This re-definition of its mission brought about a marked shift in the nature of the leverage that evaluation could exert:

namely, the use of evaluation to 'steer' policy. This it could do as a result of a sustained and protracted strategy, which began in 2000 and was finally brought to completion in 2007 with the promulgation of the Law on University Reform. In essence, strategy focused on the inter-linking and coordination of three decision-making cycles – evaluative, negotiatory and electoral – to an *a posteriori* 'chain of command'.

The chain of command was bound firmly into the institutional level by dint of the enhanced executive powers laid upon the university pres-ident. Significantly, it has not as yet entirely replaced the more classic leverage that policies developed *a priori* may exert. The presence of both modes of operating brings considerable pressure to bear upon the indi-vidual institution to fall in with the requirements of the Prince and on the terms that the Prince has laid down, terms that are all the more telling for the fact that the Prince now has efficient ways of knowing whether his will has been obeyed – or not.

What insights can we derive from the specificities of the Evalua-tive State *à la française* that are applicable to the broader issue of the Evaluative State itself?

The first is quite clearly that whilst from a technical point of view the evaluation agencies may legally and structurally, if not always finan-cially, have the status of formal independence vis-à-vis ministries with oversight for higher education and whilst indeed the criteria and dimen-sions employed in evaluation are drawn up uninfluenced by similar technical demands emanating from the ministry, such agencies are not necessarily immune to the broader shifts within the polity in values or the priorities that flow from them. The demise of the *Comité National d'Evaluation* and the rise of AERES both point to this conclusion.

The second insight is no less important. If nothing else, the saga of the Evaluative State in France justifies the distinction between *positional* autonomy and *institutional* autonomy. It also reveals with unrivalled clarity that they are not necessarily always the two sides of the same institutional coin (Bleiklie and Kogan, 2007). Indeed, the visions enter-tained for one are not necessarily shared, or even recognized as being compatible, with the vision contained in the other, which apparently justified the natural extension of the latter.

Finally, there is the vexed issue of leadership. Is strong leadership always a guarantee of institutional autonomy, particularly if institu-tional autonomy is achieved at the price of amazing reductions in the latitude and self-determination enjoyed – or put up with – by those who believe their fate is decided by what happens in the domain of *positional* autonomy? This is a far from idle question. To the wary – and even more so to those sensitive to the recent history of the Republic's universities – the Pécresse Law appears to have achieved (and admirably so) one quite astonishing feat. Whilst the uproar of 1968 put paid to what was then commonly alluded to as the *université napoléonienne*, Madame Pécresse appears to have placed a Napoleon in every university!

8
Spain: Defining Autonomy, Setting Up Evaluation

Introduction

A particularly interesting variation on the relationship between the Evaluative State and the operationalization of autonomy is to be seen in Spain. The current thrust of reform in Spanish higher education shares certain generic features with France – modification to the internal distribution of decision making, revisions to procedures for electing the university president and re-defining the mandate and responsibilities of internal governing bodies. Whilst the dimensions involved are similar, the direction of change is not. In turn, such differences reflect, on the one hand, that in Spain the construction of the Evaluative State is still in hand. On the other, the differences also reflect that the unfolding of higher education policy in Spain follows a very different trajectory from its neighbour north of the Pyrenees.

There are good reasons for including Spain in this study. Whilst the unfolding of the Spanish model of the Evaluative State follows a very different rationale and chronology, such differences serve to draw our attention to the importance that historical, political and cultural differences play in formulating policy, even if that policy has broadly the same purpose. A further consideration is also useful to bear in mind. Both Spain and Portugal have to some degree a shared historical legacy. Both were imperial powers with a seaborne empire (Boxer, 1969). Both were the pioneers in 'exporting' their 'referential models' of both schools and universities beyond the Old World. This 'outreach' began as early as 1580 in the case of Spain (Alvarez and Alvarez, 1992: 151). Even so, higher education policy in both nations tends to command less attention amongst outsiders than do other systems in Western Europe.

Nominal similarities and essential differences

Unlike France, where the notion of 'participant democracy' permeated most attempts at overhauling the university from 1968 and which recent legislation, as indeed the government that passed it, sought clearly and explicitly to disavow, the ideological strength of the corresponding ethic south of the Pyrenees is very far from having run its course. On the contrary, it is a construct that is central both to the development of the Spanish version of the Evaluative State and to the internal re-arrangements in university governance. Both in its symbolism and in its operational consequences, the Spanish strain of 'participant democracy' was – and remains – more robust by far than its French equivalent. In France, participant democracy four decades ago was the price of restoring a fragile peace to the groves of academia. For that reason, it was quarantined in the university. In Spain, the same principle served as a marker point for the future political development of the nation as a whole. It was a very real break from a regime of extreme authoritarianism and was intended to be (Coombes and Perkins, 1989; ICED, 1989; Diez Hochleitner, 1990; Garcia-Garrido, 1992; Mora and Vidal, 2007). Because participant democracy served as the bedrock of a resurrected democratic Spain, its application was not limited to the university. Nor, for that matter, did the notion of 'autonomy' as an administrative principle find its unique expression in this institution.

The Constitution of 1978, which marked the return to a democratic order, provided for autonomous regions and nationalities as the first level of government. Reform of the university followed as a direct consequence of the wider recognition of this principle. Seen from this perspective, the 1983 Law on University Reform (*Ley de reforma universitária*: LRU) merely extended the principle of autonomy, already enunciated with respect to the regions of Spain, to the university, together with the other principle formally set down in the Constitution of 1978 and developed further in the LRU: namely, academic freedom.

While the LRU is commonly interpreted as having modernized Spain's universities and adjusted them to the pressures of social demand, it may also be interpreted as the first step in bringing the university world, which was hitherto grounded in a 'Napoleonic' model of central, national control, into alignment with the developing powers and responsibilities of the new Autonomous Communities (Coombes and Perkins, 1989; Garcia-Garrido, 1992).[1] Within the concept of participation, there were, however, two dimensions: participation *within* the institution through the recognition *inter alia* of the Student

Estate on internal governing committees; and participation *outside* the institution, namely the strengthening of the specific responsibilities of the Autonomous Communities for the institutions geographically located within them. In short, revisions by the LRU centred on the internal bodies of governance – a priority seen in the creation of a Social Council (*Consejo Social*). The *Consejo Social* was externally chaired and was composed largely of lay members (ICED, 1989). Participant democracy in Spain thus had two faces and turned round this dual rationale. The participation of external interests in the university world was strengthened as part of a broader national strategy of administrative decentralization. At the same time, the first steps towards forging a 'stakeholder' relationship between Autonomous Communities and universities were put in place (Neave, 2002).

The identifying and characteristic feature that differentiated Spain from France lay in the fact that in Spain strengthening both internal and external participation predated the construction of the Evaluative State. Indeed, it may be argued that the very particular form the latter assumed in Spain was largely a continuation and a further variation on the overall strategy of administrative devolution.

Conflicting autonomies

The LRU conferred upon Spain's universities a considerable degree of latitude in such areas as budgeting, internal organization, academic appointments and course and curriculum design, together with the possibility of entering into research partnerships with private enterprises. Institutional autonomy, however, was to be counterbalanced by reinforcing the second dimension in 'participatory democracy' – namely, by the presence in the *Consejo Social* of members drawn from both the internal academic community and representatives of local political and social bodies and interests (Sanchez-Ferrer, 1997). Thus, political autonomy conferred upon the Autonomous Communities existed in a state of tension with the newly reinforced institutional autonomy that the universities now enjoyed.

Less than half a decade after the promulgation of the 1983 LRU, evidence emerged that this particular arrangement between the two 'autonomies' had already deviated from the legislator's original intent (ICED, 1989). Far from acting as a meeting point between academia and the local community, even in regions where enthusiasm for local participation was strongest, the *Consejo Social* found itself marginalized and given a very different role by the academic community, a community made all the stronger by the fact that the professionalization of institutional administration had accelerated in the meantime. Rather than representing external interests taking their place in the groves of academia, the *Consejo Social* found itself assigned another role: that of representing university interests to the private sector and in particular that of fundraising for the university (ICED, 1989; Sanchez-Ferrer, 1997). If the truth were out, the effective degree of institutional autonomy, which the strategy of internal participation bestowed on Spain's universities, cancelled out the degree of political autonomy that the LRU of 1983 placed at the disposal of the Autonomous Communities.

Spanish-style autonomy

The tensions within the academic community, which had seen its powers of self-government strengthened by the 1983 LRU on the one hand and increased responsibilities assigned to the Autonomous Communities on the other, reflected the explicit ties between the central concept of 'autonomy' as an expression of Spain's new democratic order. In the Spanish setting, however, autonomy carried with it an interpretation that differed markedly from its usage elsewhere. Autonomy was not exclusive to the university, and, by the same token, the university was not seen as standing apart from the broader implications that followed from the indissoluble bond between autonomy and democracy.

It is important then to bear the particular nature of this 'Spanish exceptionalism' in mind. As a political principle, autonomy *à l'espagnole* represents a third interpretation of this concept. It rests on a basis that is very different from being either institutional or positional. Rather, the Spanish definition views autonomy as the fundamental right of a *community* – primarily defined in cultural, linguistic and historic terms – to govern its own affairs. Precisely because the community is defined in such terms, the right to set its own educational priorities is a quintessential expression of this specific interpretation. In contrast to the situation elsewhere – in France or, for that matter, in the Netherlands – autonomy was not primarily conceived in institutional terms, though its implementation and operationalization certainly had an impact upon the institutional dimension. On the contrary, autonomy as applied to the university was seen as an extension into higher education of that self-same organic right that was applied not to the institution so much as to the 'community' within it (Mora and Vidal, 2007).

In effect, the academic 'community' – both staff and students – stood as a projected counterpart inside the university of the spatial, historical and cultural community that existed outside. And, just as in the case of the regional community, the main assumption was that, given sufficient latitude, the academic community would itself develop new initiatives for serving and servicing the larger external community. The assumption that underpinned autonomy as it applied both to regional communities and its extension into universities was that the two forms of autonomy would complement each other. Autonomy would allow the region and the university to work together in forging a new relationship between the university and society that fully took into account the interests of each. Hopes, however, are one thing; the way in which different interests interpret them is another (Mora and Vidal, 2007).

Re-distributing power and authority in decision making

Attempts to break through the deadlock between autonomy as interpreted by the academic community and the construction placed upon it by the regional communities, which also wielded major responsibility for funding Spain's system of higher education, were evident in the University Reform Law (*Ley Organica Universitaria*: LOU) of 21 December 2001. Whether the LOU was a withdrawal from oversanguine expectations or a retreat to conservatism is a matter of opinion. However, it remained abundantly clear that central government intervened strongly to re-shape the balance of power within the 'academic community'. It added three 'external personalities' to the university governing board (Mora and Vidal, 2007) and also conferred additional weight on senior members of the Academic Estate. Henceforth, only those having tenure and doctorates could hold key decision-making posts at the faculty level or at the school level. Both at the faculty and the institutional levels, all decisions on which voting was required, required full professors to be in the majority (LOU, 2001: paras 16.3 and 18.2). Electing the university rector also underwent revision in the same direction, with a corresponding reduction in the weight accorded to the Student Estate together with a new flexibility in the electoral process itself. The possibility of the direct election of the rector was introduced as an alternative to the indirect, collegial election via the Senate (*Claustro*) (LOU, 2001: para 20.3).

Re-distributing the cards in internal governance was not, however, the major thrust of reform, although as a side point, it is worthwhile noting that the move to reinforce the power of senior academics echoed similar measures undertaken some 25 years earlier in France and Germany towards the end of the 1970s. Important though it was, the shift in the balance between the Student Estate and Academic Estate, and within the Academic Estate towards seniority was far less significant than the enhanced status and responsibility placed upon the rectors of Spain's universities as 'national actors'. Here too it is possible to observe a certain parallelism with recent French initiatives inasmuch as both the Pécresse Law and the Spanish *Ley Organica Universitaria* of 12 April 2007 reinforced the key role played by institutional leaders in their function as shapers and shakers. However, the difference lay in re-defining their institutional responsibilities in France as opposed to enhancing the part they were called upon to play in shaping the national strategy in Spain.

Re-thinking national coordination

Just as the 2001 LOU modified the principle of organic autonomy, so it is equally possible to see the creation of a University Coordination Council as the highest instance within the university system for coordination and consultation (LOU, 2001: Article 28) as voicing 'second thoughts' about the appropriateness of a reinforced regional layer as the most suitable format for nation-wide coordination. The University Coordination Council drew on a national remit. It was to consult on university policy, coordination and programming advice and was to comment on proposals laid before it (LOU, Article 28). In effect, the take-up of the opportunities presented by the 1983 LRU by the 17 Autonomous Communities was spotty at best. Some, amongst them Catalonia and the Basque Country, took full advantage of the opportunities created by the legislation. Others did not.

The University Coordination Council, brought into being by the LOU of 2001, sought to alleviate the tensions between political and academic autonomy by separating one from the other. It strengthened coordination by creating a national arena for debate, discussion and development amongst the main 'social partners'.

Such an attempt to satisfy both cabbages and kings focused on the University Coordination Council acting as an over-arching national body, divided between a General Assembly on University Policy (*Conferencia General de Polítca Universitaria*) – the *political* arm, chaired by the Minister of Education, Culture and Sport – and a University Council. Membership of the former was composed of those in charge of university teaching on the Governing Councils of the Autonomous Communities. In parallel, and within the same organizational framework, legislation provided for a University Council (*Consejo de Universidades*).

The University Council was made up of the Minister acting in consultation with the rectors of Spain's universities; in effect, the *academic* arm. The University Council ensured that proposals for study programmes were within the boundaries set by the government. In addition, it had a general advisory capacity on all matters relating to higher education and the duty to submit proposals on university policy both to the government and to the General Conference. The latter exercised *political* responsibility and oversight for higher education policy generally in terms of annual and multi-annual planning for human, financial and equipment resources at the system level.

Such an arrangement underwent further modification with the 2007 *Ley Organica de Educación* (LOE). If anything, the legislator placed further emphasis on the basic bicephalous structure – political/administrative versus academic – already evident in its predecessor of 2001. The LOE abolished the University Coordination Council, but retained both the General Assembly for University Policy and the University Council as two distinct bodies.

Re-discovering the bicephalous relationship

Viewed comparatively, Spain's re-invention of what bears a remarkable similarity to the classic 'dual hierarchy' in the relationship between the government and universities is of more than just passing interest.[2] This development becomes even more interesting when one considers that the prime responsibilities allotted to each of these two bodies would seem at first sight to involve 'policy formation' by *input* measures, whereas the main thrust of policy elsewhere in Western Europe lies in shaping policy by *output* measures and by institutional performance. It is equally clear that the strengthening of what elsewhere falls under the heading of institutional autonomy is, in Spain, largely an incremental process, conducted within a very different justificatory setting, itself couched largely within, and with reference to, the canons of participant democracy.

Institutional autonomy is presented less as a uniform goal *per se* than as the outcome of successive measures, on the one hand, to build up and operationalize the interplay between universities and the Autonomous Communities and, on the other, to transfer very real operational responsibilities previously vested in central government to the institutional level. One instance of this manner of proceeding is to be seen in the 2007 LOE: the disbanding of what were, in essence, national curricular templates (*catalogo de títulos*) with the purpose of 'freeing up' and encouraging the individual universities to develop study programmes without interference from the central state.

The rise of the Evaluative State in Spain

Nor is the difference in the 'justificatory context' limited to the operational relationship between the universities, the Autonomous Communities and central government. On the contrary, this justificatory context shaped the rise of the Spanish version of the Evaluative State as well. In effect, the 'justificatory context' laid a very different purpose on this construct. It also inverted the dynamic between the Evaluative State and institutional autonomy. In Spain, constructing the Evaluative State *followed on* from the prior definition of autonomy rather than serving as an instrument for laying out the conditions under which institutional autonomy subsequently emerged, as had been the case in France and the Netherlands.

As early as 1995, a National Programme for the Assessment of Quality in Universities had been established within the general framework laid out by the 1983 LRU (Mora and Vidal, 2007). The Programme differed from corresponding moves elsewhere in two respects. Initially, the Spanish model of quality assessment did not involve a single specific 'agency of public purpose' as, for instance, had been the case in France and the Netherlands; rather, quality assessment figured as an 'add-on', assigned to the Council of Universities, a configuration that was not very different from arrangements in Sweden (Neave, 2004b). In addition, certain Autonomous Communities also set up their own evaluation agencies (de Miguel Diaz, 1999; Mora and Vidal, 2007). Thus, the moves towards the Evaluative State in Spain faithfully reflected the basic dualism that characterizes Spanish higher education policy, split between two levels – national and regional.

The same legislative thrust that in 2001 created the University Coordination Council as a series of parallel commissions was also instrumental in setting up the National Agency for Quality Assessment and Accreditation (*Agencia Nacional de Evaluación de la Calidad y Accreditación*: ANECA) initially with foundation status. Though clearly dedicated to raising quality and consolidating excellence, the upgrading of quality assessment from programme status to foundation status was not driven by domestic considerations alone. This was because, whilst no less engaged in assessing excellence, the Foundation for Evaluation and Quality was justified by a very different rhetoric: namely, the need rapidly to bring the structures and duration of degree programmes at both the undergraduate and graduate levels into line with the templates set out in the Bologna Process (Mora and Vidal, 2007; ANECA, 2007) as part of Spain's integration into the European Higher Education Area (EHEA) (ANECA, 2008).

Subsequent legislation saw the strategic importance of Spain's nascent Evaluative State strengthened even further, both in its technical capacity of quality assessment and accreditation and in its broader role of enhancing institutional accountability on the one hand and shaping the boundaries of latitude for institutional initiative on the other. Thus, under the terms of the LOE 2007, the looming outline of the Evaluative State took on a new precision. Quality and assessment were once again upgraded in terms of priority. ANECA, for its part, was re-positioned as a fully-fledged and self-standing national agency constructed around a five-year evaluative cycle. Evaluation and accreditation for courses under development at the institutional level were made compulsory.

Additional powers

However, ANECA's remit went well beyond the usual limits associated with course recognition and programme validation. It also extended to areas which in other systems fell under the rubric of the conditions of employment for academic staff. Staff accreditation is, in itself, a powerful instrument not merely in shaping the Academic Estate through determining who is qualified to embark on an academic career; it also occupies a central place in drawing up a national 'pool' of 'recognized teachers' from which the individual university may pick and choose in relation to its particular vacancies.

Whilst unusual when viewed from outside Spain, a 'national list of recognized teachers' was not, as has been pointed out, unknown. Indeed, it found its exact counterpart in France and for this reason could be seen as one of the last vestiges of Spain's version of the Napoleonic university. Whilst the function of identifying a 'national list of recognized teachers', known in France as the *'liste d'aptitude'*, replicated a long-established French practice, in Spain it involved a slightly different procedure, which related to a complex and demanding series of public, national competitions (*oposiciónes*). In their original form, the Spanish *oposiciónes* were competitions for nomination to a particular post, itself a task that had previously been carried out by the national administration (McNair, 1984). In France, as has been noted, inclusion on the *liste d'aptitude* was a prior condition to appointment to a particular post, which took place as a subsequent and separate act.[3] Furthermore, as mentioned in Chapter 7, France, unlike Spain, did not hand over the procedures associated with drawing up the *liste d'aptitude* to the tender mercies of AERES; it remained in the hands of the National Council for Higher Education and Research (CNESER).

By making staff accreditation part of ANECA's responsibility, rather than, as had previously been the case, the responsibility of the Ministry of Education, a number of highly significant changes were introduced. Recognition of suitability for senior professorial appointments was transferred to a national process of peer review, thus replacing the public disputation, which was held to be both opaque and inefficient (Mora, 1997).[4] More important was the *de facto* dissociation of senior academic staff from their traditional status as servants of the state brought about by the fact that academic and staff appointments would henceforth come under civil law, as opposed to administrative law (section 48.1 of the LOE). This was a step fraught with significance for the historical status of academic employment. It meant that academics ceased being public servants and instead became private employees.

Staff accreditation was heralded as a substantial move in improving the individual university's ability to select its staff – a task previously undertaken by central government – and as such as a major element in enhancing institutional self-determination.

Nevertheless, the fact that ANECA is in charge of what amounts to a national evaluation system of the individual 'fitness for purpose' as well as the subsequent performance of individual members of academic staff in Spain stands as a further characteristic that marks out the Spanish version of the Evaluative State from its counterparts elsewhere. Based on a six-year cycle, individual evaluation using this mechanism is indispensable not only for the individual's promotion in the academic ladder, it is also a *conditio sine qua non* for being recognized as qualified to undertake research and to submit research projects to national agencies. The difference does not lie in the fact that individual performance is evaluated; rather, it lies in the fact that it is undertaken by the same agency that accredits institutions.

The Evaluative State: an exercise in prudence and caution

A number of points follow from the way in which the Evaluative State has emerged in Spain. The first is the incremental nature of the exercise. It was spread out over some 12 years, passing through three distinct phases: from programme to foundation and from foundation to national agency. Seen from this perspective, the drive towards focusing the Evaluative State around a single 'agency of public purpose' in Spain appears both hesitant and certainly cautious. At the present time, however, it remains unclear how far such prudence was dictated by the functional dualism present in ANECA's mandate – on the one hand, to cooperate with its regional counterparts already active in some of the Autonomous Communities whilst, on the other, filling the void for those communities that had not set up regional accreditation agencies.

There would appear to be an element of potential 'mission ambiguity' implicit in what appears to be a central responsibility for overseeing those regions without their own agencies and the devolved responsibility of coordinating with those that did possess their own agencies. In turn, the situation poses, though in a different domain, the same basic issue of 'complementarity' that was present earlier and that bedevilled the issue of 'political' versus 'academic' autonomy between regions and universities. Potentially, this remains a matter of major importance.

The issue of 'complementarity', as was noted earlier,[5] is built into any system of higher education where the main burden of policy seeks to strengthen the 'regional' or 'intermediary' layer between the national central administration and the institutional level. It becomes particularly pressing when, as ANECA made plain in a recent mission statement, it envisages its future role as the major source of information for monitoring the current condition of higher education to provide benchmarks for decision making at regional and national levels and to serve as the main intermediary between agency networks operating at regional, national and international levels (ANECA, 2008).

Conclusion

What conclusion – an interim one to be sure – may we draw from the Spanish experience in strengthening autonomy on the one hand and in constructing the first stage of the Evaluative State on the other? Clearly, the 'autonomy of communities' provided an over-arching vision, the operationalization of which had direct consequences for both institutional and positional autonomy. As a principle that is fundamental to democracy in Spain, autonomy has been subject to sustained definition and adjustment, with the intention both of giving reality to the particular political order Spain has opted for and, within the more limited confines of higher education, creating a closer and more appropriate 'go between' for higher education, society and newly defined stakeholders.

Defining the 'autonomy of communities' has altered the legal status of academic staff and research personnel. As elsewhere, it has placed greater weight upon leadership and management both in the individual institution and on the national landscape. The concentration of Spanish higher education policy upon shaping the 'autonomy of communities' in turn shaped the initial outline of the Evaluative State, a radically different causal direction. Indeed, it appears to reverse the dynamic visible elsewhere in Western Europe.

The working relationship underpinned by the Evaluative State in Spain is determined by the operational consequences that follow from defining the 'autonomy of communities', not, as was the case for instance in France and the Netherlands, *a contrario*. From this it follows that the current stage of development of the Evaluative State in Spain would appear to still be in a state of transition when set against the situation in France or, for that matter, the Netherlands. Such a transition is if anything more delicate given the presence of two spheres or levels of authority engaged in the shaping of a federal system of higher education. Though the move away from the unitary state cannot be denied, key functions still remain vested in the federal authority. Research policy and funding is one such function. Student grants and scholarships are another. For their part, individual Autonomous Communities fund higher education just as they also exercise oversight for the setting up of new study programmes.

This dual level of responsibility is reflected in the relative complexity of the organizational model on which the Spanish version of the Evaluative State rests. At the federal level, strategic responsibility has been conferred upon ANECA. It is clear from the agency's own statement of its role and future ambitions that the part it will come to play will involve it in providing all constituencies – academia and administration, students and leadership as well as external stakeholders, both regional and national – with an evidence-based and up-to-the-minute portrait of higher education's achievement and performance across the historical or cultural nations that make up Spain.

What remains rather less clear is how far the duality of ANECA's role, balanced between cooperating with those Autonomous Communities that already have their own evaluation agencies and shaping the criteria to evaluate those Communities that lack such agencies, will settle down to assume a viable and stable function in the medium term. Given the enduring tensions between the principles of 'complementarity' and 'competition' that appear ever-present between the national, regional and institutional decision-making levels in Spain, this tension is unlikely to be resolved simply by putting in place the makings of the Evaluative State. A more likely – though highly undesirable – scenario may well see these forces of potential conflict injected into the workings of the Evaluative State itself.

Part III

Portugal: A Focused Account

9
Portugal: Laying out the Higher Education Landscape

Introduction

The return to democracy through revolution or through the delinquent behaviour of an Ancien Regime have been central in opening up the EU to the countries of East and Central Europe just as the collapse of the Berlin Wall also marked the bicentenary of the French Revolution of 1789. Yet this pattern of dramatic change was first ushered in a quarter of a century earlier, with the Portuguese Carnation Revolution in 1974 (*la Révolution des Oeillets*), although today Portugal's place as the first to act in this way is sometimes overlooked.

However, the Carnation Revolution was no less important in re-shaping the mission and purpose of Portugal's higher education system (Neave and Amaral, 2011, pp. 3–42). Thus, 15 years prior to the demolition of the Berlin Wall, the forcible closing down of an authoritarian order in Portugal generated a broadly similar response as it was later to do in the one-time Marcher lands of the now defunct Soviet Empire. It unleashed social demand for higher education and speeded up structural change, which had already been contemplated in the case of the polytechnic sector. In short, the nation embarked resolutely on a path towards massification that was to be amongst the most spectacular in Western Europe. With a gross participation rate of some 7 per cent of the 18–24 age group attending higher education in the mid-1970s, 24 years later, the corresponding statistic for 2000 hovered around 50 per cent (Amaral and Magalhães, 2007: 20). Nor is such spectacular growth the sole feature in differentiating Portugal from many of its fellow EU Member States in Western Europe. For while the major systems of higher education in Western Europe went through two distinct phases in the drive towards massification – the earlier phase taking place during the

1960s and early 1970s, and the later phase during the 1980s and early 1990s – Portugal's drive towards massification was confined to one large, single detonation that echoed and rolled across the 1980s and 1990s.

Putting the forces in place: the Constitution of 1976

From the outset, the issue of institutional autonomy found its place in the Constitution of 1976 as part of the new and radical mission that the newly retrieved democracy assigned to higher education. Under Article 76 of the Constitution, universities and other higher education were given the explicit task of guaranteeing equal opportunities for all and, no less ambitious, the democratization of the education system (Amaral and Carvalho, 2008). The same article laid down two main conditions for the universities of Portugal in fulfilling this mission. Universities were to be autonomous in drawing up their internal regulations and they were to enjoy 'scientific, educational, administrative and financial autonomy' within the framework of the law and in keeping with whatever system of quality assessment might be devised.

These were radical conditions indeed. They reflected the spirit of the moment and more particularly the influence that the Portuguese Communist Party wielded in drawing up the Constitution. However, their significance lies less in their source of political inspiration than in the fact that they reflected a situation of intent rather than serving as a statement of the current condition of higher education. Article 76 may thus be interpreted as a monument to future purpose, a mission to be realized without prejudice to the nation's capacity to execute it immediately. Indeed, as Amaral and Carvalho have pointed out, more than a dozen years were to elapse before enabling legislation was passed in the shape of the Act of 1988 on university autonomy and its counterpart dealing with the status and autonomy of polytechnic higher education institutions, which was promulgated in 1990 (Amaral and Carvalho, 2008).

The unbearable wisdom of hindsight

Working with the wisdom that hindsight always confers, the lapse of some 12 years between the statement of intent, principle and vision on the one hand and the capacity to implement the policy that gives such vision operational teeth on the other appears as an inbuilt feature of higher education policy in Portugal from the start. More to the point, the dissonance between intent and capacity was to coalesce into a central and structural feature in the interplay between the government, central administration and the nation's system of higher education. As the military dictum has it, intention does not imply the capacity to act any more than the capacity to act implies the will to do so.

Still, the statement of intent contained in Article 76 deserves closer scrutiny, both on its own account and also because the insight it affords is central to setting the overall context in which 'policy style' (Premfors, 1981) has evolved in Portugal and very specifically so in the two domains of institutional autonomy and the rise of the Evaluative State.

Three remarkable features of the 1976 Constitution

The first feature of Article 76 that strikes an attentive observer is the role conferred on universities as agencies of democratization, an interesting homage to the central thesis of the day, much bruited abroad in the 1990s by student radicals from Amsterdam to Berlin and from Paris to Stockholm; a priority that stood in contrast to the more official and consensual line of policy upheld by governments which, from the mid-1960s onwards, placed this key responsibility upon upper secondary education (OECD, 1969).

The second feature involved a fundamentally new interpretation of the concept of legal homogeneity. As with most systems of higher education in Europe, legal homogeneity has played – and continues to play today – a major part in legislative change in Portugal. Since this issue has been extensively developed earlier in this analysis, we will not encourage tedium by repeating it here.[1] Article 76 introduced a significant revision to legal homogeneity, one that the current state of scholarship in this field suggests has unfolded only in Portugal. For whereas in its usual construct, legal homogeneity – as its name implies – imposed the same conditions on all institutions within a specific sector of the higher education system (Neave and van Vught, 1994a; Neave, 2007; Teichler, 2007; Neave, 2009a), Article 76 drew an interesting distinction between, on the one hand, operational regulations that were institutionally defined and drawn up and, on the other, the general legal framework into which they fitted.

This is of more than passing interest. It shows clearly that in the minds of the fathers of the Constitution of 1976, legal homogeneity had two distinct elements. Together, they provided the formal legal framework – others have sometimes alluded to 'frame factors' (Dahllöf, Lofgren and Willén, 1979) – that apply uniformly across the appropriate sector. Second, within the formal national legal framework, there was to be a degree of discretion – or institutional latitude – conferred upon the individual establishment to draw up its own internal regulations that adapted and applied the essential characteristics of national legislation to the particular circumstances prevailing in the individual university. Such a construct is important for two reasons: first, it imparts a further refinement to the notion of legal homogeneity; and, second, it confers upon legal homogeneity as a *modus legislandi* a degree of adaptability that in turn suggests that legal homogeneity as a policy instrument can be reconciled with some degree of institutional autonomy or self-determination, in contrast with the original edition of such a construct, which tended on balance to sacrifice institutional discretion to sectoral uniformity. This particular interpretation of legal homogeneity was to prove singularly important in shaping the relationship between the universities and the government in Portugal, and was to play an essential part in shaping the systemic development of Portuguese higher education.

The third feature to emerge from a close reading of Article 76 is the juxtaposition and implicit conditionality between the various operational dimensions to which autonomy may be applied – scientific, educational, administrative and financial – and 'the appropriate assessment of the quality of education' (para 2 of Article 76). If we consider that the issues of quality and assessment were to become the identifying activities of the Evaluative State (Neave and van Vught, 1994b) and that the concept of the Evaluative State itself did not emerge as an analytical perspective until the late 1980s (Neave, 1988), the association of these two issues so early on is a remarkable example of foresight and anticipation, if not that rarest of all qualities in human endeavour, divination!

A Portuguese exception? The interplay between institutional autonomy and the Evaluative State

The juxtaposition of two issues that were to be central and strategic elements in shaping Portuguese higher education over the 20 years from 1988 onwards, however fortuitous, nevertheless sets Portugal apart from other systems which, *grosso modo*, were embroiled in broadly similar undertakings. Whether the way in which the government and the universities of Portugal went about adjusting to frenzied social demand on the home front, to European integration, to globalization or to the siren song of the knowledge economy should be seen as an example of 'national exceptionalism' remains, for the moment at least, a moot point.

Even so, what remains clear is that the interplay between institutional autonomy and the Evaluative State in the Portuguese context is markedly different in terms of timing, phasing and the dynamic interplay that these two issues assumed elsewhere in Western Europe. In France, defining institutional autonomy was a final *mise-en-scène*, following on from the testing, running and expansion of the Evaluative State. In Spain, the dynamic that emerges is very different. The Spanish Evaluative State put its head above the parapet only after the issue of institutional autonomy achieved a *modus vivendi* with the basic political order within Spain, based as it is on a more extensive notion of autonomy, namely the autonomy of communities.[2] In Portugal, by contrast, the two tasks of reconstructing higher education are pursued simultaneously. The one interacts with the other. Indeed, it is not an exaggeration to suggest that shaping institutional autonomy and the launching of the Evaluative State are interwoven points. Initiatives in one area spark off moves in the other. Of course, such an interactive and dynamic shaping of higher education policy begs an explanation. Why? How?

Government, administration and universities

A number of clues are to be found in Amaral and Carvalho's succinct analysis of the background and general context surrounding the drive towards institutional autonomy. Others are to be found in a recent OECD review of tertiary education in Portugal, which dates from 2007. The former concentrated on the technical capacity of the national administration to develop additional skills associated with running an increasingly complex system of higher education, among others monitoring its current status and its ability to deal with the sheer volume of work that expansion and reform both generated. Amaral and Carvalho point out that such capacities were vital, especially at a time of rapid growth in the higher education system and most certainly given the increasing complexity that inevitably followed in the wake of rapid sectorialization along binary lines and with the burgeoning of a private sector across both universities and polytechnics (Amaral and Carvalho, 2008).

Amaral and Carvalho suggested that the root cause of the incapacity to develop an adequate system of oversight lay in the limited technical skills of permanent civil servants and, more to the point, the apparent inability of the ministry to deal in a timely way with new demands flooding in from an increasingly complex system. Though Amaral and Carvalho did not use this exact terminology, it is clear nevertheless that for them the root cause lay in the inability of central administration to 'think outside the box' of legal homogeneity.

For its part, the OECD focused not on the shortcomings of the central administration so much as on the general capacity for shaping Portugal's higher education system. Delicate as always, the OECD placed the weight of its diagnosis on measures, not on men – or women. It noted the haphazard expansion of higher education, and the absence of clear priorities. It identified six 'problem areas' that required rapid action. These were as follows:

1) System steering and management.
2) System growth and the need to stimulate long-term demand in line with 'market forces'.
3) Coordination and rationalization at the system level.
4) The binary divide and more particularly how to achieve an appropriate diversity.
5) The place of the private sector.
6) The instrumentality of steering, funding contracts, accreditation procedures and formula-based funding (OECD, 2007: Chapter 7, paras 7.9, 7.11–7.29).

The 'snapshot' versus the long term

As is customary with OECD reviews, the diagnosis was tied closely to the condition of Portuguese higher education at the time the report was written. It fitted into a specific moment. Its recommendations for strengthening *institutional* leadership reflected in part its own special *Weltanschauung* of neoliberalism and 'New Public Management' (Amaral and Neave, 2009). In part, because that is the agreement between the host country and visitors, the review also took into account the current views of the government and the national administration. As will be shown later, this latter consideration was not without consequence for the recommendations that the review came up with.

'Snapshot' reports, even if of a 'one-off' nature, nevertheless contain (though they do not necessarily identify them as such) issues whose causes very often continue to endure and have long been a sore trial to those having to deal with them. After all, issues that emerge in the short term do not always require outsiders to address them or to come up with a remedy. That is the business of the national authorities. However, those issues that do require remedy tend to be precisely those that have remained unsolved over the years. Once we bear this apparent paradox in mind, a very good case can be made for seeing the six points that the OECD report regarded as being in need of pressing reform not simply in terms of a one-off diagnosis but as an account that also highlighted in part the long-term, enduring and generic shortcomings of higher education policy in Portugal. Nevertheless, the OECD examination did not deal with what is best represented as the historic dynamic or the way in which the issues it identified shaped the higher education system over time. In all fairness, this perspective was not part of its remit. However, if we are to grasp the factors that shaped institutional autonomy and the Evaluative State in Portugal, such an approach is not negotiable.

10
The Dynamic in Portugal's Higher Education Policy

Introduction

One way to bring home the dynamic in the unfolding of autonomy on the one hand and the shaping of the Evaluative State on the other is to do so in terms of the predominant issues that preceded them and the policy themes that debate between universities and the polity threw up. Such an approach serves a number of uses. It sets the broader backdrop against which autonomy and the Evaluative State may be set. It also provides an introductory tableau for their subsequent and more detailed dissection. Seen from this admittedly historical perspective, these two focal issues arguably fall neatly into three chronological phases, each of which may be characterized by a dominant theme. These phases are as follows:

1) 1980–93: balancing complexity and instability.
2) 1994–2002: intention versus capacity.
3) 2003–8: institutional autonomy or managerial freedom?

1980–93: balancing complexity and instability

The Portuguese University Autonomy Act of 1988 was a many-splendoured thing. As others have noted, together with the Polytechnical Higher Education Act passed two years later, it injected 'a considerable degree' of autonomy into Portuguese higher education, principally in the areas of finance, administration and responsibility for the upkeep and maintenance of university buildings (Amaral and Carvalho, 2008). For the universities, the 1988 Act also endowed them with 'pedagogical autonomy' – that is, the right to develop and run new study programmes without requiring final clearance from the ministry. By conferring 'pedagogical autonomy' on the university, the Portuguese quest for institutional autonomy began where its Spanish counterpart ended.

However, what may be seen as giving final expression to the intentions contained in the Constitution of 1976 had, over the intervening years, assumed a very different context and significance. In the first place, if both acts are viewed together as an example of system change by legislative means, it is instantly clear that they underpinned a strategy of 'sectoral differentiation'. Both polytechnics and private sector institutions remained firmly under the oversight of the ministry for the formal validation of their courses. If, in the first phase of extending institutional autonomy, all higher education institutions received a greater degree of latitude and responsibility, some – and the universities in particular, like the characters in George Orwell's *Animal Farm* – were more autonomous than others! In the second place and following the same line of reasoning, the fundamental instrumentality of system coordination through legal homogeneity was substantially modified in respect of the universities.

The anatomy of system instability

Why the universities were granted this particular treatment was not simply the government's belated recognition that it was finally in a position to apply one of the principles outlined in the Constitution of 1976. Other considerations were also present. Prime amongst them were growing difficulties associated with that basic issue posed by switching the prime driving force in higher education from social demand to 'market forces', and especially so given that this transformation coincided with both financial stringency and with spiralling levels of student demand (Amaral and Magalhães, 2008).

For obvious reasons, this conjuncture, which was delicate in itself, caused growing dismay amongst a powerful group of long-serving university rectors. However, their disquiet was not confined to student numbers or solely to institutional budgets. It went further, taking on a more strategic perspective and particularly an unease with the seeming incapacity of central administration to ensure system cohesion in policy making, an incapacity compounded on the one hand by the rapid succession of ministers responsible for higher education and on the other by the practice of re-defining 'delegated responsibilities' that were the prerogative of each incoming minister (Amaral and Carvalho, 2008).

Delegated responsibilities

'Delegated responsibilities' are a uniquely Portuguese institution. Each incoming minister has the task of assigning to different posts and administrative divisions in his or her ministry the various functions that correspond to the political priorities for which he or she is responsible. However, these are not confined to the inner workings of the ministry or to setting the administrative agenda of individual directors or divisions within the ministry according to the minister's interpretation of his or her mandate. Delegated responsibility also sees some of these functions, largely those of a technical nature – for example, drawing up work contracts for ministerial approval or drafting the text of legal enactments – delegated to 'experts' within the universities.[1]

Ministerial instability had direct consequences for this 'outsourced' part of the administrative agenda and especially so since there was no guarantee that the administrative priorities and distribution of tasks set by one minister would be continued in exactly the same way by his or her successor (Amaral and Carvalho, 2008). Put succinctly and seen from the standpoint of the universities, ministerial instability was not compensated by administrative continuity (Soulier, 1939). On the contrary, it amplified both administrative discontinuities on the one hand and thus fuelled system inefficiency on the other.

Reinterpreting the 1988 University Autonomy Act

Against this backdrop, the 1988 University Autonomy Act takes on a very different light. For, whilst the satisfaction of rectors is readily understandable given that the Act extended the boundaries of institutional latitude and discretion – which are significant in themselves – its importance lay in a very different domain indeed. In effect, system coordination by legal homogeneity, particularly when student demand and budgetary compression went hand in hand, has direct – and often dire – consequences for higher education's capacity to adapt rapidly and efficiently to the new situation.

System adaptation was largely determined by the capacity of central administration to act expeditiously, an expedition in turn determined by the formal requirement for legislative enactment that conferred authority on universities to act and to implement measures. In truth, a system grounded in the principle of legal homogeneity tends to follow the rule well known to convoy captains: a convoy moves at the speed of its slowest ship – or in this case the higher education system evolves at the speed of the ministry's most punctilious legal draftsman!

Vigorous lobbying by university rectors for 'some degree' of institutional autonomy may certainly be interpreted as an excellent example of 'the Law of Anticipated Results' (Amaral and Rosa, 2008; Neave, 1996b).[2] However, these results were not seen as limited to institutional initiative. From the perspective of the leadership of the universities, extending institutional latitude was but one side of the coin. The obverse of this same agenda lay in two main objectives: first, to impart continuity – and thus a new impetus – to the broader, strategic issue of system-wide reform by placing certain elements that were previously located within the short-term and temporary practice of outsourced 'delegated responsibilities' on a permanent footing within the institution; and, second, universities by taking over certain functions hitherto vested in the ministry in charge of higher education would hopefully lighten the ministry's burden as an anticipated prior condition to the *ministry* showing enhanced performance. Here was a neat reversal of the expectations that elsewhere accompanied a similar process in the UK, France and the Netherlands – namely, that ministries hoped to see improvements in *university* efficiency!

Clearly, seen in this light, the 1988 University Autonomy Act raised issues beyond simply taking the first steps down the long road to institutional autonomy. Nor, for that matter, was the issue of institutional autonomy the sole and unique aspect that bade fair to place the relationship between the universities, the national administration and the government on a radically different footing. As suggested earlier, the 1988 Act profoundly modified the integrity of legal homogeneity. It acknowledged, if only tacitly, the view strongly held by the leadership of the universities that to strengthen the effectiveness of higher education policy making required the 'offloading' of those functions that could readily be taken over by the universities the better to allow the ministry to concentrate on outstanding strategic priorities – the future shape of the higher education system and particularly the place of the rising polytechnics and private universities within this.

That the leadership of the universities appears to have been the main driving force behind 'offloading' the responsibility for finance, building maintenance and programme development in Portugal is an interesting refinement to our understanding of the same phenomenon that was visible elsewhere in Western Europe from the early 1990s onwards and was often presented in terms of the 'offloading state' (Wielemans and Roth van der Werf, 1997). Whereas in France, the Netherlands and Spain, corresponding policies are usually presented as 'top-down' measures, in Portugal, the initiative was 'bottom-up', with the paradox that whilst these issues reflected the relative weakness of the central state, the legislation of 1988 and 1990 sought if not to strengthen the state then at least to raise its level of effectiveness by formally reducing its detailed scope.

1994–2002: intention versus capacity

Subsequent developments suggest that the stance taken by the university rectors was very far from being either opportunistic or reactive, even less short term. It was, on the contrary, a strategic posture extending to other lines of policy and particularly to the crucial areas of evaluation and accreditation. It must, for the moment, remain a matter of speculation as to how far the leadership of the universities deliberately set out to reinforce consensus-building mechanisms within its own ranks as a preliminary to testing out an evaluation system. Even so, it is significant that the university's equivalent of the 'Party of Movement',[3] having secured room for manoeuvre for itself at the institutional level – one of the more evident blessings that flowed from the 1988 University Autonomy Act – set about creating a permanent institutional basis to undertake amongst its own ranks further exploration of the issues that Portuguese higher education faced. Such coordination took the form of the *Fundacão das Universidades Portuguesas* (Foundation of the Portuguese Universities: FUP).

The FUP is a laterally operating intermediary body. It acts, under private law, as an independent and permanent sounding board for the leadership of *public* universities to explore on its own terms, initiative and definition matters of mutual concern, which its members perceive as the strategic issues confronting Portuguese higher education in general and the university sector in particular. Created by the rectors in July 1993, the FUP is a foundation whose membership today extends to 14 public universities plus the private sector Catholic University. It runs in parallel to the official Council of Rectors of the Portuguese Universities (CRUP). Its role is then complementary to the Council whilst enjoying the freedom to define its own agenda, to explore without hindrance the implications that result from an open-ended approach to developing higher education rather than being tied to a formal agenda set by the ministry.

Dualism in Portuguese politics and higher education strategy

From 1994 to 1998, the FUP effectively fulfilled a purpose which underpinned a proactive stance on the part of university rectors, particularly in elaborating the groundwork strategy for the development of higher education in Portugal, and later by taking on a policy-analytic capacity with the founding of the *Centro de Investigação de Políticas de Ensino Superior* (CIPES) in 1998. Yet, the university 'Party of Movement', by assuming the initiative, underscored (although in a different way) a deep-seated duality within Portuguese politics, namely the phenomenon of the 'parallel state' (Santos, 1990 and 1993, cited in Amaral and Carvalho, 2008). In its classic form, this feature emerges in a dual attitude on the part of the state, which, on the one hand, insists on the formalities of 'progressive legality' whilst, on the other hand, being prepared to put up with a regular and blatant disregard of these same legal provisions (Amaral and Carvalho, 2008).

The notion of a 'parallel state', perhaps better described as policy's equivalent of cognitive dissonance, is held to be a prime explanation for the apparent ineffectualness of the Portuguese state. However, from a comparative perspective, it is fair to say that if the way in which these contradictions emerged in Portugal is indeed specific to Portuguese policy – academic drift amongst polytechnics and, at times, a strange inventiveness in interpreting the law by certain private sector universities – the root cause is evident elsewhere as part of the rigidities inherent in legal homogeneity itself.[4] By creating a 'counter coordinating centre' within the university world, rector proactivity arguably introduced dualism in a new and strategic form between the 'Party of Movement' and other interests, in both the private and the polytechnic sectors, not to mention the central administration, which, together and by the same token, constituted a 'Party of Order'.

The duality in strategy was equally visible in other dimensions as well. Its dividing lines marked a second division between the 'Party of Movement' and the 'Party of Order' in higher education policy. The former looked *outside* Portugal. From amongst the policies that were then current, it sought developments and practices that could be taken over both to modernize the nation's higher education system and at the same time bring it more closely into line with trends visible in other Member States of the EU. However, the Party of Order sought to protect its recent gains from the 1988 Act on Pedagogical Autonomy. The polarization that resulted acquired all the weight of a central and vexatious feature of the politics of higher education in Portugal.

The Portuguese model of the Evaluative State

The Evaluative State welds together a triple helix constructed from evaluating institutional performance, operationalizing, identifying and accrediting quality and, finally, rationalizing both system and institutional management. It is the Archimedes' lever for re-engineering higher education in Europe. Its potency as an instrument for change in Portugal was, on paper at least, immense and was regarded as such.

The Decree Act 38/94 of 21 November 1994 set out the legal framework for a quality assurance system (ENQA, 2006). It was, in effect, the first step towards establishing the Evaluative State *à la portugaise* and thus, at least in intent, moving system coordination from its historical mode of state control to what some have identified as creating a 'facilitatory' or 'surveillance' relationship between the central administration and higher education institutions (Neave and van Vught, 1994a). Portugal was fortunate, however, in having a number of functioning 'models' already in place from which to choose – British, Dutch or French. Each entailed a different strategy and each gave held out a very different relationship between the universities and the central administration.[5] Opting for the Dutch model is then interesting *per se*. However, the choice between the various national templates has to be seen against the backdrop of the specific strategy already launched by the 'Party of Movement'.

First stage: 'going Dutch'

The main features of the Dutch model lay, as we have seen,[6] in its ownership and in its location. Evaluation and its procedures were the responsibility of the Dutch universities. They were located in the Association of Dutch Universities (*Vereeniging der Samenwerkende Nederlandse Universiteiten*: VSNU), the Dutch universities' official interlocutor and representative organization vis-à-vis government and civil society in the areas of research, education, funding and personnel policy (VSNU, 2009).

Why the 'Party of Movement' opted for the Dutch model of evaluation is not difficult to grasp. In the first place, the Dutch 'model' gave further weight, substance and reality to the 'pedagogic autonomy' recently conferred upon the universities precisely because its 'ownership' lay in the hands of the universities. A similar arrangement in Portugal would serve to consolidate the 'pedagogic autonomy' that already exercised under the 1988 Law. In the second place, by setting evaluation within the framework of the FUP, this body took on official responsibility for piloting evaluation at the national level – a function all the more weighty for being backed by administrative law. Having a remit under administrative law boosted the legitimacy of the FUP, which up to that point had rested solely on private law. In the third place and viewed from a slightly different perspective, adding evaluation to the FUP's original 'exploratory remit' further enhanced its potential as the universities' spearhead for change in Portuguese higher education.

Second stage: frustration, fragmentation and exceptionalism

The second stage in developing the Portuguese model of the Evaluative State was reached with the promulgation of Decree Law 205/98 of 11 July 1998. This set up the National Council for the Evaluation of Higher Education (*Conselho Nacional de Avaliação do Ensino Superior*: CNAVES) as a 'delegated responsibility' – that is, the National Council acted as a delegated agency outside the Ministry of Higher Education, but under its oversight. The Law put an end to the pilot exercise within the university sphere of influence. It assigned evaluation to a self-standing coordinating agency (ENQA, 2006). It also substantially revised the organizational framework that the mission carried out by the FUP implicitly sought to advance. The decision, though technical in nature, had a very specific political dimension. Making the National Council a 'delegated responsibility' under the Ministry of Higher Education sought to allay a certain unease and sensitivity that had grown up around piloting evaluation under the auspices of the FUP. In effect, the FUP brought together only public sector universities. It embraced neither public sector polytechnics nor private sector universities and still less private sector polytechnics. This was not the only source of disquiet; there was another. The basic template on which the FUP sought to develop a national evaluation system itself rested on a referential framework, which subscribed to a unitary model – namely, the Dutch model.

The prospect of extending such an arrangement beyond the boundaries of the public university was not greeted with cries of acclaim either by the private sector as a whole or by those polytechnics that fell within the public sector. On the contrary, to inject a unitary model of evaluation, tested solely by an organization that was intimately and symbiotically linked to the leadership of public sector universities, into the remaining sectors of the Portuguese higher education system was looked upon with great misgivings. The private sector universities looked upon a unitary model as simply reinforcing the hegemony that the public sector university enjoyed over its private sector counterparts. From the perspective of the polytechnics, to project the FUP's unitary scheme merely piled new advantages on top of those the public sector universities already enjoyed, not least of which was pedagogic autonomy. Withholding this boon from polytechnics still rankled. From the viewpoint of the other sectoral interests in Portuguese higher education, the unitary model was not popular, much less acceptable – except to public sector universities.

Creative destruction

Despite these tensions, Decree Law 205/98 put in place the makings of an Evaluative State in Portugal. However, it did so by throwing out all notion of basing it on a purely unitary model. Whilst the government accepted the principle of evaluating higher education, it was at pains to avoid accepting the detailed proposal of the 'Party of Movement' amongst the rectors of public sector universities. The 'solution' retained by the government was very different from the Dutch unitary model that had attracted the 'Party of Movement'. The government opted for a two-tier arrangement that closely followed the structural segmentation of the nation's system of higher education. Evaluation bodies with oversight for specific sectors formed a second tier. The first tier took the shape of an overall coordinating agency – an umbrella organization – that straddled a second tier of sectorially based committees with the overall edifice being brought together as CNAVES.

Under this two-tier model, to the FUP went the responsibility for evaluating the public university sector. For the public polytechnic sector, a similar remit was laid on the *Associação de Institutios Superiores Portuguesas* (Association of Portuguese Polytechnical Institutions: ADISPOR). Overall evaluation of the private sector – covering both universities and polytechnics – was handed to the *Associação Portuguesa do Ensino Superior Privada* (Portuguese Association for Private Higher Education: APESP).

This two-tier arrangement is interesting on its own account for a number of reasons. It stands as a remarkably clear illustration of what may best be described as the 'politics of evaluation'.[7] As such, it is an example of the way in which 'technical solutions' may be mediated; purists may see this as an example of 'nuancing' or adjusting technical solutions to the realities of power and influence, an inevitable process which often takes place as the technical issue reaches the arena of national politics after being worked out in the corridors of power. In addition, and taking into account the predominant patterns then to be seen in higher education systems where evaluation was already in place, a case can very certainly be made for interpreting this segmented structure as a further pointer to Portuguese 'exceptionalism'.

Structuring the Evaluative State

Such exceptionalism applies to two aspects in particular. First, though two-tier arrangements are not in themselves exceptional, they tend (as was pointed out earlier)[8] to reflect a country's political structure with multi-tier models most in evidence in federations – as in the case of Belgium, Germany and Spain[9] – or in the case where a high degree of regional self-government has been put in place. This, for instance, is the case with the four regionally based funding agencies in the UK. Second, it does not always follow that unitary states *eo ipso* drive towards a unitary model when setting up the Evaluative State. There are, as has been pointed out in Chapter 1, a number of exceptions – amongst them Austria, Ireland and the Netherlands – where unitary states later opt for a multi-level, multi-agency evaluation system. This latter trend has recently extended to Sweden with the establishment in October 2009 of an agency for evaluating vocationally based education and training as a complementary and parallel body to the Swedish Higher Education Agency (*Hogskolverket*) which focuses on universities and university colleges.

The particular Portuguese dynamic

However, so furious a multiplication in the number of agencies within the evolving structure of the Evaluative State is precisely that. It evolves on and out of what, at the beginning, was largely a single agency base. Nevertheless, it is here that Portuguese exceptionalism is most in evidence. In 1998, when the Portuguese Decree Law put the two-tier evaluative model in place, there were few unitary systems that had moved over to a multi-agency model, though clearly some chose to do so later. The outstanding feature of the Portuguese model of the Evaluative State lay in its starting off on a two-tier basis, despite being located in a unitary state.

The initial model of the Evaluative State in Portugal was, in effect, asymmetrical. It explicitly distinguished between public and private universities on the one hand and between universities and polytechnics within the public sector on the other. Furthermore, it subscribed to both the binary principle within the public sector and at the same time appeared to endorse the unitary principle when extended to the private sector. The interests it sought either to recognize or to reconcile must for the moment at least remain a matter of speculation, though intuition suggests that the particular treatment accorded to public sector polytechnics certainly reflected their formal differentiation from universities in terms of their mission. However, that this logic was not carried across to the private sector suggests that other considerations were also at play, not least the wish on the part of the government to pacify the private sector.

There is, however, another possibility, which drives in a different direction. This second supposition – and at the time of writing it can be no more than that – would explain such a tripartite arrangement as echoing a tactic that could earlier be observed in the UK: namely, the wish to temper the influence that universities *stricto sensu* had wielded up to that point over the design and definition of basic evaluative procedures. In the UK, the take-over of auditing and evaluation, first developed by and within the Committee of Vice-Chancellors and Principals with the advent of the Quality Assurance Agency in 1994, was plucked out of the hands of British universities and given over to the mercies of that 'agency of public purpose'. Similarly, whether the move to create CNAVES was a gesture to the polytechnic interest or a token of growing distrust between the leadership of the universities and the government must for the moment remain shrouded in discretion!

Organizing the Evaluative State: round 1

From an organizational perspective, CNAVES bore a certain generic similarity to its Spanish counterpart. It too rested on a two-tier pattern, though, as we have seen, the tiered arrangement in the Spanish model of the Evaluative State reflected differences in levels of government rather than differences between legal status *and* institutional mission. CNAVES acted as a coordinating centre for three evaluation councils (ENQA, 2006: 22). This is an original configuration, for whilst such a division may be justified on the grounds of difference in purpose and public mission between universities and polytechnics, differences in terms of ethical outlook are rather more questionable when viewed from the viewpoint of objectivity in performance and institutional achievement, which is what evaluation is about.

The only conclusion that may be drawn is that CNAVES stood less as a bid to leverage system coherence than to effectively accommodate the forces of potential fragmentation. By the same reasoning, since CNAVES was the child of the polity, it was indeed a faithful mirror of its parent's feebleness! Its short existence – Decree 369/2007 of 5 November 2007 put paid to it with extreme prejudice – provided a tragic illustration of the dictum that in truth political intention may all too often serve to dilute both technical intent and capacity. Indeed, CNAVES prolonged one significant gap in Portuguese higher education policy: no complete overall evaluation of higher education was ever presented, despite its nine years *in situ* (ENQA, 2006: 65).

Frustration explained

Why political intent should have lead to so miserable a performance deserves an explanation at the very least. For the members of the ENQA Review Panel, who were invited in 2005 to report to the Portuguese government, CNAVES was the victim of the extended scope of institutional autonomy granted a decade earlier. The reviewers believed that neither universities nor polytechnics were willing to see a newly conferred autonomy reduced by dint of external evaluations (ENQA, 2006: 23–4). Another explanation laid part of the blame on resistance from the private university sector (ENQA, 2006: 29) – a splendid paradox in itself inasmuch as CNAVES' structure bent over backwards to give private sector universities separate recognition and status against all commonly acknowledged canons of rigour that evaluation supposedly engages.

There is, however, another explanation. Whilst it is not incompatible with those advanced by the ENQA Review Panel, it goes beyond the very specific domain – evaluation and accreditation – which the team was called upon to assess, although it is only right to note that passing allusion was made to it in the course of the Panel's report. The ENQA review team suggested that one reason for the distrust expressed in relation to evaluation was that private sector universities saw their public sector counterparts holding the whip hand in CNAVES and thus in shaping institutional evaluation in general (ENQA, 2006: 24). The implication was that since evaluation procedures had been 'piloted' by an agency set up by the leadership of public universities, for that very reason evaluation could only be to the detriment of the private sector. In short, CNAVES was not, in the eyes of private sector universities, sufficiently independent.

Such suspicions brought the first bid to install the Evaluative State in Portugal to a grinding halt. The pedagogical autonomy of the universities was rescinded by Law 26/2000 of 23 August 2000, which itself was subsequently revoked and then upheld by Law 1/2003 three years later (Amaral and Carvalho, 2008: 6). This outstanding example of policy as a derivative of the hesitation waltz showed the crisis to be no passing thing. It was arguably neither coincidental nor conjunctural.

The 'Party of Order' and the defence of legal homogeneity

It is a moot point as to whether the distrust of public evaluation felt by private sector universities drew on a more general sense of rivalry with the public sector or whether evaluation merely provided the occasion to express that rivalry in an ostensibly technical rather than by outright ideological discourse. It is clear, however, that just as the 'Party of Movement' amongst the leadership of the public universities had pressed forward with testing the technical and procedural dimensions of the Evaluative State, so the 'Party of Order' in both the polytechnic and in the private university sectors sought with equal vehemence to defend the principle of legal homogeneity. Agreed, an interpretation in these exact terms has so far found little if any echo in the scholarly literature. If, however, a closer look is taken at the reasons for dissent amongst the polytechnic sector, this view becomes rather more credible.

The polytechnic sector never accepted being deprived of the principle of 'pedagogic autonomy'. Its lobbying was instrumental in the government's decision in 2000 to revoke it (Amaral and Carvalho, 2008: 6). The grounds for the objection by the polytechnics may be – and certainly were – presented in terms of equity and fair treatment. However, the reason for contesting the legitimacy of the decision to grant pedagogical autonomy to public sector universities was precisely because polytechnics remained subject to the undiluted rigours of legal homogeneity. More specifically, they remained shackled to the requirement to secure ministry approval for the validation and recognition of their courses. Public sector universities did not. The difference in treatment was then held by the polytechnics to be in contradiction with legal homogeneity as the central principle to Portugal's higher education system, though it has to be said that these terms were never employed, even if the thrust of their argument came very close to this latter frame of discourse.

Restoring legal homogeneity entailed one of two possibilities, both of which fulfilled the demands of the polytechnic cause: either 'pedagogic autonomy' was extended to the polytechnics or it was removed from the universities. Either way, the principle of legal homogeneity would once again reign supreme. That the government of the day opted for the latter course was an explicit acknowledgement of the degree of mobilization that the 'Party of Order' had built up and brought to bear against what appeared to be the licentious departure from the principle of legal homogeneity.

2003–8: institutional autonomy or managerial freedom?

Portugal's first attempt to move towards the Evaluative State foundered because it was equated with the particular interests of the public university, the dominant sector of higher education. What remains obscure, however, is whether the decision of the government to restore the rigidities, together with the legitimacy that legal homogeneity appeared to command, reflected vacillation on its part or the inability of the central administration to fully activate the instrumentality required to change the basis of system coordination from state control to state surveillance (Neave and van Vught, 1994a; Amaral and Rosa, 2008: 7). There are other possibilities: that failure reflected the strength of dissent or that moving evaluation from the sphere of influence exercised by the 'Party of Movement' also corresponded to a change in the composition of the latter, for though academic leadership abides, its leaders pass. Functions endure whilst individuals go marching resolutely on. In all likelihood, all these factors each played their part.

Organizing the Evaluative State: round 2

Either way, the reassertion of legal homogeneity had direct repercussions on the manner in which the Evaluative State and with it the setting down of new conditions and justifications for advancing institutional autonomy were pursued. Whereas the first bid to move towards the promised land of the Evaluative State sought to build evaluation around the internal, disciplinary dynamic inherent to universities (Metzger, 1987; Clark, 1994) – that is, control *through* knowledge rather than using control *over* knowledge, the former being the salient feature of the Dutch model – the second attempt deliberately and expressly aligned itself around external criteria of efficiency, effectiveness and quality. This was far from fortuitous. In the opinion of Amaral and Carvalho:

> the creation of competitive environments within the public sector organisations and non-government competitors … an increased emphasis on accountability for results … [gave rise to] a management environment which better matches authority and responsibility. (Amaral and Carvalho, 2008: 7)

Authority and responsibility were certainly issues at stake, but these qualities are not desirable only within the individual institution; they are also a necessary prior condition if 'system cohesion' is to be ensured. There is in short a dialectical relationship between their grounding within the individual university or polytechnic just as there is between the degree of responsiveness by, and compliance of, these institutions to the will of the Prince. What is important to look at, *en premier lieu*, are not the instrumentalities incorporated into and resulting from evaluation and accreditation. Still less should immediate attention dwell on responsibility and authority *per se*, for these qualities assume very different meanings and consequences depending on who one's interlocutor is. However, what is of excruciating importance is the end purpose that these installed qualities and their operational concomitants are held to serve. The shared purpose of authority and responsibility across both institutional autonomy and across the three formative dimensions of the Evaluative State – operationalizing quality, identifying its location and maintaining its upkeep – is to ensure that institutional governance aligns institutional priorities with the national purpose, as the OECD recently pointed out (OECD, 2008: 4).

More speed, less haste

The renewed attempt to set the Evaluative State on a more solid base drew on a dynamic that was very different from its unfortunate predecessor. The task of 'making the running' shifted away from the 'Party of Movement' in public universities and moved firmly back to central government. The latter had ruled out any attempt to move beyond legal homogeneity. Nevertheless, both institutional autonomy and the shaping of the Evaluative State were seen by ministers as the obverse and the reverse of a new national agenda to raise institutional efficiency and to sharpen higher education's national purpose. Such a resolution ushered in a spate of major legislation, which fuelled the view that, far from placing greater initiative in the hands of higher education, central government was now determined to strengthen the powers of intervention of the central ministry (Amaral and Magalhães, 2007: 63–76; Amaral and Carvalho, 2008: 7).

Nor was the second drive towards the Evaluative State distinguished from its predecessor by legislative haste alone. True, 2006 and 2007 were remarkable years in this respect: Decree Law 74/2006, passed on 24 March 2006, set out the legal framework for implementing the Bologna Process, while Law 38/2007 of 16 August 2007 and its decree of application 369/2007 promulgated on 5 November 2007 laid down the conditions establishing the *Agência de Avaliação e Acreditação do Ensino Superior* (Agency for Assessment and Accreditation of Higher Education: A3ES). The Agency's operational mission was to take charge of external assessment across all sectors of higher education, to inform the public and to develop a 'culture of quality' (Portugal Law 38/2007, Articles 11.2, 5.C). Not only was evaluation made compulsory; it was to take place 'within the framework of the European system of quality assurance in higher education' (MCTES, 2009 Law

38/2007, Article 8). This stipulation closely followed the recommendations that ENQA made in the study that the Portuguese government commissioned from it. On 10 September of that same year, Law 62/2007 laid down a new legal framework for all higher education institutions.

Government as a 'galvanized Party of Movement'...

Here was executive haste of a high order. The sheer volume, complexity and scope of the legislation promulgated in the space of two years, the priority accorded both to re-engineering the higher education system in its totality and to setting down the operational basis for the Evaluative State, were all faithfully reflected in the precipitation unleashed! Here too the intertwining and bonding of system overhaul with the press to set up the Evaluative State – a feature which, as has been argued earlier, was an abiding issue of higher education policy in Portugal – emerged with indisputable clarity.

However, to suggest that both the government and the central administration sought to demonstrate a pleasing capacity for initiative, if only to give the lie to accusations of inefficiency, vacillation and weakness by unveiling a wondrous and suddenly acquired energy, would be intolerably cynical. And yet, compared to the two previous phases in the unfolding of higher education policy in Portugal, to qualify the third as 'galvanic' is not unmerited.

The government and the national administration seemed to take over the role hitherto played by the 'Party of Movement'. In its earlier assumption of this role, the leadership of the universities had sought inspiration from empirical models and established practices abroad. In addition, the central administration turned to outside sources as much for good counsel as for the enhanced legitimacy, standing and external approval that were to be garnered from the recommendations that international organisations, both non-governmental and intergovernmental, could come up with. These political benefits, which were important in themselves, came in addition to suggestions of a technical nature that bore on the general field of governance, as well as the accompanying examples and recommended models for coordination, instrumentality and shaping opinion (Amaral and Neave, 2008; Martens and Wolf, 2009).

... 'with a little help from their friends'

Just as it had been in the logic of the leadership of the universities to look to their fellow university organizations abroad – to the

Netherlands in this case[10] – so the ministry turned to the OECD for advice on re-engineering the higher education system and to ENQA for the appropriate structures, methods and criteria for tracking quality and assessing institutional achievement.

Faced with the naturally sensitive and complex issues that root-and-branch system change demands, it is of more than passing interest to note the time which elapsed between the moment reports from ENQA and the OECD were presented to the government and the subsequent legislative enactment to which they were an input. ENQA's report appeared at the end of 2006. The OECD presented its conclusions to the Portuguese authorities in December of the same year (OECD, Press Release, 13 December 2006) – that is, 11 months and 10 months respectively before legislation was passed.

Covert pressures

To be in a position to legislate so soon after receiving two sets of comprehensive recommendations was a remarkable achievement. However, the possibility cannot entirely be ruled out that rapid acceptance and equally rapid action may both have owed much to the government's need to press forward. This is because, unlike the earlier quest for the Evaluative State, the government itself was under considerable pressure, above all pressure from outside Portugal, to put in place those reforms which clearly demonstrated the nation's determination both to modernize its higher education system and to do so in ways that brooked no doubt about its commitment to European integration. That the first item to spring forth from the legislative onslaught – Decree Law 74/2006, promulgated on 24 March 2006 – integrated Portuguese higher education into the Bologna Process confirms this impression. So too did the explicit commitment to align the activities of A3ES upon the supranational 'European model' which was then being busily hawked about by ENQA.

11
Re-focusing Institutional Autonomy: The Portuguese Decree Law of 2007

Introduction

To analyse so complex and widely ranging a piece of legislation as an Act that re-defines the legal framework of a higher education system *in toto* is a task that is doughty in the extreme. It is no less so when this analysis has to take account of the continuities and changes introduced by the Act. Agreed, there is always an easy way out. In this case, the *solution de facilité* would be to concentrate wholly, specifically and exclusively on those elements which touch upon institutional and positional autonomy. However, such an approach is far from satisfactory. On sheer pragmatic grounds, the fact remains – and it has been observed in countless studies on the kaleidoscopic face of autonomy in higher education – that changes brought to bear on, and in operationalizing, autonomy have a 'knock- on' effect in other areas of an institution's activities. These areas are not always directly involved or strictly a part of the dimensions that determine both the nature and the extent of autonomy itself. Thus, the observer does well indeed to be exceedingly chary of the pitfalls that lie in wait for him or her! They are many and they are subtle.

Mindful of these traps, the analysis undertaken here of Decree Law 62/2007, the Legal Framework of Higher Education Institutions, passed on 10 September 2007, is split into two parts. The first focuses on the general thrust and strategy and how both fit in with the ongoing saga of higher education policy in Portugal from a long-term perspective, while the second focuses on the changes it introduced at the system level.

Continuity and change

Decree Law 62/2007 drew heavily on the recommendations of the OECD, which was then currently engaged on a far more wide-ranging exercise in re-stating the boundaries of post-school education, an exercise which shifted this referential universe from higher to tertiary education (Amaral and Neave, 2009: 82–99). Precisely because the OECD report was so close in time to the Act's promulgation, it is important to set the legislation overhauling higher education both within a Portuguese context and also within the context of the evolving stance of the OECD itself.

The OECD was not engaged in exploring tertiary education alone. It had also embarked on setting a new mid-term agenda, which flowed from its own analysis of the current state of tertiary education in some 24 systems across the world. This exercise, of which Portugal was part, generated an impressive range of recommendations and prescriptions, strategies and policy models. Amongst the key dimensions the OECD built upon were the expansion and diversity of higher education, changes in ways of funding it, enhanced accountability and performance, new models of institutional governance and global networking (OECD, 2008). Given the OECD's steadfast allegiance to neoliberalism as a social and economic doctrine, there is good reason for seeing tertiary education as a form of conceptual Gladstone bag. Its purpose lay in extending the scope of application of neoliberalism to a broader range of pragmatic issues, thereby enhancing the validity – or the relevance – of the doctrine itself. Such a manner of proceeding has been qualified in certain quarters as 'ideological consolidation' (Amaral and Neave, 2009: 14–16).

By bringing the OECD in to review the state of higher education in Portugal and to make recommendations, it was largely a foregone conclusion that the reconstruction of higher education would reflect both the ethics and justification of neoliberalism. It was also a foregone conclusion that the thrust of reconstruction it would propose would largely fall in with the canons of its main administrative and operational template – New Public Management (Pollitt and Bouckaert, 2004).[1]

Continuity *in* change

As was pointed out earlier,[2] the OECD focused on six major areas. However, these areas entailed a particular rationale, namely to draw up structures and procedures that established 'system cohesion' on a new basis. This basis rested on enlarged institutional responsibility and on strengthened institutional leadership, together with what appears to be a greater degree of diversity within the public and private, university and polytechnic sectors.

The 'policy problem' and its solutions

To propose the 'offloading' of functions previously exercised by the central ministry was not in itself novel. As a policy, it took up once again the same strategy that had underpinned the 1988 University Autonomy Act, a strategy that had served as the guiding light for that part of the leadership of the universities that was then acting as the 'Party of Movement'. Both the OECD's recommendations and the particular strategy the leadership of the universities had earlier sought to advance were remarkably similar. The difference, and it was significant, lay in the justification behind them. For 'the Party of Movement' amongst rectors, the main issue at stake lay in solving the problem of an 'overloaded' central administration. Offloading, which the 1988 Act undertook, may be seen as driving towards a more 'modest' central administration – a notion that was certainly radical at the time but was more akin to the empirical theory developed by the French sociologist of organizations, Michel Crozier. Crozier's argument called for a voluntaristic and politically driven reform of public services. It saw a 'modest state' as a way of re-building a more free-flowing and sensitive articulation between the administration and *administrés* as a condition that was desirable on its own account (Crozier, 1987).

For the OECD, imbued with the tenets of neoliberalism, the same 'solution' was itself an integral part of a wider ideological and ethical shift to be injected into a nation's institutions and for which the OECD stood as one of the main mouthpieces. 'Rolling back the frontiers of the state' was not only a slogan that is more hostile by far to the very notion of the state than Crozier's 'modest state';[3] it was also the means through which society is placed on a new ethical grounding, one where 'market forces', competition between individuals and, by extension, between institutions shape a world that is economically driven rather than politically answerable. Thus, though the 'policy problem' remained constant over the 17 years between rectoral initiative and the OECD recommendations, the ideological justification did not. 'The policy problem' was now tackled by applying liberal economic theory as the solution, a feature that recent commentators have identified as the hallmark of the OECD's 'policy style' (Porter and Webb, 2007: 4).

Different directions in the reforming impulse

However, there remains one other salient feature in the approaches brought to bear in modernizing Portugal's higher education system. It provides a final example of change *in the midst of* continuity. It relates particularly to what is best understood as the 'locus' or the point of concentration around which the reforming impulse centres. Given the differences in interest, it cannot be very surprising that whilst reforming rectors saw reform in terms of inner change, of academia 'putting its own house in order' and, by so doing, riding to save the state from itself, the OECD took a line that was diametrically opposed to that pursued by university leadership during the early 1990s. Far from seeing the universities as part of the solution, which had been the implicit assumption of the 'Party of Movement', the OECD review team held the universities to be part of the problem. Thus, distrust moved from focusing on the central national administration and instead latched on to higher education as the *causus malorum*. In the opinion of the OECD: 'The institutions [of higher education] are too academic [sic] and inward-looking. There is a high degree of insularity and inbreeding' (OECD, 2007: para 7.62).

For the OECD, the reforming impulse was clearly *external* to higher education. Reform should drive from outside and work inwards through two channels of leverage: first, by developing a relationship between the system and the central ministry based on the instrumentality of 'contractualization' (OECD, 2007: para 7.31), that is, institutional performance agreements, a practice which had effectively been pioneered in France (Chevaillier, 2002); and, second, by using a strengthened leadership to generate and sustain the momentum of reform within the institution (OECD, 2007: paras 7.31–7.34).

Strong leadership: freedom for what to do whom?

The place occupied by externally driven reform in the swathe of the OECD's recommendations formed a constant theme: more sustained ties between higher education and the local community, more weight upon regional development and, last but not least, a structural overhaul designed to amplify the virtues of strong 'outwardly looking' leadership. Changes in governance were the touchstone of this strategy. The Review Panel came down heavily in favour of appointed – not elected – rectors together with the injection into the heartland of academia of deans and heads of department to be appointed by the governing authority rather than remaining elected posts (OECD,

2007: para 7.34). What may be queried here is less the construction of this top-down chain of command, which was intended to strengthen leadership, so much as the form of leadership it entailed. Was leadership to be managerial or academic? Could it, even with the most elastic stretch of the imagination and terminology, be said to be democratic at all in the way in which decisions were to be carried out?

To this latter insolence, an indirect answer was indeed to hand in the way in which the Review Panel justified its most innovative recommendation: the foundation university. Foundation universities were proposed as self-governing entities, supported by the government, but under private law.[4] Revealingly, the freedom that foundation universities were held by the OECD to enjoy and to represent was managerial, not academic – a distinction that tends to put a very different construct indeed on institutional autonomy. In the minds of the Review Panel, the distinguishing feature that ought to set the foundation university apart from the classic public university should lie in the former being an establishment where '*managerial* freedom should be the norm' (OECD, 2007: para 7.33, emphasis added) – a truly Orwellian statement, worthy of Napoleon the pig himself.

Change at the system level

Decree Law 62/2007 of 10 September 2007 is a 'framework law'. In other words, it outlines the contours and the profile that the higher education system is to assume. Some of the stipulations laid out have immediate legal effect. Others emerge in the fullness of time, unless specific mention has been made about the timing and details of their implementation. But 'framework laws' have another characteristic and it is important to bear it in mind: they make provision for further – more detailed – legislation to be included subsequently should the need arise. In summary, framework laws are dynamic. They are intended to impart that dynamism to the system to which they apply. In this respect, they are more akin to what in the inimitable jargon of the European Commission at Brussels is termed 'an action programme' (Neave, 1987). As its name suggests, a framework or guideline law (*Loi d'Orientation*) starts the process of reform off. It sets out the priorities within the range of tasks included. It does not necessarily include datelines for implementation. For this reason, a guideline law is best viewed as a particular form of 'open-ended' legislation.

From a comparative perspective, Decree Law 62/2007 falls fully within that practice of broad-spectrum reform through system-wide legislation seen elsewhere in Western Europe. Such an approach emerged from the various *Lois d'Orientation* that have marked higher education policy in France since 1968, in Germany since the 1976 *Hochschulrahmengesetz* and its successors, and in Austria in the form of the 1976 *Universitaetsorganizationsgesetz* and its subsequent revisions. The 1993 version of the *Universitaetsorganizationsgesetz* is particularly interesting since its Portuguese counterpart was to draw on a number of its features (Peschar, 2003: 108–15).

The Higher Education Guideline Law of 2007: two perspectives

By and large, changes at the system level introduced by the Portuguese Higher Education Guideline Law of 2007 may be divided into two broad themes: on the one hand, remedy and redress and, on the other, putting in place structures and new conditions for system development in the future. The first obeyed the rationale of ensuring a greater 'system cohesion'. It clarified and consolidated the boundaries between the four sectors of the Portuguese higher education system – between universities and polytechnics and between the public and the private sectors. The second put new forms of institutional governance into place, together with new and more flexible procedures and instruments for shaping higher education in the short to medium term. Amongst the latter, A3ES may be included. Strictly speaking, the law that brought A3ES into existence (Decree Law 38/2007 of 16 August 2007) preceded the Higher Education Guideline Law of 2007 by less than a month. The former enactment is best seen as a step in the policy sub-set, developed in parallel to the system overhaul, namely the firming up of a strategy of quality assurance. This latter policy was already underway. It began with the promulgation of Decree Law 74/2006, which revised the structure of Portuguese diplomas and brought them into line with the Bologna Process. In dealing with qualification structures, it also contributed directly to clarifying some of the differences in status and condition between universities and polytechnics. Whilst universities were free to choose between programmes carrying either 180 or 240 European Credit Transfer System (ECTS) Credit Units, polytechnics, unless they were able to demonstrate express need, were limited to programmes carrying 180 credits. Standardization around the Bologna model of study duration effectively cut the polytechnics off from Master's programmes that led to research training and to higher degrees.

Remedy, redress and system cohesion

Amongst the more outstanding issues that fell into the category of 'remedy and redress' was the status of the polytechnics, very particularly the issue of 'academic drift' and the pressure exerted by polytechnics to teach higher degrees. The Higher Education Guideline Law rejected this claim, thus underlining the restrictions already set out in Decree Law 74/2006. The Guideline Law re-defined the mission of polytechnics as concentrating on advanced vocational and professionally oriented technical training (Portugal, 2008: Article 3.1). Polytechnics were restricted in the number of cycles they were allowed to cover at first degree – that is, at *Licentiatura* – level. They were, in effect, limited to two laboratory cycles out of four (Portugal, 2008: Article 43A, paras i–iii).

To be recognized as a polytechnic, an establishment required, first, accreditation by A3ES, the national accreditation agency, and to teach at least four first cycles, two being technical laboratory cycles. Subject to polytechnics submitting to normal accreditation procedures, the Guideline Law permitted them to award *Licenciado* (first cycle) and Master's (second cycle) degrees (Portugal, 2008: Article 7). However, the monopoly on doctoral level studies remained firmly with the universities (Portugal, 2008: Article 7).

Distinctions in terms of mission and curricular orientation – effectively system cohesion – were not the only dimensions to reinforce differences between polytechnics and universities contained in the Higher Education Guideline Law. Career categories were no less important if only because similarity in the formal terminology used to designate rank and status between university and non-university establishments had fuelled 'academic drift' in the non-university sector, not only in Portugal but in France, Norway and the UK as well (Kyvik, 1981; Pratt and Burgess, 1974; Doumenc and Gilly, 1977). The creation of the title of 'specialist' was central in preserving the boundary between the two institutional types. Not only was it reserved exclusively for the polytechnic sector, it was also to be conferred by decree law upon individuals of 'quality and skill of particular relevance and recognized professional experience in a particular area' (Portugal, 2008: Article 48, para 1b). This singular honour welded the polytechnic staffing structure firmly to the vocational and technical fields, now inseparable as the prime identifiers of that institutional type. By the same token, since the title of 'specialist' was unique to the polytechnics, it marked a further distinction between them and universities.

These were not the only elements to address the delicate boundary issue between the two institutions. Another equally pressing concern was the question of pedagogic autonomy, that is, the right to develop programmes without prior clearance from the central ministry. Formally, the Higher Education Guideline Law went back on previous legislation by granting pedagogic autonomy to *all* higher education establishments in the public sector as part of a more comprehensive policy (Portugal, 2008: Article 9.7). By so doing, it accomplished what from the polytechnics' perspective may be seen as a final act of redress in an issue that had poisoned relationships between universities and polytechnics for nigh on two decades.

Granting pedagogical autonomy – that is, the freedom to launch new programmes and courses without prior clearance from the central authority – was a handsome gesture to the polytechnic cause. It was also a singularly empty one. For what the Prince conceded generously with his right hand, through the provisions of the Guideline Law, he had already snatched away with his left with the legislation that created A3ES. By requiring that all new programmes, whatever their institutional origins, had compulsorily to be assessed and accredited by this new agency, pedagogic autonomy, in the original meaning set down in the 1988 Law and reiterated in the Guideline Law, was less generous than it appeared at first sight.

It would be unkind to suggest that pedagogic autonomy now possessed a certain similarity to the legendary Dead Sea fruit. If the Scriptures are to be believed, this fruit, despite an initial allure, turns to dust and ashes in the eating! What remains no less evident, however, is that defining – or, in the case of Portugal, re-defining – the Evaluative State was indeed a powerful prior condition in shaping the scope of institutional autonomy.[5] Nevertheless, pedagogic autonomy was only one among a series of responsibilities to be delegated to the institutional level. In doing so, what may be seen as 'the balance of responsibility' at the systemic level between public sector universities and polytechnics was profoundly altered, which is why these initiatives have been scrutinized.

Institutional autonomy: different viewpoints

Endowing higher education with what the Guideline Law laid down in terms of statutory, pedagogic, scientific, cultural, administrative, financial and disciplinary autonomy vis-à-vis the central state (Portugal, 2008: Article 11.1) may be analysed in different contexts: first, as a Portuguese instance of a broader process that was visible elsewhere in Western Europe – that of 'offloading' part of the burden that had hitherto been the lot of the central ministry; second, as an example of reinforced institutional autonomy, which tends to be the most-often used presentational discourse; or, third, as illustrating the setting down of conditions necessary for re-launching the Evaluative State. All three interpretations are equally fruitful.

However, there remains one further angle of attack. This is to see the delegating of a multi-faceted autonomy as part of the ongoing historical dynamic in the higher education policy of Portugal. Such a perspective builds on the leitmotif that has been developed in terms of the continuities and recurrent issues that have arisen in the past two decades. Within this setting, a reasonable case may be made for examining the provisions in the Guideline Law and more specifically institutional autonomy as building forward from an earlier rationale, the origins of which may be traced back to Law 108/88 of 1988, the first example in Portuguese legislation of the principles of university autonomy being translated into practice grounded in the university. This is a fruitful exercise in many ways. It opens up new dimensions to the theme of continuity and change in Portuguese higher education. It also puts the issue of institutional autonomy very specifically and very firmly in a Portuguese context. Finally, it sheds new light on the way in which institutional autonomy is usually presented. Arguably, the appropriateness of this approach has already been demonstrated in the way in which some of the recommendations in the OECD Review on Tertiary Education in Portugal appear in a new light. Precisely because the report has been re-inserted within the long-term perspective provided by the 1988 Law, the OECD report takes on a significance even beyond that which its draftsmen had originally entertained.[6]

One final point remains. Using the 1988 University Autonomy Act as a reference point – as a marker in Portugal's history of higher education policy – against which elements can be singled out and followed through, a similar revision occurs in the very particular status of Decree Law 62/2007 as a Guideline Law. It brings our attention back once again to the very particular interpretation of legal homogeneity in Portugal. This interpretation deserves closer attention.

Definitions of autonomy tend to be either implicit or, in other words, to have a residual status. Autonomy exists in the interstices of legal codification. The Higher Education Guideline Law, by contrast, defined the boundaries of institutional autonomy with considerable precision and explicitness. It defined autonomy as the right for the university to take decisions in the scientific, cultural, administrative, financial and disciplinary spheres. In a very real way the Guideline Law also *extended* the principle of institutional latitude. This it did by re-iterating a singular and remarkable provision that had already existed two decades earlier in the Portuguese University Autonomy Act of 1988. The 1988 Act granted the freedom to a university to draw up its own internal bylaws, one of its particular features.[7] This provision was retained in the 2007 Higher

Education Guideline Law. However, by allowing the *institution* to 'fill in the details', it also conferred an additional dimension to the very notion of a Guideline Law, one that was not found in comparable legislation elsewhere.

What set the Portuguese version of guideline legislation off from its counterparts in France and Germany, for example, is not the possibility for including later, further and more detailed elements. This feature is built into guideline laws as it is in their Austrian, French and German counterparts. It is what distinguishes a Guideline Law from other types of legislation. As its name implies, a Guideline Law provides a framework, orientation or general direction to which further detail may subsequently and at a later date be added. However, in its classic form, the opportunity for filling in further detail is reserved for the *government* and for the legislator. In the Portuguese case, this provision is certainly present. But latitude in respect of detail to be completed is extended to the *individual institution of higher education* so that it may subsequently align and accommodate its specific mission and objectives as well as modify its internal regulations and bylaws that embed the institution into the broader general framework that the law first sets out. This discretionary element of institutional initiative contained in the Portuguese Guideline Law is very different from the usual construction such legislation entails elsewhere and which, elsewhere, amounts to giving a second bite of the cherry to the legislator or the ministry. In effect, the Portuguese version of Guideline Laws was itself a practical example of institutional autonomy in action.

Re-engineering the higher education system

The tidying up of boundaries between sectors – university and non-university, public and private – and the clarifying of the mission, important though they are in modernizing higher education for Portugal, are better seen as the necessary concentration, the indispensable precondition to setting higher education on a new path. However, remedying previous shortcomings does not always guarantee the will to move in new directions, even if the capacity to do so has been both improved and enhanced by assigning and 'offloading' new responsibilities to the individual institution. Strengthening leadership, institutional latitude or both is certainly necessary. Equally significant, however, is a mobilizing force, a strategy that at one and the same time places an obvious premium on the ability to respond rapidly to 'the forces of the market' and to have sufficient flexibility and the formally recognized right to do so.

Changes in the structure of institutional governance may, from a purely analytic standpoint, fulfil both purposes. It is true that reform in the balance of power at the institutional level most certainly affects that same balance of power at the system level, and this will be tackled in Chapter 12, which examines the impact of the Guideline Law in re-shaping governance at the *institutional* level.

Two major innovations

The Guideline Law's strategy for the development of a self-adjusting system of higher education rested on two major innovations and, no less important, on the final linking up between regular institutionally-based performance assessment with contract-based financing, with the central role falling to A3ES. The two innovations contained in Decree Law 62/2007 provided for the creation of 'foundation universities' (Portugal, 2008: Chapter IV, Article 129, English translation) as well as for enhanced collaboration within and between the university/non-university sectors at the level of organizational research units (Portugal, 2008: Articles 13, 14, 16). Taken at face value, these two options are of considerable importance. Not only were they levers for restructuring higher education, they also placed the onus for re-structuring on the individual university or polytechnic. In short, they opened the path up to what may be described as 'organic restructuring', driven from within the higher education system and subsequently recognized – or rejected – by the ministry, the minister or, if and when it ceases to have a purely metaphysical status, by the Council for Higher Education which, whilst envisaged, has yet to be implemented.

This is a very different dynamic indeed from the classic 'top-down' approach that has long held sway in the Portuguese higher education system. Such a 'within system' dynamic does not deprive central government of the ultimate responsibility for shaping higher education, but it bids fair to place the government in a reactive rather than in a proactive posture. With such options in place, from the standpoint of central government, higher education is bent to national purpose and priorities less by the handing down of directives than by the rejection of those elements in an institution's strategic development programme which do *not* so correspond. Shaping higher education thus becomes a matter of institutional initiative and ministerial veto. This might be called 'remote steering' (van Vught, 1989; 1997: 80–104). From the viewpoint of the government, it is also 'reverse steering'.

Reform from within: a strategic objective

Viewed as a strategic whole, these four dimensions represent more than simply extending institutional latitude to individual universities and polytechnics. In essence, what is involved is the ability of individual establishments to shape not merely their own place and profile within the system of higher education but, by the same token, to also shape the contours of the system itself. This potential for reform driven 'from within' is a highly significant step. Though it in no way compromises the right and duty of the ministry or an equivalent such as a Council for Higher Education to recognize the initiatives taken, even so, it is clear that by opening up the possibility for public universities to convert to a 'foundation university', a high degree of the initiative for 'system development' moves from central government down to the individual establishment. The same process of 're-siting' initiatives on a less grand, but no less crucial, area of inter-institutional collaboration to make optimum use of human, financial or equipment resources in effect performs the same function – that of rationalizing the existing provision in the light of possible changes in demand upon it. In either case, whether opting for 'foundation' status, which appears at the moment to be more of an experiment,[8] or creating inter-institutional links for teaching and R&D, the boundaries of institutional self-determination are greatly extended.

In the matter of 'foundation universities', the Higher Education Guideline Law followed the OECD recommendations, though it is only fair to point out that the emergence of such 'hybrid' establishments was visible in Western Europe well before the OECD Review Panel even set foot in Portugal. Sweden and Germany, for instance, have been particularly active in this regard (Neave, 2008: 61–3; 2009b). More to the point, however, it would appear that the role of foundation universities, largely as a result of the greater latitude that is held to come from a combination of concentrated structures of management and more diverse sources of funding,[9] is to act as the catalysing agent to self-driven 'inner reform' for both the public sector from which it comes and for the private sector to which it resembles in being governed by private law.

Re-configuring the Evaluative State

Just as the unfolding strategic purpose behind the Higher Education Guideline Law sought to impart an enhanced capacity for institutional 'self-adjustment' and potentially to accelerate the dynamic of system change from within, so the institutional latitude necessary for realizing these aims was balanced out by strengthening external procedures of verification. In setting out the enabling Act for evaluating higher education, the legislator introduced a number of changes. The first placed A3ES on a very different footing from its predecessor, CNAVES. Compulsory and regular external assessments for quality of performance and the task of accreditation for all sectors of higher education were brought together under a single-tier national agency in place of its predecessor's passably baroque structure (Portugal, Law 38/2007: Chapter I, Article 2).

Re-defining the nature of the Evaluative State in Portugal deserves close attention, not simply because, as with its counterparts in other systems of higher education in Western Europe, it went through a number of phases of development. It deserves closer attention for one very simple reason: its evolutionary dynamic was very different indeed from that of its counterparts elsewhere. Whereas the first phase of its developmental trajectory in the form of CNAVES placed particular weight on what is best described as a 'balance between contending interests', the second stage, which saw CNAVES abolished[10] and replaced by A3ES, set very particular store on concentrating the processes of assessment and accreditation into one single body. At the very time when other systems – those in Germany, Ireland and Spain, for example – were engaged in adding to the agencies associated with the Evaluative State and, by so doing, created multi-level, multi-agency systems of evaluation, Portugal went in the opposite direction. A3ES saw the Evaluative State in Portugal revert to the very same single agency model from which others had subsequently moved on. As such, it returned to an arrangement that was remarkably akin to the original proposal, developed and outlined by the rectoral 'Party of Movement' which the government had rejected earlier. As a unitary state, Portugal reverted to the unitary model for both evaluation and accreditation.

With its dual responsibility for assessing the performance of higher education and for ascertaining how far individual institutions fulfilled their mission in the light of operational performance indicators (Portugal, Law 38/2007: Chapter II, Article 3.1) allied with the process of accreditation, clearly in the mind of the legislators, A3ES stood at the 'commanding heights' of a performance-based system.

A3ES is a foundation under private law. It is independent of both the political sphere and of establishments of higher education (Portugal, Decree Law 369/2007, 5 November 2007: 3). All higher education establishments are subject to its procedures of assessment and accreditation (Decree Law 369/2007: Article 3, para 2). Finally, A3ES was given the exclusive right to grant accreditation for professional purposes to any higher education establishment or any study cycle (Article 7, para 8). Other 'entities' are expressly forbidden to act in an accrediting capacity, which explicitly excludes the possibility of individual higher education establishments seeking accreditation from non-national, external bodies.

The heart of the Portuguese Evaluative State: monitoring and intelligence

It is evident that the keystone in Portugal's definitive move towards the Evaluative State was now in place. It is also equally obvious that the potential range of influence that A3ES may come to wield will have repercussions well beyond its remit of evaluating and assessing, verifying and accrediting institutional performance and achievement. If A3ES' remit is to develop a 'culture of quality' and to give official weight and cognisance to institutional self-evaluation, it will also possess the influence indirectly to shape the higher education system. This, it is reasonable to suggest, given its independent status vis-à-vis both the ministry and the higher education system, will emerge at two levels. Both levels reflect the fact that institutional evaluations on a compulsory and regular basis are effectively a form of monitoring which, at the disaggregated level, focuses on the achievements of the individual university or polytechnic. At the same time, such achievements, once aggregated up, open the way for regular and ongoing accounts on the condition of higher education at the national level.

Thus, the functions of A3ES, from a policy perspective, place it at the crossroads between two streams of 'intelligence'. Both are vital. Both are indispensable to the basic task of ensuring at one and the same time that institutional and system adjustment on a continuous basis – a quality earlier described in terms of 'organic restructuring' – have meaning and, more to the point, convey the information necessary to translate meaning into action. A3ES stands, on the one hand, at the 'feedback' point to the individual higher education establishment about its own specific condition, acknowledged capacities and achievements – or their notorious absence! On the other hand, it also stands at the 'feed-forward' point by independently presenting reports on the 'state of the nation' to the ministry and the government. It provides the gold coin of up-to-date information on the basis of which national policy may assess its own progress in the light of the goals it has set itself. Such information flows ought to allow the national administration, where necessary, to undertake 'mid-course corrections' or to launch new initiatives.

The presence of a 'dual-stream' intelligence and monitoring system, which in effect is what A3ES provides for quality and accreditation, may also bring with it – potentially at least – a 'solution' to one of the abiding issues that has bedevilled Portuguese higher education for the best part of quarter of a century: administrative overload at the centre. If the role and place of A3ES is scrutinized from within this specific *problématique*, it is clear – at least on paper – that its 'feedback' function is the *conditio sine qua non* thanks to which much of the burden of detecting short-term and detailed blockages or non-responsiveness to rapidly changing external demand for programmes, projects, courses or for administrative efficiency – and, most important of all, rapidly coming up with an appropriate remedy – can be 'outsourced' from the ministry to the individual university and polytechnic.

Evaluation as the key to a new division of academic labour

One of the most important functions that A3ES may fulfil is to allow a clear division between the tactics of adjustment and the strategy of reform. Monitoring and feedback to the individual institution ought, in principle, to 'outsource' the former to the exact point in the particular institutional setting where remedy is required and where the institution has both power and authority to take it in hand. By the same logic, such 'offloading', taken in conjunction with A3ES' role of 'feeding-forward' system-level trends to the ministry and the government, ought to allow both administration and the *pays politique* to concentrate on the latter perspective.

Such a re-distribution of tasks lies at the heart of the rationale for the Evaluative State and has been justified both in terms of diminishing the heavy hand of the central administration and raising its level of strategic effectiveness by concentrating its attention on shaping medium-term priorities. This 'new' *modus operandi* has been described in various ways: as 'remote steering' (van Vught, 1989; 1997: 80–104) when viewed from the perspective of the central administration or 'New Public Management' when viewed from the its operational consequences upon the re-distribution of tasks – and thus responsibility and authority – within the public service sector (Pollit, 1995: 130–54) or, in this case, when injected into the fabric of higher education.

Less clear, however, is the degree of leverage that A3ES may exercise in stimulating competition between institutions. For whilst competition occupies a much-publicized place as the basic driver behind the wheel of neoliberalism, it does not necessarily follow that evaluation and assessment always have to endorse this form of manipulation and persuasion (HSV, 2003) any more than it follows that the Evaluative State is exclusively, uniquely and monogamously wedded to neoliberalism, though there are many who would have us believe that this is so (Amaral and Neave, 2009).

A3ES, the Evaluative State and value allocation

The Evaluative State may certainly be used as a vehicle to embed the dimensions of institutional behaviour – competition being the most evident – as an integral feature in higher education systems. But it is equally possible to apply similar techniques of evaluation and judgement in another ideological context entirely: for instance, one in which weight is placed on cooperation, solidarity and working together, which are no less efficient means of sharing scarce resources (SVR, 2008: 1(6)–6(6)). It is significant in this regard that A3ES' unhappy predecessor foreswore both league tables and presenting its reports in ways that would lend themselves to the tempting approach of comparison by public ranking. Such a stance cannot entirely prevent abuse. Nor, for that matter, can it prevent individuals and institutions from re-interpreting their achievements in this way. Still, it is worth noting that other evaluation systems, notably the Swedish system, have hitherto been no less adamant in resisting the temptation posed by league tables (HSV, 2005a: 15). However, it must be admitted that ranking is a powerful device, both in installing compliance – not always a desirable quality in human endeavour – and in racheting up the speed of institutional response.[11]

In this respect, A3ES as the focal point of the Evaluative State in Portugal faces some very crucial decisions. Verifying performance and granting validation to courses and programmes is never an end in itself. Behind performance and achievement are purpose and values. Today's institutional efficiency is often held up as endorsing the economic doctrine of the moment, sometimes alluded to with elegance, customary to the French, as '*la pensée unique*'. Certainly, this task of defining the values that performance is to sustain may be left to the institutional leadership to determine pragmatically as the implications of the way in which performance is weighed up emerge. Yet, however 'neutral' the technical procedures and however 'independent' the status of A3ES, the issue of values conveyed, whether ostensibly or covertly, remains. Irrespective of whether the decision is to be taken expeditiously or incrementally, A3ES will, sooner or later, have to choose between whether it is to be perceived or whether in reality it is to act as a channel for verifying not merely the attainment of national goals and the fulfilment of the institutional mission, but both set against the public good. It will, in short, have to decide whether it is to reflect the single doctrine of contemporary neoliberalism or, on the contrary, to sustain a certain doctrinal diversity and eclecticism. Brutally expressed, the issue is whether in assessing performance, A3ES is to sustain the 'Old Testament' of the OECD and neoliberalism or whether it is to act as the vehicle by which that latter is either modified, bypassed or surpassed.

Precisely because A3ES stands at the commanding heights in a performance-driven higher education system, it occupies a position of authority and responsibility. Thus, it has an implicit function of 'value allocation' (Easton, 1965). This it exercises through verification, evaluation and accreditation. And authority, as was argued earlier, is inseparable from the vision, values and therefore the relationship – whether one of primacy or subordination – between the economic or social dimensions in human affairs which evaluation shapes and embeds into higher education.

12
Reform at the Cutting Edge: The Institutional Level

Introduction

It is one of the more outlandish paradoxes of our day that, at the very moment when the sheer administrative and managerial complexity of 'post-modern' higher education systems reaches such a pitch, the best minds in the nation's permanent civil service elite throw up their hands and confess themselves unable to master it. It is scarcely less paradoxical that at the same time, executive decision making should be 'handed over' and concentrated in the hands of individuals who are not simply external to the university, but are part-timers to boot! The rise of the 'external' president in the Netherlands or Chairman of the General Council in Portuguese universities, and the extension of the 'pool' from which chairmen are drawn to 'outside personalities' are not, of course exclusive to Portugal. Indeed, the Higher Education Guideline Law of 2007 moved in the same direction (Portugal, 2008: Article 82, para 1). Similar measures, which have already been discussed, are evident from recent and current initiatives in France, Denmark and the Netherlands, among others.[1]

Policy as perversity

In truth, the paradox is never-ending. For it is no less bizarre that decision-making responsibility should be concentrated in even fewer hands at the very moment when the range of responsibilities 'offloaded' from the national administration to individual universities and polytechnics multiply fast and furiously. Even if the scope of institutional responsibility remained unchanged, to have fewer 'leaders' involved holds out little promise other than sure and certain 'administrative overload' being transferred from the ministry to the university. Administrative overload is far from conducive – save for Stakhanovites and workaholics – to efficiency, to the quality of service rendered and, even less so, to satisfaction amongst those who bestow and those who receive such services! Yet, by its very nature, what is presented as 'institutional autonomy' most assuredly does not reduce the range of functions and responsibilities. Rather the contrary. In circumstances such as these, to limit, as the Portuguese Higher Education Guideline Law stipulated, the numbers making up the General Council of the university, reducing it to between 15 and 35 individuals, depending on the size of university involved (Portugal, 2008: Article 81, para 1), appears perverse in the extreme. In truth, under such conditions 'strong' leadership is necessary if only because only the strong are likely to survive!

Amazing reductions, wondrous shrinkage

Cutting back the membership of key executive bodies, the relegation of others to advisory status, a fate that the Higher Education Guideline Law meted out to university Senates[2] (Portugal, 2008: Article 77), is a pattern echoed outside Portugal, in France, the Netherlands, the UK and beyond. In the case of the UK, shrinkage accompanied the introduction of a 'corporate' management structure to the governance of 'new universities', summoned into being by the Higher Education Act of 1992. This Act elevated one-time polytechnics to full university status (Williams, 1996: 39–56). Similarly amazing reductions marked the efforts of the French Minister for Higher Education and Technology[3] and the Dutch legislation dating from March 1996 (de Boer, 2003: 253–5).

However, strengthening governance and strengthening leadership are two distinct elements in the overall drive to 'rationalize' university management, a process that parades under a number of different flags – the 'rise of managerialism' (Daalder and Shils, 1982; Kogan, 2004) comprising the application of the canons of 'New Public Management' to the university world being the most common. Within these boundaries, the exercise of re-engineering higher education at the institutional level takes place precisely because 'managerialism' relates to organizing knowledge as a saleable product. This nexus forms the basis – which is predominantly commercial in nature – of the services that the university may negotiate with the 'knowledge society'. It also determines the nature of the emerging relationship between higher education, the economy and, incidentally, society.

Broad is the path that leads to managerialism

If all paths to institutional autonomy head towards managerialism or appear to subscribe to the canons of New Public Management, this does not mean that the underlying purpose is always the same. Nor does it mean that those who find themselves dragged along the road of 'faith-based policies' as 'fellow travellers' perceive the journey towards such new operational, ethical and administrative models in the same way (Santiago, Carvalho, Amaral and Meek, 2006). Finally, even if the internal reform of institutions is legitimated by evoking successful examples of systems elsewhere that have dutifully plodded along such a road and happily reached New Public Management's safe and efficient haven, it does not follow that all share the same motives for travelling the same weary highway.

The metamorphosis of the university *sensu lato* from being the home of shared collegiality to being the place of 'managed professionals' (Rhoades, 1998; Scott, 1998) fulfilled different purposes, obeyed different priorities and proceeded down different avenues. Thus, for instance, the end purpose of strengthening executive power in British universities has been justified in terms of that ultimate in operational reductionism and self-distortion – working better with business and industry (Smith, Adams and Mount, 2007: 8). In France, by contrast, strengthening the 'external presence' is seen as a lever to gain greater purchase over reform internal to a university that has long shown little enthusiasm for the whims of ministers or the wiles of presidents! In Spain, however, closer external ties have a broader and more diffuse end – strengthening the regional economy, certainly, but doing so as a means of dealing with a broader issue: namely, to sustain the viability of regional cultures. By focusing on procedures, structures and instrumentalities in a desperate effort to show divergence or convergence around a particular model, itself a pilgrimage towards the normative and the orthodox, we tend to blind ourselves to the very different purposes and the very different strategies to which they are put – a classic example of confounding means with ends, if not a reversal of them both.[4]

Some stops along the way

Along the road that takes a university away from collegiality and towards 'managerialism' lie a number of intermediary stops: the growth and expansion of the Administrative Estate, the internal re-distribution of tasks, the drive towards 'professionalizing' management and the strengthening of leadership. Broadly speaking, the first two stages – the expansion of the Administrative Estate and the internal re-distribution of tasks – are internal to the individual university. They may then be considered as part of the process alluded to earlier as 'organic growth'. However, the latter two analytical stages – the professionlization of management and the strengthening of leadership – are qualitatively different. They are different because in those systems where higher education is rooted in legal codification and legal homogeneity, the latter two developments require formal enactment if they are to be recognized by the appropriate authority and thus have a formal recognized existence. For this reason, these two dimensions may be considered as 'externalizing the process of institutional re-engineering'. They are external in two respects: first, by dint of the fact that authorization is required from external authority; and, second, because once authorization is granted, what was hitherto an internal practice of pragmatic accommodation and adjustment is transformed into a formal and permanent structure and/or procedure.[5]

Collegiality and esprit de corps: *central concepts*

The difference between these two stages is crucial to our understanding the basic *prise de position* amongst members of the Academic Estate taken up willy-nilly into this particular institutional dynamic. The difference is useful in that it reveals a pragmatic and structural underpinning to that most emotive of all symbols, the dissolving of 'collegiality' as a real and working ethic *in saecula saeculorum*. As most academics will admit, collegiality embraces far more than professional relationships. It is far greater than a professional ethic or *déontologie*. As the *Weltanschauung* of the Academic Estate, collegiality encompasses collective and individual identity, status, personal worth, personal honour, institutional authenticity and honorability, and thus binds together personal, collective and institutional standing and esteem in the national community – qualities that are literally non-negotiable without denying them and non-separable without compromising the whole.

There are, naturally, nuances and contextual variations that modify what literally amounts to a 'mystery'. This particular term has nothing whatsoever to do with superstition or with a supernatural presence in the groves of academia. Rather, it relates back directly to the original medieval quality that, in turn, harks back to the Latin '*mysterium*' and which emerges in modern French as both '*métier*' (trade or occupation) and as '*maîtrise*' (mastery).

Academia as a 'mystery' is the common and unifying trait between 'collegiality' – the Anglo-Saxon interpretation of academia's collective mindset – and, for instance, its French counterpart, which is (again literally) an *'esprit de corps'*. Such differences in terminology reflect the equally basic difference between the view of academia as a stand-alone 'profession' in the Anglo-Saxon world and the opposing vision, which was until very recently dominant in mainland Europe, of academia as a key body in the state's provision of public services – which, in France for instance, emerges in the untranslatable term *'corps de l'Etat'* (Neave and Edelstein, 1987: 211ff.).

Thus, collegiality carries with it the same overtones for American and British academics as *'esprit de corps'* does for their French colleagues who, officially and until the recent vexations of Madame Pécresse,[6] could still count (although for how long is highly problematic) on formally being part of the *'corps universitaire'* (Kessler, 1986).

The dynamics behind the rise of the Administrative Estate

So long as 're-engineering' the institution remains within the limits of the first two stages, collegiality is not necessarily seen by the Academic Estate to be under threat; in fact, quite the contrary. In its initial stages, the growth of the Administrative Estate[7] can relieve the burden on its academic colleagues, above all in such areas as student services and financial assistance, 'support services' that do not bear directly on the definition or the content of teaching and learning. An expansion in the numbers of the Administrative Estate thus shades over and begins the dynamic process of internal 'task re-distribution'. What marks this second stage off from the third – the 'professionalization' of the Administrative Estate – lies in the re-distribution of tasks that takes place during the second stage, which tends to be largely pragmatic and hand to mouth. The 'collegium' chooses to 'hand over' activities of a routine and, it has to be admitted, often of a fastidious nature. Within the institution, such 'delegated responsibilities' are not held by the 'collegium' or the 'corps' to be central to teaching, learning or research. They do not, for this very reason, determine either collective or individual status and ranking for either 'corps' or 'college'. In the second stage, the Administrative Estate 'services' the Academic Estate. The historical pattern of what the British sociologist A.H. Halsey termed 'Donnish Dominion' continues and is thus preserved (Halsey, 1995).

The third stage, identified here by the 'professionalization' of the Administrative Estate, is, however, a very different matter. 'Professionalization' involves a dual dynamic as a development that is both internal and external to the individual higher education institute.

The emergence of, and the coalescence around, a self-conscious collective identity amongst those individuals whose skills are subject to direction by others is the classic intrinsic explanation of professionalization.[8] Far more weighty in the Administrative Estate's rapid drive towards professional status have been such external events as a reduction in the national budget for higher education, the drive for cost-effectiveness by governments and the imperative necessity for higher education to demonstrate and to prove its efficient use of human, monetary and equipment resources. To this it is fair to add the rise of the Evaluative State, for it expands the scope of those things for which the institution is answerable by adding quality and performance to the accounts required. By doing so, it acts as a final catalysis to the process of administrative professionalization.

Inverting the relationship between the Academic and Administrative Estates

Both the shift from accounting to accountability and the obligation to demonstrate the veracity of claims of efficiency indelibly alter the function and thus the status of the Administrative Estate. The services it discharges are no longer subordinate to the requirements of the Academic Estate. With the rise of conditional financing and the practice of 'contractualization',[9] the press to generate diversified sources of funding and the need to 'market' the university are not just an *Umwertung aller Werten* of the historical self-concept of the university, they are often and literally the price of its survival. For this reason, they bring about an inversion in status between the Academic and Administrative Estates. The conditions upon which academia may continue to discharge *its* functions of teaching and learning, research and local community servicing are directly related to, determined by and *subordinated to* the unchallengeable priority of ensuring the overall financial health of the institution – an inevitable consequence of neoliberalism's application of the cash nexus as the prime yardstick of human and thus institutional achievement! Hence, as with the Anglican litany, so with the respective relationship between the Academic and Administrative Estates: 'He hath put down the Mighty from their Seat and hath exalted Them of Low Degree!'

However, the pressure from outside upon the institution is only part of the saga. Two other sub-dynamics play an equally significant role in inverting the relationship between the two Estates. They are best illustrated by referring to two procedures that are well known to the practitioners of military skulduggery: ex-filtration and in-filtration.

1) Ex-filtration

Ex-filtration is the process by which individuals with permanent tenure and who are officially employed as full-time members of the academic staff assume administrative and managerial functions in parallel to their primary task as teachers and/or researchers. In itself, ex-filtration is far from being either novel or even innovative. On the contrary, it is – and has long been – an inescapable part of academia's lot. Those chosen are then primarily members of the Academic Estate but also have executive responsibilities at the base unit level (faculty, school or department) (Premfors, 1989: 5–22). This posting, though temporary, confers on them a dual status. Though recognized as full-time academics, these 'draftees' are, in effect, 'ex-filtrated' from the Academic Estate to perform 'service tasks' on behalf of their colleagues within the framework of the Administrative Estate. Not untypical in this regard is the departmental chairman in British academia or, to draw on an even more exotic source, the 'Prefekt' in Swedish universities (Institute for International Education, 2001: 7). In both cases, their function is executive. 'Intellectual leadership', however, remains with the senior full professor in the department (Moodie, 1986: 43–56). Like their American counterparts, who were the source of inspiration for the practice of the non-professorial chairman, departmental chairmen do not necessarily enjoy senior status. Their positioning in the formal academic hierarchy appears to be relatively eclectic, not to say plainly ambiguous. Scholarship today equates them with 'middle management' (Santiago, Carvalho, Amaral and Meek, 2006: 215–50). One could not hope for a more revealing illustration of the eclectic identity conferred by 'ex-filtration', not to mention validating the judiciousness of the concept and its appellation!

Whilst such 'dual-status' figures and thus the dual functions their status reflects are routine in the university world, they are a particularly sensitive pointer to the changing balance of power between the Academic and Administrative Estates. They are, in effect, at the point of intersection of the bottom-driven academic hierarchy and the top-down line management of the administrative hierarchy. However, the question remains as to whether they are the upward emanation of the Academic Estate or a downward expression of the Administrative Estate. That the common convention in higher education studies is to rank them as 'middle management' hints at the enhanced responsibilities now falling to the Administrative Estate, not least in its role as coordinator of institutional purpose. Whether it is reasonable to suggest that this shift in the balance of power is wholly to the benefit of the Administrative Estate is, of course, to risk implying that the relationship between the two is largely a zero-sum game.

2) In-filtration

However, weakening the Academic Estate by dint of a temporary and lateral assimilation of some of its members into the arcana of administration is not the only dynamic present. 'In-filtration' is no less a potent process. Nevertheless, whereas ex-filtration inserts the professional academic as an amateur administrator into the managerial chain of command, in-filtration obeys a reverse logic. It injects professional career administrators into the base units, with the responsibility euphemistically presented as 'coordination' or 'leadership'. Whether it is either charitable or accurate to describe such individuals as 'amateur academics' is very probably unkind and certainly gratuitous! Just as it was pointed out that the notion of departmental 'middle management' derived much from well-established practices in North American universities, here the origins of professional administrators spring from the same source (de Boer and Goedegebuure, 2009).

In American universities, the Dean wields powers far more extensive than, for instance, his or her British, French or Spanish fellows did. Answerable for planning and budgeting at the faculty level and for general strategic development, his or her remit also includes recruiting, negotiating conditions of remuneration for all academic staff under his or her responsibility and appointing new academic staff. The American Dean has direct 'line management' responsibility to the Provost in charge of academic affairs in the university's central administration (Read, 2000). In contrast to the well-established practice in Europe's universities, his or her position is less the senior elected member at the faculty level and hence a projection of the *ascending* academic hierarchy so much as the executive arm of the *descending* administrative nexus reaching out and down into the base units at the faculty level.[10]

However, examples of 'in-filtration' are rather less frequent. The only instances to my knowledge where so far the figure of the 'European' Dean has been metamorphosed along the lines of his or her American colleague are to be found in Ireland and the Netherlands (Maassen, 2002: 449–64). There, full-time professional administrators, some lured away from previous posts in hospital administration or from the private sector, have been brought in with the purpose of streamlining operations and introducing to academia the benefits of the managerial rigour acquired in large-scale and complex institutions in both the public and private sectors. Significantly, higher education scholars usually allude to them either as 'the Manager Dean' (de Boer and Goedegebuure, 2009) or as the 'Professional Dean' (van Welie, 2000), the latter being not overly tender of their predecessors' abilities!

Nevertheless, the person of the 'Professional Dean' is a neat illustration of the process of 'in-filtration' as a second dynamic that contributes to inverting the roles of the Academic and Administrative Estates. In-filtration, it may be suggested, effectively curtails the upward reach of the academic hierarchy. It does so by extending the central core of executive power down into the base units. At the same time, by re-designating the profile of the 'Professional Dean' as an *administrative* professional, power is placed in the hands of an individual whose professional identity is shaped less by a commonalty of values that stem – or have been 'indoctrinated' is perhaps the most appropriate term – from having once studied an academic discipline currently practised by those whom he or she administers; rather, this referential commonalty has a different focus – the mastery and possession of a range of administrative techniques that serve to assert a professional identity shared with the institution's central administration.

Envoi

It has been suggested that in-filtration and ex-filtration are not only present, they are also powerful in re-shaping the relationship between the Academic and Administrative Estates in the university. Managerialism has emerged as a way to re-engineer the capacity of Europe's universities to cope with pressure on resources and to come up with 'solutions' to the insistent pressure from the government, acting in the name of external interests, to have higher education respond rapidly to demands, whether real or perceived (European Commission 2006, quoted in de Boer and Goedegebuure, 2009). There are arguably good reasons, quite apart from personal sensitivities, to see the 'professionalization' of the Academic Estate as a dissolvent to the spirit of collegiality, previously the prime vehicle of academic and, by extension, institutional cohesion. What cannot be foreseen with any degree of confidence, let alone accuracy, is whether the mechanisms analysed here to account for the triumph of the Administrative

Estate may not evolve further, and even less so the direction that they will take.

Having laid out a broad backdrop, the following chapter returns to the specific issue of how Portugal's system of higher education has adjusted its internal governance in response to generically similar issues.

13
Portuguese Higher Education Reform: Four Key Dimensions

Introduction

It is a cliché of the most abominable sort to say that reform introduces 'efficiency' and 'effectiveness', for if these two qualities were absent from what is to be changed, there would be no point in reforming in the first place. In truth, there are very few if any changes in higher education that ultimately cannot be boosted without invoking these two perfectly meaningless terms. Still, they have their uses. They suggest that the measures taken are to be pragmatic rather than idealistic, utilitarian rather than moral, though disagreement on what is useful is often as acrimonious as disagreement over what is moral! More important by far are such questions as what has to be changed? To what purpose? How are they perceived by those affected? And, finally, how have they worked out?

Crucial though these questions are, by their nature, not all of them can be answered by the legislator, who is concerned with initial intent and purpose.[1] The latter two questions, for instance, though important, can only be answered either by the action of interested parties, by subsequent scholarship or the former being evaluated by the latter, which has been one of the roles of scholarship before the Evaluative State took this task over. Succinctly stated, it is entirely within the scope of human endeavour that what is initially conceived and presented as efficient and effective, like military planning, does not always survive the first contact with the enemy or, in this case, with institutional reality.

Four dimensions in the Higher Education Guideline Law

Seen by an outside observer, the Portuguese Higher Education Guideline Law of 2007 introduced four key provisions. These were of paramount significance to the individual higher education establishments. They were as follows:

1) The representation of outside interests on Governing Councils.
2) The definition of institutional autonomy as functional and operationally multi-faceted.
3) The provision for an experimental institutional model that is radically different in its structures (legal, financial and governance).
4) The possibility of extensive cross-institutional collaboration and resource usage at the level of organizational units.

In examining these four provisions, which are key to the institutional re-engineering of Portugal's higher education system, two main approaches are employed. The first focuses on the national context and particularly on the advance that current change represents in comparison with what went before. The second places the thrust of current legislation against similar developments in Europe. The two approaches are complementary to one another, but they do not necessarily yield the same outcome or support the same assessment, still less the same conclusion. What appears to be radical when viewed from inside Portugal and in terms of the unfolding saga of the nation's policies in higher education is not necessarily so when set against parallel initiatives elsewhere.

1) Injecting the outside interest

The Portuguese Higher Education Guideline Law of 2007 introduced a new form of representation into the universities and polytechnics in the shape of the General Council. In turn, the General Council acts as a vehicle for change across four dimensions. In the first place, it opened the way for individuals 'of merit with relevant knowledge and experience not belonging to the institution' (Portugal, 2008: Article 81, para 2c) to be co-opted onto the Council. Co-option entailed a two-stage process: first, the support of one-third of the Council after hearing a 'justified proposal'; and, second, an absolute majority. In the second place, outside interests account for 30 per cent of the General Council's total membership (Portugal, 2008: Article 81, paras 5a and 5b). In the third place, the chairman of the General Council is elected from the ranks of external personalities (Portugal, 2008: Article 82, para 1). In the fourth place, eligibility for election to the post of rector is open to external candidates drawn from the ranks of academia from other establishments or research institutes, whether

Portuguese or foreign (Portugal, 2008: Article 86, para 3). This particular stipulation broke with the tradition of choosing the rector solely from internal candidates. Similar provision was made for polytechnics, with the difference that presidents/directors were to be drawn from individuals of 'recognized professional experience' (Portugal, 2008: Article 86, para 4b).

The General Council

The term of the General Council is for four years, except for student representatives, whose term lasts two years (Portugal, 2008: Article 81, para 8). Meeting four times a year (Portugal, 2008: Article 84, para 1), the General Council exercises what is best described as strategic oversight, which covers such duties as approving the university's medium-term planning, the general guidelines dealing with pedagogic, scientific and financial matters, the sale or acquisition of assets as well as approving budget proposals and the annual consolidated account (Portugal, 2008: Article 82, para 2f). The decision to set up, close or alter the status of organizational units also falls within its responsibility. (Portugal, 2008: Article 82, para 2c).

Strengthening the external interest is innovatory when seen from within Portuguese higher education and certainly so in the reduction in the numbers of committee members. This latter development, as has been pointed out earlier,[2] is far from being without precedent when attention turns further afield. Wizened though it might seem compared to its earlier composition, the General Council still retains direct lines of communication and responsibility with the base units. In this respect, it appears to retain clear ties with the institutional fabric rather than being a semi-hermetic, largely closed off body, like its French counterpart, the *Conseil d'Administration*.[3] Though the General Council possesses a certain similarity to its Dutch counterpart in the duumvirate of the external chairman and the internal rector, in Portugal the formal relationship between these two representative personalities seems to be on a more equal footing. The rector does not report to the chairman but rather to the General Council *en tant que tel*.[4]

What may strike insiders as innovatory within the national setting appears relatively modest when set against developments in other systems. But bodies exercising strategic oversight do not provide a full grasp of what is involved. Executive bodies are equally important and in particular the workings of the Management Board which appears to act as a headquarters staff to the Rector.

The Management Board

The Management Board has five members, appointed and chosen by the Rector, including a vice-rector and a director from one of the organizational units (Portugal, 2008: Article 94). It is responsible for 'the administrative, asset and financial management of the institution, in addition to the management of human resources' (Portugal, 2008: Article 95, para 1). Also amongst its responsibilities are drawing up charges and salaries (Portugal, 2008: Article 95, para 2).

The Management Board may be seen as concentrating and coordinating management around manifest institutional leadership, a pronounced development visible in the UK (Whitchurch, 2006) and France, for instance. However, the formal powers available to the Rector to shape the university in Portugal through the appointment of key leadership figures seem unequalled elsewhere. That vice-rectors are still 'freely appointed' by the Rector, which has been the case since 1986, that the rector is not confined in the choice of individuals to those already part of the rectorial kingdom but may look outside (Portugal, 2008: Article 88, paras 3 and 4) generates a degree of patronage – and potential leverage – that would cause great covetousness indeed amongst fellow vice-chancellors, presidents and principals. So too would the Rector's power to dismiss vice-rectors, which is also amongst his or her prerogatives (Portugal, 2008: Article 88, para 3).

A new construction dissected

Constructing institutional autonomy in Portugal, viewed simply from the functions and distribution of power within the two major bodies responsible for strategic oversight and leadership, starts from a very different base. In theory at least, it appears to lend itself to a far greater concentration around institutional leadership *qua* individual personalities than would seem possible elsewhere. There is, so it would appear to a foreign observer, one feature in particular to emerge from a close perusal of those provisions of the Higher Education Guideline Law relating to outside interests and internal leadership. New though the presence of an 'external constituency' is, it does not appear to bring into question the very real strength that has accumulated around the Rector as the *summum* of magnificence in the ascending academic hierarchy. Indeed, the impression given is that responsibility handed down to the institutional level serves not to dilute the primacy of either the Rector or the academic hierarchy so much as to consolidate both.

If, for a moment, we hark back to the dynamic between the Academic and Administrative Estates,[5] whilst limiting our gaze to the two highest organs of internal governance alone, there does not appear to be evidence to suggest that the curtailment of the academic hierarchy through what has been termed 'in-filtration' from the administrative hierarchy has taken place – yet.

2) Defining institutional autonomy

The Higher Education Guideline Law entered into considerable detail when setting out the various dimensions of autonomy. Vis-à-vis the state, higher education was granted not one, but a series of 'autonomies' – pedagogical, scientific, cultural, administrative, asset and disciplinary autonomy (Portugal, 2008: Article 11, para 1) – thus finally promulgating the conditions originally set out in the Constitution of 1976. There was, however, a second level of autonomy granted that related not to the *type* of institution – university and polytechnic, public or private – so much as to the *individual* establishment. This 'second layer' of autonomy recognized that each establishment could draw up individual internal statutes to define its mission, its objectives and to 'establish [its] autonomy and define [its] organizational structure' (Portugal, 2008: Article 11, para 1).

As has been noted at various points in this analysis, this 'second layer' of autonomy had direct implications for the relationship between the state and the higher education system, and particularly in relation to the modification it introduced to the fundamental concept of legal homogeneity, as well as the unusual twist it gave to a more commonplace understanding of the basic concept of a Guideline Law.[6]

Yet the interesting aspect of the way in which the Higher Education Guideline Law dealt with institutional autonomy is precisely in its refusal to follow conventional wisdom. It did not see autonomy as a unitary, even metaphysical, principle. Still less did it abide by the usual distinction between institutional autonomy on the one hand and positional or personal autonomy on the other (de Groof, Neave and Svec, 1998). Nor, unlike Spanish legislation, did it make mention of linking either principle or the institution explicitly to supporting democracy or re-affirming the values for which it stood. Such aspects are not absent; rather, they are implied indirectly by the fact that the Law grew expressly out of the 1976 Constitution where such vital issues figured with obvious prominence.

Autonomies in the plural were, in effect, functional definitions with direct operational consequences, sometimes across all levels of the institution and sometimes laying down conditions under which specific organizational entities were to operate. Thus, for instance, the granting of academic and pedagogical autonomy entailed the setting up of pedagogical and scientific Boards of Management in the university as well as their creation at the level of organizational units – that is to say, the base units at faculty level and below, schools included (Portugal, 2008: Article 40, para e).

A careful review of the clauses in the Higher Education Guideline Law that set out the framework conditions for organizational units suggests they were 'twice armoured'; first, by their inclusion in the Law itself; and, second, by dint of their being endowed with managerial autonomy under the statutes of the individual establishment (Portugal, 2008: Article 96, paras 1 and 2). This is also the case for the Pedagogical and Scientific Councils (Portugal, 2008: Article 102, paras 1a and 1b) which are institution-wide boards.

Organizational units, as their name implies, operate at the school and faculty level. In both instances, the internal statutes and regulations of the individual university or polytechnic define their remit (Portugal, 2008: Article 98). They are chaired by an elected president or director, whose mandate cannot exceed eight years and who represents the unit both inside and outside the establishment (Portugal, 2008: Article 100, para a).

The heartland of collegiality

This is the heartland of collegiality. The Higher Education Guideline Law defines the electoral constituency for Scientific Councils, Pedagogical Councils and the boards of the organizational units in a way that clearly reflects the commitment to the spirit of 'participative democracy' that pervaded the 1976 Constitution. The Scientific Council (called a Technical Scientific Council in polytechnics), together with the Pedagogical Council, has a minimum of 25 members (Portugal, 2008: Article 102, para 6), 60 per cent of whom are drawn from the ranks of professors, professional research staff and other full-time staff who hold doctorates and who have been employed in the establishment for at least one year (Portugal, 2008: Article 102, para 1a). 'Representatives of recognized researchers that have been positively assessed' account for between 20 and 40 per cent of the Council's membership (Portugal, 2008: Article 100, para 1b).

Governance structures for organizational units differ in several respects. Their membership is limited to 15, 60 per cent being made up of teaching staff and researchers together with student representation. Organizational units may, if they so wish, include representatives from non-teaching staff and even representation from outside the establishment (Portugal, 2008: Article 97, paras a and b(i)–b(iv)). Their president or director serves for an eight-year term (Portugal, 2008: Article 101).

Institutional autonomy, institutional dualism

That structures of governance, which provide coordination across the institution in the domains central to *academic* endeavour and also at the level of the base units, are still clearly underpinned by the outward and formal trappings of 'participation' is interesting indeed. In Portuguese higher education, at least in the public sector, institutional autonomy may well serve to strengthen a form of dichotomy between boards and councils. Those which come under the direct pressure of outside interests and have the weight of public policy bearing down on them may well be induced to move down the lines of New Public Management. Counterbalancing this, however, are those that choose to focus on 'the academic enterprise', upholding the long-acquired right of freedom to learn and to teach. Conferring institutional autonomy, operational and multi-faceted as it is, may well – and given the present state of our knowledge we can say no more than that – strengthen what appears at the institutional level to be a replication of a feature already noted at other levels of the Portuguese system of higher education.

The division of interests between the Party of Movement and the Party of Order has, as we have already seen,[7] been a central feature in the influence wielded by institutional leaders in shaping *national* policy. Interestingly, some scholars have detected the coalescence of a similar line-up *inside* institutions instead of *between* them. If the role remains the same, the actors differ. Institutional leadership and the upper echelons of administration take their cue as the Party of Movement. The Party of Order draws its strength from lecturers and researchers who are less fired by enthusiasm for the changes that the Guideline Law has ushered in (Magalhães and Amaral, 2007: 1–24).

Collegiality versus managerialism

This in its turn brings us back to the four stages of development, which earlier were held to be instrumental in shaping the relationship between the Academic and Administrative Estates. A recent study undertaken before the Guideline Law was enacted provides some purchase on this issue. It examined the perceptions amongst those academics seconded to temporary administrative duties, those who in terms of the concept developed earlier were 'ex-filtrated'.[8]

The analysis by Santiago and his colleagues is revealing for two reasons: first, because it provides empirical evidence for the state of tension between the values associated with 'collegiality' on the one hand and 'managerial' rigour on the other; and, second, because it shows very clearly the extent to which 'ex-filtration' is not merely underway but serves as a vehicle for inseminating the operational attitudes of New Public Management into the 'collegium' (Santiago, Carvalho, Amaral and Meek, 2007: 215–50). Their conclusions are worth citing:

> In Portuguese HEIs, there is increasing pressure over those in charge of departments/schools and faculties to assume a more managerialist attitude. This pressure may deepen the gap between the 'traditional' academic roles and the management/administration responsibilities of those who head basic academic units. (Santiago, Carvalho, Amaral and Meek, 2007: 243)

A flawed Law?

However, what remains uncertain is how far the implicit endorsement of the principle of participant democracy evoked by the Higher Education Guideline Law being conjoined to the 1976 Constitution may be made to lie down with the multiple and varied operational definitions of institutional autonomy in that self-same Guideline Law – definitions which drew their inspiration from the canons of New Public Management. This is a serious matter because it suggests that, inasmuch as the spirit of the Law appears to be contradicted by the letter of the Law, that Law is fundamentally flawed. When a law is flawed, it is by no means easy for contending interests, which in both cases are subject to that law, to reconcile their differences; rather, the temptation for each to justify their different stances becomes all the greater for the fact that each can justify its action by referring either to the letter, to the framework or to the spirit of that law. This is not greatly conducive to peace in the amphitheatres or quiet confidence in the rector's suite!

Finally, if we bear in mind that the study by Santiago *et al.* was undertaken *prior* to the Higher Education Guideline Law being enacted, whether these contradictions have served to make relations between the administrative Party of Movement and the academic Party of Order better or worse is of the utmost importance, because in respect of the impact that the Guideline Law has had on these already tense relations, we know nothing whatsoever.

3) Provision for an experimental model

The drive towards managerialism in the higher education systems of Western Europe shines largely by the absence of experimentation, as it does by the equally sparse evaluation of that experimentation, *prior* to the forcible injection of the organizational rationale into the fabric of higher education. Yet, since the early nineteenth century, if not before, the university has been the temple of verified, replicable and therefore scientific knowledge, as opposed to knowledge as an authoritative doxology, along the lines once expounded by the medieval schoolmen (Ben David, 1978: 33–5). In girding up their loins to meet the variously described 'demands' of the 'knowledge society' or of the 'knowledge economy' (Sorlin and Vessuri, 2007), Europe's universities committed what, from the standpoint of the criteria explicit in the type of knowledge in which they dealt, must surely be the most unforgivable sin of all: they suspended disbelief and, in the absence of prior and incontrovertible evidence as to precisely how the various 'managerial models' available to business and industry would perform in higher education, launched themselves onto the fathomless waters of faith-based policy making.

Both New Public Management and managerialism are grounded in values and practices current in, and redolent of, the corporate sector, large-scale industry and commerce. That such ways of doing things were practised at all seems to have been judged sufficient on their own account for universities to take them on lock, stock and barrel, despite the very obvious fact that only with the greatest stretch of the meanest imagination and with disbelief suspended to a similar degree could a university be said to resemble a large firm, save in the most irrelevant dimension of all, size! On such a criterion, a good case could surely have been made for rationalizing the university along the lines found in the military!

It is then of more than passing interest that Portugal's Higher Education Guideline Law should make provision for what may be qualified as an 'experimental' form of 'foundation university'.[9] It is possible to speculate about the motives that lay behind this decision: an idea whose time had come? The wish in some way to defuse the intense rivalry between the public and private sectors of higher education by persuading some already-established public sector establishments to shift their legal basis from public to private law? A sudden determination to push further on the front of 'financial off-loading'? The notion to open up new avenues for proceeding incrementally towards a closer alignment of higher learning with some of the more pronounced features of neoliberal policy (Carrera Fernandes, 2009) – an initiative which may be urged on in the public sector only at great cost and at the price of no little strife? To put in place a means to accelerate the overall programme of re-engineering higher education at a pace beyond the capacity of establishments that were already in place to keep up with developments that were visible elsewhere? All these motives are within the realms of possibility.[10]

Apart from their difference in legal status, foundation universities have a very specific governance structure in comparison with their public sector counterparts. The fact that this feature figures in the Guideline Law suggests that the search for alternative arrangements in this specific domain is amongst the more important priorities for which the foundation university serves as a 'test bed'.

Foundation universities: key characteristics

The key characteristic which sets the foundation university apart from its one-time public counterparts lies in its Council of Trustees, a body which combines a higher degree of concentration with a broader scope of responsibility than, for instance, the General Council in public universities. Since, to date, establishments that have opted for foundation status were public universities, their decision clearly marks a further concentration around the twin principles of leadership and management powers reinforced over and above the restrictions already imposed by the Guideline Law on the organs of governance in the remaining sectors. The Board of Trustees of foundation universities draws on 'five individuals of exceptional merit with professional experience recognized as exceptionally relevant' (Portugal, 2008: Article 131, para 1). The five-person body is appointed by the government on the recommendation of the university (Portugal, 2008: Article 131, para 2). It sits for a five-year term, which is renewable once (Portugal, 2008: Article 131, para 4).

The Council of Trustees is responsible for appointing the Managerial Board on the recommendations made by the Rector (Portugal, 2008: Article 133, para 2a). It ratifies the decision taken by the General Council to appoint or to dismiss the Rector (Portugal, 2008; Article 132, para 2b). In short, as the American sociologist of higher education Burton Clark observed several decades ago, 'Trusteeship means supervision of an *enterprise* by outsiders' (Clark, 1983: 116, emphasis added).

'Strong leadership' and its concomitants

The Board of Trustees stands at the pinnacle of the governance structure of foundation universities, which otherwise follow the council and board pattern for higher education establishments in the public sector (Portugal, 2008: Article 132, para 4). It is especially revealing in respect of what are held to be the concomitants of 'strong leadership', although in this it is not devoid of certain ambiguities. If analysed in terms of its formal structure, membership composition and responsibilities, the Board of Trustees is clearly a co-opted oligarchy. Its members are not subject to the electoral process. Furthermore, it appears to wield a countervailing power to that of the Rector inasmuch as appointments made to the Management Board, which in its earlier form acted as the Rector's headquarters staff and was appointed at the discretion of the Rector, are now brought under the purlieu of the Trustees.

This latter responsibility lends itself to a certain interpretive creativity, depending on how the function of Rector is perceived: as the splendid termination to the ascending academic hierarchy or as an eminence in its descending administrative counterpart. If it is the former, then it is obvious that the Board of Trustees strengthens leadership by imposing what appears to be an independent body of oversight as a possible offset to the academic hierarchy. If, however, the Rector's place is viewed as at the top of the *administrative* hierarchy, then it is fair to suggest that the Board of Trustees serves to reinforce the administrative hierarchy by extending it above and beyond the General Council. Less plain by far, given the part of the government in appointing members to the Board of Trustees, is whether 'strong leadership' is not a euphemism, a coded phrase for restoring the government's power to intervene through the bias of confirming appointments.

Implications for staffing and salary structure

The fact that foundation universities function under private law has direct consequences for both financial assets and staff management. As regards the latter, foundation universities individually assume the power to set up their own staffing structure for teaching, research and other members of staff in *parallel* to arrangements for public sector higher education (Portugal, 2008: Article 134). However, a parallel staffing structure is not the same thing as a similar *salary* structure and in this regard it remains unclear whether pay scales and increments fall under the particular establishment's internal regulations. This possibility would seem to imply that the prospect of inter-establishment differentials cannot wholly be ruled out and indeed would appear to be in the offing. Why this should be so stems from the way that the state will fund foundation universities. The Guideline Law makes very clear that state finance will be conditional, based on a cycle of negotiation of 'not less than three years'. Funding will be made according to the objectives to be reached (Portugal, 2008: Article 136, para 1).

Flagships for innovation?

These are the immediate differences that set foundation universities apart from their peers in both the public and private sectors. More interesting, however, is their precise role as harbingers of system change driven in the first instance from within individual establishments. Even more interesting is whether foundation universities are to limit themselves to testing those innovations given to them by the Guideline Law or whether they are to take on the role of 'permanent testing grounds' for innovation. This latter possibility would see them acting as semi-permanent 'flagships for innovation'. *En passant*, it also has to be asked whether the system of a minimum three-year contracts, which regulate their financial base, is sufficient for innovation to be devised, tried, weighed up and finally embedded.

The reasoning that prompts this suggestion is grounded in the financial conditions that the government has placed on foundation universities and particularly the requirement that foundation universities raise half their annual income from non-state sources. However this is to be achieved – whether by developing new skills amongst existing administrative staff, by taking into administration academics who have shown talent in the fields of fundraising nationally or internationally, or, alternatively inveigling their colleagues who have developed new forms of cost control at the base unit level – these tactics in theory figure amongst the many possibilities that put themselves forward.

Task re-distribution: a retake

Regardless of which of these avenues may emerge as the most productive, the conclusion is obvious. The constant quest for foundation universities 'to go forth on the highways and byways and compel them to come in so that their coffers may be filled' will very certainly bring about a new spate of internal 'task re-distribution'. In all probability, it will be as radical and as far-reaching as that which the Portuguese Evaluative State will most assuredly bring in its wake, but with one difference: whereas the Evaluative State will make itself felt primarily within the area of academic performance and quality, not to mention institutional survival in certain instances, the repercussions arising from the former will in all likelihood bear down on administrative performance and efficiency. Whether, in so doing, it will speed up the process of 'ex-filtration' – the leakage from academia over to *administration* – is difficult to say, though intuition suggests that it will.

Foundation universities will be forced to turn their hand to developing new forms of internal verification and internal cost control, together with the formal procedures to sustain them and the organization to carry them forward. Yet, such changes can be embedded in the institutional tissue only on condition that new job profiles – even sub-professions – are created to give them permanency. Thus, the lot of foundation universities is, in all likelihood, to find themselves faced with a situation of permanent adaptation and experimentation. What follows from this is not difficult to foresee. Even though some may argue that the legislator in no way saw foundation universities explicitly as 'hot houses' for innovation of a financial and an administrative nature, that is what lies in store for them, given the terms on which they are now funded.

Institutional example: the driver of systems adaptation

The issue that this situation poses goes far beyond the foundation university itself. In reality, it ties in with the broader issue not of *institutional* adaptation so much as *system* adaptation. Should the managerial initiatives or managerial re-engineering that foundations universities devise for themselves, whatever they are, turn out to be successful, will the force of their example be sufficient to persuade other establishments in either the public or the private sector to take them up? This is no idle question. On the contrary, it lies at the heart of institutional autonomy. This is because, as it is instrumentalized today, institutional autonomy is related to institutional self-adaptation – organic change – as an alternative that substitutes for government intervention in shaping the nation's system of higher education. That this role may fall on Portugal's foundation universities, irrespective of whether such a role was explicitly foreseen or is simply the result of purely fortuitous circumstances, is not very important. What is important, however, is the presence within a system of higher education of clear examples of innovation and internal adjustment, examples which can be taken up and adapted further by others within that system.

To put a finer point on it, institutional autonomy has been granted precisely on one over-riding assumption, which is that institutional autonomy provides the conditions for rapid adaptation. There is, however, a correlative assumption, which is as follows: that other universities and polytechnics are, as the song says, 'readily, willing and able' to profit from *their* autonomy to follow the inspiring example. Thus, theoretically at least, institutional autonomy, once aggregated up, should serve to raise both the speed of take-up and the alertness of individual institutions to do so. *Institutional* autonomy aggregated up is the Archimedes' lever of *system* adjustment. And, no less weighty at a time when the twin imperatives of accountability and performance are the shibboleths of the moment, it is most certainly in the interest of higher education to be able to sustain and demonstrate to the public and to its authoritative representatives its ability to adapt by assimilating the best practices that individual establishments have developed and others have acted upon.

Organizational units: the basic building blocks for system adjustment

Even when they deal with similar issues – for example, 're-distributing tasks' – not surprisingly, different systems assign it with different priorities and a different place in the chronology in the general agenda of reform. Thus, the Dutch began re-shaping their system of higher education in the wake of the neo-Keynesian consensus breaking up during the early 1980s. Task re-distribution occupied second place in adapting the structure of higher education to the new practicalities of being driven by market forces (White Paper, 1983). Not only did 'task re-distribution' emerge later in Portugal; the basic issue – how to ensure that higher education institutions had sufficient flexibility to come up with appropriate measures to deal with unforeseen developments – assumed a very different form. Policy in Portugal has not cast aside the shaping hand of national administration as an addition to the Invisible Hand of Adam Smith's market – far from it.

The key issue: key initiatives

Key to the strategy outlined by the Higher Education Guideline Law was to instil at the institutional level the capacity for what we have called 'organic restructuring'. But 'organic restructuring' – in essence the ability of the individual institution to continually adjust in the areas of teaching, learning, research and service to the community – in turn depends on the institution's ability to make micro-adjustments. Micro-adjustments are the prior condition for ensuring adaptation is sustained – and sustainable!

For Burton R. Clark, one of the shaping minds of comparative higher education, base units are 'the building blocks of the higher education enterprise' (Clark, 1983: 133). The Higher Education Guideline Law granted 'organizational units' (that is, faculties, schools and departments), the legislator's translation of base units, one specific margin for initiative. This revolved around the various forms of external cooperation in teaching or in research with other higher education institutions within Portugal and abroad (Portugal, 2008: Article 16). Arguably, setting up associations and consortia with other universities or, to put them on a more permanent footing in the form of a foundation, was simply the legislator recognizing and taking into account a time-honoured practice that was inseparable from academic work and had long been the norm in 'big science' (medicine, physics, biology, genetics and engineering). Inter-institutional collaboration, spurred on by the European Higher Education Area and the European Research Area, is now an integral although fluctuating feature for all fields and disciplines.[11]

Thus, at the level of the base units, the Higher Education Guideline Law explicitly opened up an avenue for further initiative, the natural complement to innovation in the administrative domain that has just been examined. By laying out new conditions for inter-institutional cooperation, the issue of 'task re-distribution' was injected directly into the academic domain. However, it went well beyond the straightforward creation of inter-institutional links and partnerships. This is because whilst provision anticipated a re-distribution in tasks between the participating interests – and thus served as a powerful spur for the cross-flow of ideas, students and researchers – such opportunities carried with them the seeds of a more wide-ranging agenda still, one of continual mobilization. Launched from within the base units, this 'mobilizing impulse' was intended to serve as a direct agent for re-contouring higher education at the system level. Furthermore, the development of teaching and research collaboration was not limited to within sectors. On the contrary, the Guideline Law was at pains to emphasize that organizational units could work together across the binary divide just as they could transcend the legal differences and boundaries between the public and private sectors (Portugal, 2008: Article 129, para 2; Article 14, para 2; Article 17, para 1).

An ongoing agenda

Whilst rooted in disciplinary affinity in order to better generate quality, this aspect of the Portuguese version of task re-distribution was construed instead as the *first* step down a broader road towards institutional restructuring. Organizational units could subsequently evolve into new forms of institutions (Portugal, 2008: Article 129, para 2). Groupings that had evolved into 'consortiums' could push their development further. Once authorization had been secured from the General Councils of their participating home bases and from the supervising minister, they could assume the title of a university institute or a polytechnic institute (Portugal, 2008: Article 129, para 8). It must for the moment remain a moot point as to whether the drive towards such 'hybrid' institutions, which explicitly encompass both public and private self-standing establishments engaged in R&D as well as research, was deliberately conceived to 'soften' the boundaries between the public and private sectors. The intention cannot entirely be ruled out.

At first sight, this dynamic vision of new institutional cross-sectoral patterns growing out of the organizational units validates in the Portuguese context Clark's observation of a quarter of a century ago that the power of base units contributes to the 'bottom-heavy' nature of higher education (Clark, 1983: 127). But, as Clark himself pointed out, when his gaze turned to mainland Europe, higher education is 'top-heavy' as well and especially so when formal responsibility for coordination at the national level lies in the hands of a major ministry (Clark, 1983: 126–7, 134). To this can be added the unrivalled leverage a ministry possesses when the dominant mode of system coordination is still grounded in legal homogeneity *en attendant des jours meilleurs*.

Giving Adam Smith a helping hand ...

However, a close scrutiny of the provisions in the Higher Education Guideline Law that laid out the structures and conditions under which the base units could work together across institutional boundaries suggests that this was not the only way of proceeding. As with most legislatively enacted systems, such initiatives require both the approval of the supervising ministry as well as permission to move ahead being given and final recognition granted to the arrangements proposed by institutional authorities, usually the university's Governing Council. Such procedures are the norm in legislatively driven systems. Yet, not without significance, the Guideline Law also provided that the government would continue to exercise an initiatory role. The government could also create new foundations and bring together base units or other entities with a similar remit, activity or status. This rider applied principally to independent research institutes formally operating outside or on the margins of the higher education system (Portugal, 2008: Article 11). Here, as was hinted at earlier, we see another example of the 'two-handed approach' in shaping the future contours of higher education. The hand of government did not deprive itself of the opportunity to help the ghostly appendage of market forces! And although the Guideline Law gave every encouragement to universities to take initiatives, it made equally plain that the government retained the whip hand, if necessary by spurring on competition through its ability to create alternative arrangements at the other interface – between research, R&D, business and industry (Heitor and Horta, 2011).

...and how that may be interpreted

Evidence to sustain this interpretation emerges clearly from the negotiations between the ministry and the public sector universities that assumed foundation status. Negotiations turned principally on the minister's determination to strengthen the national research base in the science sector by bringing certain research and R&D-based independent institutes within the purview of the university.

Sorting out the motives behind this initiative is delicate. Many possibilities exist. Prime amongst them was the improvement of Portugal's competitive ranking in the European Higher Education Area and more particularly in the European Research Area (Heitor and Horta, 2011), which is one strategic consideration. There is another: the dynamic of 'system adjustment' ought not to rest wholly on the universities. The Ministry of Science, Technology and Higher Education appeared to be marking a boundary between system development reflecting strategic national priorities and, if necessary, corrective measures within this framework as against institutional initiatives seen as its executive fulfilment. If Portugal's higher education was to be dynamic, there was a world of difference between a dynamic national strategy and the dynamism that institutions showed – or failed to show – in the tactical and institutional take-up of the strategy. In other words, here was an example of 'ministerial steering' before steering itself became 'remote' and before 'within-system' self-adjustment became embedded in institutional practice. The Ministry's two-handed initiative sprang from the view that the Higher Education Guideline Law was not the end or even the completion of previous policy objectives; rather, it was the start of a transformation, which, by dint of the degree of institutional autonomy it would introduce, would in all probability be less amenable to earlier modes and instruments of coordination. Like every good card-player, the minister played his aces knowing the pack was about to be re-cut and re-shuffled!

There is, however, a fourth perspective to be placed on ministerial enterprise. It casts a very different light on the previous suggestions, which take an optimistic view in assuming that central steering by the ministry will become 'remote' and that, like the faith of Dr Pangloss in Voltaire's *Candide*, 'all will be for the best in the best of all possible worlds'.

Envoi

What if things do not turn out to be for 'the best in all possible worlds'? This question sends us back to the nature of a Guideline Law.[12] What if the minister was not acting as policy's equivalent of the elegant and canny card-player but was in fact acting within that 'reserve capacity' that every Guideline Law entails? If this was so, it raises a very different prospect indeed. This prospect hints at an implicit and continuing dualism in the scope of intervention and thus in higher education policy. Whilst 'self-adjustment' within the higher education system has been given a premium by extending the variously defined dimensions of institutional autonomy to the individual universities and polytechnics to build from beneath, system-wide, macro-decisions for shaping higher education from above nevertheless continue as part of central government's reserve powers. As with all questions of this nature, the knotty problem turns on boundary conditions: where does the ministry's responsibility end? Where does that of the university begin? Whilst the capacity for universities and above all foundation universities to adapt has been enhanced on paper, there are now two very separate dynamics in system change. One drives within higher education from the bottom up. The second acts in the traditional mode from the top down. It drives towards interface research units on the margins between higher education and industry. In the medium term, the issue is posed foursquare as to how these two dynamics can be made to function together in harmony rather than as antagonists or as an oscillating equilibrium.

Part IV

The Promise of the Evaluative State Evaluated

14
A Flight over the Evolving Evaluative State

Introduction

In weighing up the impact that the Evaluative State has on institutional autonomy, three systems of higher education in particular have been scrutinized, two of them in considerable detail. Not surprisingly, the way in which the saga of the Evaluative State has unfolded in France, Spain and Portugal shows immense variety. It is different in chronology. It differs in the stances taken by the principal actors. It differs too in terms of the degree of continuity and the readiness of the Evaluative State to build upon or to break with those earlier conventions and observed practices that underpinned the triangular relationship between government, higher education and society.

The instrumentality and the nexus

Irrespective of the exact circumstances and the political, economic, historical or cultural context which surround the forging of the Evaluative State, it has a generic purpose. This purpose is to provide a specialized intelligence, sometimes formally independent of and sometimes located in the government, to weigh in the balance the level of performance by the individual university. This it does in the light of the priorities set by – or negotiated between – the nation's authoritative representatives, acting through the appropriate ministry and their counterparts in higher education. The instrumentality that the Evaluative State brings with it is immensely powerful, deeply pervasive and a very substantial lever for ensuring that performance criteria should be met. That they are met, however, does not simply reflect material penalties that may come with the failure to fulfil publicly agreed objectives, benchmarks or norms. Nor, for that matter, is it necessary for the Evaluative State to explicitly and formally link institutional performance with levels of funding, though one or two have done so.

The Evaluative State rarely works through the cash nexus alone. It also acts through a dimension that is largely psychological in nature. This dimension wields an equally powerful influence. If anything, it is subtler and no less telling an instrument precisely because it bears down upon what Clark termed 'the gold coin of academic excellence' (Clark, 1983: 183). In effect, the instrumentality of the Evaluative State directly engages a second nexus. This second nexus is of extreme sensitivity. It is also of supreme importance to all members of higher education's three Constituent Orders: the Academic, Administrative and Student Estates. To the Academic Estate, the 'second nexus' stands as the ultimate justification for autonomy, though whether it is institutional or positional is, as we have shown, largely a matter of national circumstance. To the Administrative Estate, it is the gauge of efficiency demonstrated. To the Student Estate, it is a pointer to the 'quality of service' it receives. So central is the 'second nexus', focused on reputation and standing, that no university, save perhaps the most irretrievably despairing and despondent, can knowingly ignore it.

Threats and facts

Threats tend to be more telling than facts. And, when regularly repeated and regularly revealed to the public, they are most certainly so. Thus, rankings and league tables that flow from institutional evaluation, whether national or *a fortiori*, cross-system or international are no less powerful. They combine the renewal of threat with the likelihood – itself a threat – that those who view the ratings may perceive them as fact.

In the world of higher education, the Evaluative State acts in a very similar way to notation agencies, that other nemesis of judgement in the netherworld of stockbroking on a global scale. The Evaluative State rates the credit of universities and polytechnics and, by extension, the credibility of the claims they make on their own behalf. However, it does so by weighing up their individual 'cultural' or, more precisely, their demonstrated ability to generate, exchange and accumulate 'knowledge' capital. This it does under the rubric of quality assurance, sometimes in conjunction with validating (the British term) or accrediting (its American equivalent) programmes and degree courses.

Within the bounds this study has set itself, the 'second nexus' is doubly significant: first, because it shows a direct relationship between the Evaluative State and what the Prince presents as 'institutional autonomy'; and, second, because the association between the two is not necessarily wholly or, for that matter, singly to do with enlarging institutional self-determination, initiative or discretion. Those of a Manichean disposition may well see institutional autonomy as the Prince acting as an optimist in the matter of higher education development. By being granted greater formal latitude, universities and polytechnics now have the capacity on their own 'to respond to outside demands' with greater alacrity since they have greater freedom to do so. However, true to his – or her – belief, the Manichean cannot fail to realize that the Prince also has a dark side to his nature. The Evaluative State, if not always an expression of the Prince's pessimistic side, nevertheless allows him 'to hedge his bets' by putting in place the means to check on whether his optimism is literally justifiable – and justified! To mix the metaphor, the Prince is truly ambidextrous: what he gives with his left hand, he retains the power to alter with his right. Thus, the relationship between the Evaluative State and higher education, whilst certainly no longer philanthropic (Williams, 2004), is alterable and therefore dynamic as well as conditional.

Two central themes

To round off this part in the exploration of the Evaluative State, this chapter pursues two central themes. The first draws on all three case studies. It set out the various dimensions that have accompanied the dynamic of the Evaluative State as the central instrumentality shaping higher education today.

From the outset, the mission of the Evaluative State was to 'galvanize' higher education, to speed up its 'estimated time of implementation' (Neave, forthcoming) primarily by driving the university through 'external forces', alternatively presented by economists as 'marketization' (Teixeira and Dill, 2011: 7–10). However, appealing though it might be, dynamism has many faces. Homing in on the most important is thus a way of drawing together what the three case studies reveal about the models of the Evaluative State analysed here. What in general do they tell us about the thrust of changes in the relationship between the government, higher education and the nation?

The dynamics of the Evaluative State

The first phase

In essence, a dynamic is the energy released by objects in motion and, by extension, the process of continuous change. Change, however, is largely meaningless in the absence of a chronological framework or of a basic condition that serves as the datum point against which subsequent motion – whether progressive or regressive – may be plotted. The chronology of the rise of the Evaluative State varies enormously from system to system: it is most protracted in France, where it was launched by the 1984 Higher Education Guideline Law, and it is most compressed in Portugal and Spain, where the first glimmerings were to be seen ten and eleven years respectively after its first manifestation. It is, however, purely coincidental that in all three systems, 2007 saw legislation passed which set the Evaluative State in its current configuration.

1) The political dynamic

What is self-evident in the rise of the Evaluative State when viewed comparatively is the very different political context in which it was initiated. The Evaluative State in its earliest manifestation was not associated either with neoliberalism or, for that matter, with what has come to be identified as New Public Management in France and even less so in Spain and Portugal. This is not to say that subsequently it did not shuffle – or was driven – in those directions in France and Portugal, though rather more indirectly in Spain. Thus, the French model of the Evaluative State was part of the government's response, as it was in Portugal and Spain, to unbridled growth in the Student Estate. Yet, its guiding ethic remained rooted in the general consensus of higher education as a public service. Far from being inquisitorial, the Evaluative State could be seen as a gentle prod to encourage France's universities to be bolder in their response to changes in student demand and to assume fully the responsibilities that already fell on them.

In Portugal and, in a different way, in Spain as well, the push towards the Evaluative State followed on from the definition of the bounds of autonomy, a more delicate and protracted process in the case of the latter and, in the case of the former, one of the consequences that followed the 1988 Law that granted the universities pedagogical autonomy. Portugal differed in terms of both the source of inspiration of and the justification for moving towards the Evaluative State. Not only did the happy notion come from university leadership, it was an initiative launched by leadership of the universities as a means to raise the *efficiency of the state* through a system of monitoring and intelligence to give the state a better technical purchase over the condition of higher education. Portugal's early moves towards the Evaluative State are of more than passing interest. They cast a very different light on the process sometimes known as the 'offloading state' (Neave, 2009: 45). They suggest that 'offloading' is not always a policy that is elaborated solely within the confines of the national administration out of enlightened self-interest. It may even be from 'getting a little help from their friends'.

2) Independence and oversight

A close scrutiny of the early phase in the construction of the Evaluative State saw it variously located. Sometimes it took its initial form in bodies affiliated to universities. The Dutch and British models were good examples of this, the first being located in the VSNU and the second in an audit unit inside the now defunct Committee of Vice-Chancellors and Principals. A further variant placed the embryonic form of what was to mature as the fully-fledged Evaluative State in foundations specially set up but remaining within the university sphere. Such was the case in Portugal and Spain. A third variant emerged in the case of the French *Comité National d'Evaluation*, a self-standing body, formally independent of universities, and reporting not to the Minister of Higher Education, but directly to the President of the Republic as head of state.

Administrative distance or detachment from the main conduits of national decision making stood as both a public and a symbolic statement about the independent role that the Evaluative State was expected to assume and the disinterested judgements it was expected to pass. Whilst casting what was to become the Evaluative State as honest broker between the government and higher education, this status too was subject to dynamism, though of a rather different sort. Independence of evaluation by dint of being associated with universities was not always regarded in the same positive light as independence from government – above all not by the government. Indeed, in the Portuguese case, when the government finally 'uploaded' the pilot project stage of the Evaluative State in 1998, it also re-set the internal balance of interests. CNAVES,[1] Portugal's first bid to put the Evaluative State in place, saw what some sectors of higher education regarded as the over-weaning influence of public universities being pruned severely. Not dissimilar motives lay behind the removal of the prototype form of the British Evaluative State from the Committee of Vice-Chancellors and Principals in 1994. It was subsequently vested in a unitary agency with oversight for institutional evaluation in the shape of the Quality Assurance Agency. The Prince looked upon the labour of his university subjects and found it to be good. But, as Georges Clémenceau, France's *'père la Victoire'* of the First World War, once remarked, 'War is too important to be left to Generals'. Similarly, evaluation was too important an instrumentality to be left solely to higher education.

The second phase

Thus, if we look at the years that followed the launch phase of the Evaluative State up to what may be presented as the great legislative climax of 2007, the build-up of another dynamic dimension stands forth. This dimension, though present in all three of the systems examined here, assumed a very different form. It also showed a very different cadence in each case. Whilst it forms the second stage in building the Evaluative State, the process brought together three distinct developments. The first involved introducing new functions, contractualization being the most significant, aligned on and around the basic intelligence made available by the Evaluative State. The second may be seen in terms of a shift in policy ethics, more particularly by having recourse to the power of justification that came with neoliberalism to re-define the university's purpose and thus to re-set the terms of the relationship between the government, higher education and the economy. The third development involved the extension of the infrastructure of the Evaluative State.

1) From honest broker to Evaluative State

Taken together, these three processes may be interpreted from a number of different perspectives. Of these, two are the most interesting, though they may also be seen as two sides of the same coin. The first may be seen as injecting intermediary agencies to provide feedback on institutional performance and behaviour at the interface between the government and higher education. The second sees this same development as the appropriation of those agencies by the government, in effect moving them on towards a 'parastatal' role and function. A 'parastatal' organization is one that has some political power and is indirectly controlled by the government. It is, in effect, at this point in the developmental dynamic of the Evaluative State that it embarks on the acquisition of those functions of definition, standard setting and operationalization entailed in evaluating performance, setting out benchmarks or assessing programmes for recognition and accreditation. Moreover, it does so under the full oversight of the government. By moving beyond its initial 'ownership' by the university, assessment and short-term system intelligence procedures take on the formal trappings of the Evaluative State.

The change in status from honest broker to Evaluative State poses two questions: first, when precisely did it take place?; and, second, how did it take place? The answer to the first is reasonably precise. In the

UK, the transfer of evaluation to a single-purpose agency was made in 1994, while in Portugal it occurred in 1998 with the establishment of CNAVES, in Spain it occurred in 2001 with the creation of ANECA[2] and in France it took place in 2007 with the establishment of AERES.[3] The rapidity with which the task of evaluation was taken over by the government also shows variation. For Portugal, it only took four years for the transformation to be accomplished. However, when introduced, CNAVES displayed little, if any, resemblance to the Dutch model that the leadership of the universities had originally envisaged. In Spain, this process, which was made more complex by the basic dualism that lay at the heart of the Spanish state – at the regional as well as at the central government level – took some six years to effect. Yet, the brisk pace set by Spain and Portugal in drawing up their version of the Evaluative State stood in marked contrast to France, where the equivalent process was incremental in the extreme.

France's pioneering élan settled down into a policy cadence that was all the more curious for the fact that from the start the *Comité National d'Evaluation* combined both the role of honest broker with the place and functions of an operational parastatal body. France did not share exactly the same starting block as its two southern neighbours. Nor did it display either their boldness or their precipitation. Instead, firming up the Evaluative State in France resembled a form of 'shell game'. In a 'shell game' one player seeks to move a shell from one spot to another without the other players detecting either the move made or the direction in which it proceeds. Excellent if not compelling reasons lay behind this approach. The higher education policy in France has long been hostage to the volatility and the readiness of two of its Constituent Orders – the Academic and the Student Estates – to mobilize (if not always effectively) to veto government initiatives.

2) Restoring the Prince to his seat

Thus, the French approach to strengthening the Evaluative State took the shape of an 'indirect strategy'. It turned around a series of parallel moves that were dispersed over time and pursued in areas that were formally separate from the role and function of the Evaluative State, and which gradually reasserted the traditional dirigisme of central government.[4] The restoration of the Prince to his seat was thus achieved by the Law on University Reform passed in 2007. The Law was thus the keystone in a long-drawn out process, which gradually slotted together national and institutional policy cycles. This had been achieved by setting a similar timing on the three cycles of evaluation, the negotiation of the university 'contract' and the election of the university president. And, finally, the remit of the Evaluative State was extended by combining both research assessment and institutional evaluation into a single agency. By laying upon AERES the responsibility to make recommendations for national policy, the agency was firmly and directly integrated into the national process of policy formation rather than standing as honest broker to one side of it.

The third phase

Incrementalism set a different rhythm to the unfolding of the Evaluative State in France. The same caution could be seen when it came to evoking the basic justification for the radicalism of the measures introduced. Thus, unlike either the UK or, for that matter, Portugal, the appeal to neoliberalism and the justification of the Evaluative State as higher education's spearhead towards New Public Management (though no less marked a shift in terms of policy ethics) emerged in France as a process of 'infiltration' rather than as the 'firm smack of government'. In short, the final transformation into the Evaluative State set it both symbolically and operationally as the instrument for the verification of neoliberalism in higher education. In Portugal and Spain, the injection of neoliberalism into the Evaluative State required a third phrase, which was largely obviated by France's incrementalist policy 'style'. In the case of Portugal, the third phase, which culminated in the 2007 Higher Education Guideline Law, carried with it a further interpretation – that of a government having second thoughts.

1) Portugal: swimming with and against the tide

In Portugal, the third phase in the evolution of the Evaluative State was thus at one and the same time a corrective and the rapid importation of neoliberalism to justify such a corrective. Other developments during this latter phase set Portugal apart from the broader trends visible elsewhere. The replacement of CNAVES by A3ES in effect saw Portugal swimming *against* the tide of fashion as policy. However, its rapid embrace of neoliberalism as the ideological driver and rationale to justify this corrective saw the Portuguese government moving enthusiastically *with* the ideological flood tide, a trend that was also visible in France at the same time.

Yet, the way in which the Evaluative State took shape during its third phase in Portugal was no less exceptional. Whilst other systems of higher education saw the Evaluative State evolving from its basic unitary model towards a multi-level arrangement in the case of Spain or

Germany (Kehm, 2007: 139–48) or to a multi-sector model in the case of the Netherlands[5] and Ireland (Clancy, 2007: 111–18), Portugal proceeded in the opposite direction. The structural dynamic that emerged during the third phase saw Portugal reverting to a unitary model that was not very different from the original vision outlined 13 years earlier by the leadership of the public universities.

2) Regime change: settling neoliberalism in

Regardless of the differences in timing, overall strategy and the organizational re-shaping that took place during the third phase of the evolution of the Evaluative State, one common theme emerges clearly from 2000 onwards. This common theme is to be seen in the rapid espousal by governments of neoliberalism and 'managerialism' as the ideological and operational vehicles of reform. With this in mind, attention now shifts to the second dimension explored by this study, namely the dynamic the Evaluative State was set up to impart in respect of institutional autonomy.

From positional to institutional autonomy

The transmutation of referential values

Institutional autonomy can very certainly be – and often is – justified on much the same grounds as its earlier 'Humboldtian' construct. It brings together the necessary and conducive conditions for sustained, creative and original thought which, when maintained at a consistently high level and over time, ought to lead to excellence. There is, however, a great difference between autonomy interpreted as positional and its present-day definition as institutional. The difference lies in the following distinction: positional autonomy applies in a differential manner to individuals – the more senior the individual, the greater the personal or positional autonomy enjoyed. The second applies to the institution. Institutional autonomy, like positional or personal autonomy, is likewise differentiated. This differentiation emerges principally in the inversion of the historic relationship between two of higher education's Constituent Orders: the Academic and Administrative Estates. Likewise, the grounds on which such differentiation is justified also differ. Whereas positional autonomy was justified in terms of maturity in excellence – *the maîtrise* of the *métier* that lay at the heart of the academic 'mystery'[6] – its contemporary re-definition in Western Europe reposes on managerial responsibility.

Since the purpose of higher education is now conceived primarily as *economic*, the ancient *mysterium* as the predominant 'referential value' that determines individual status and rank is transferred to 'managerialism' as the central organizing rationale within the individual university. Thus, institutional authority is detached from its association with the historic identifying and unifying ethic of the Academic Estate. Rather, institutional authority now lies with the Administrative Estate in the skein of 'line responsibility'. Added to this is the 'hollowing out' – the evacuation of significance, both real and symbolic – from the academic 'mystery' as a one-time source of authority inside the university (Neave, 2011b: 261–98). 'Hollowing out' reflects a fundamental change in the notion of knowledge. It has mutated from the 'gift relationship' *gratis et pro Deo*, which higher education as part of the welfare state took over from the university's ecclesiastical origins as an integral part of the academic ethic. Knowledge today is regarded both as a commodity and as a legitimately saleable product, an essential form of capital in the knowledge economy and in 'knowledge production'. Precisely because it is the basic, renewable and most valuable resource in the knowledge economy, it requires formal organization, not to mention management and measurement (Sorlin and Vessuri, 2007; Heitor and Horta, 2011)!

Benefits bestowed: a questionable autonomy

However, when we look at precisely what benefits have been bestowed or, in the case of France, Spain and Portugal, are in process of being bestowed by the transition from an academic 'ethic' to a management rationale, the question that inevitably springs to mind is does this procedure for transferring authority amount to any form of 'autonomy' at all? As scholars have noted (Amaral and Magalhães, 2007: 63–76), the rhetoric of 'rolling back the frontiers of the state' has had precisely the opposite result. They have rolled forward in the shape of juridification, the multiplication of regulations to de-regulate and a degree of intervention through the intermediary of the Evaluative State, which is if anything more pervasive because it is regular, let alone the impact such intervention may have on institutional stability. Amaral's Paradox, the rolling forward of regulation to supposedly roll back intervention by central government and thus to de-regulate (Neave, 2011a: 15–36), is so widespread in Western Europe that it is to all intents and purposes a generic feature in higher education policy, as well as being a glaring contradiction between the ostensible ends and the means through which those ends are to be achieved!

Rolling forward verification, regulation and detailed oversight the better to expedite institutional decision making does not stop at the outer fringes of the groves of academia. For the price of installing academia's equivalent of 'just in time delivery methods' for the 'products' of higher education – that is, students qualified, researchers trained and lecturers effective in what they teach and research – is as high as it is evident and as evident as it is contradictory. This is because if the frontiers of internal regulation have been rolled forward to put in place the benefits of 'strong leadership', the boundaries of that very ancient governing ethic – collegiality, together with its more recent addition, participant democracy – have been rolled back as fast as ever opportunity and opportunism permit. Collective decision making, once permeating across individual establishments, has reduced and mutated. It has shrunk around a few 'portal personages', some of whom are co-opted from outside and for the form confirmed by election. Collegiality mutates into a latter-day Caesarism (Fuller, 2006: 362–8) or, depending on which country and thus which political culture is involved, as Bonapartism resuscitated! None will deny that Caesarism and Bonapartism are 'modes of leadership' and styles to which 'strong' leadership has an undeniable kinship.

In the three systems examined, one thing is clear: institutional autonomy is neither primarily nor directly applied to the Academic Estate. This is not to say that the Academic Estate enjoys a blessed and enviable immunity. However, it is safe to say that the Academic Estate was largely a second-order consideration. The *prima mobile* for what is described as 'institutional autonomy' is to strengthen the executive powers of leadership in the first instance and the managerial function of the Administrative Estate in the second. Institutional autonomy is thus coterminous with managerial freedom, just as managerial freedom goes hand in glove with academic accountability and enhanced performance.

Re-engineering the university

This does not bode well for those who argue that institutional autonomy builds on and out from the principles of academic or positional autonomy. Still less would it seem to back those who hold that institutional and positional autonomy are part and parcel of the same construct (Bleiklie and Kogan, 2007: 477–94). Indeed, the separation between the two, together with the conviction amongst the French Academic Estate that institutional autonomy involved the sacrifice of positional autonomy, was precisely the 'provocative act' that brought France's Academic

Estate onto the streets. Nor, given that institutional autonomy focuses primarily on administrative and procedural re-organization rather than pedagogical or curricular change, does it appear to extend the boundaries of positional autonomy. There is, on the contrary, some evidence from Portugal which suggests that 'hollowing out' is deeply rooted and has begun to bear down on those base units once held as both the essence and place where positional autonomy was both real and active (Santiago, Carvalho, Amaral and Meek, 2006: 215–50).

Despite the nominal and linguistic similarity implied by the term, institutional autonomy today bears little substantive resemblance to its previous form. That governments and their servants choose to stick the label of 'institutional autonomy' on a particular range of activities does not necessarily mean that what *they* mean – or have in mind – conforms exactly with what previous practice or conventional and common understanding once attached to the now cunningly-chosen phrase (Neave, 2006b: 21).

Other labels can be attached to the process of 're-engineering the university', which are revealing. For instance, the OECD, in its review of Portuguese higher education, saw reform at the institutional level not in terms of 'institutional autonomy' so much as 'managerial freedom' (OECD, 2007). Another label, drawn from the UK, saw institutional reform resulting in 'corporative freedom' (Shattock, 2003). Viewed from the history of certain nations in Western Europe, such a term is inadvertently most unfortunate in the associations it drags clanking behind it and certainly when it is explicitly coupled with the 'leadership principle'. Admittedly, the terminology employed by British and American scholars is happily without that intolerable stench of a past best forgotten, which is probably why they can apply the adjective 'corporative' to describe the thrust of reform and do so without the slightest blush! To Anglo-Saxon ears, the adjective 'corporative' carries with it the uncompromising overtones of brisk and business-like efficiency. It brings with it legal overtones of being self-governing whilst also formally accountable. Indeed, some British scholars see the atrophying of governing boards in the 'new' universities as evidence of a 'corporative model' of governance being put in place (Wiliams, 2004).

Envoi

The margin for misunderstanding between the basic categories of 'institutional autonomy', 'institutional freedoms' in the plural and 'institutional freedom' in the singular, not to mention some of the current terms employed as substitutes for them, is sufficient for creative confusion to flourish. Confusion or ambiguity both multiply furiously when extended to 'academic' or positional autonomy. It does so for the simple and evident reason that the way in which academic autonomy is viewed and the duties and obligations that attach to it reflect not just differences in terms of the 'conceptual framework' that tend to accompany academic autonomy as it crosses the frontiers of nation-state systems of higher education. Academic autonomy is firmly grounded in linguistic, legal and historical conventions that grew up organically and coalesced around the university itself. The three studies of France, Spain and Portugal revealed this with great clarity.

However, for the past two centuries or so, *institutional* autonomy in the public higher education systems of Western Europe shone largely by its absence.[7] This remained the case, until that felicitous descriptor was attached by governments to the process of re-engineering higher education around the canons of neoliberalism, managerialism and New Public Management. For most of mainland Europe's systems of higher education, no precedent existed that could allow them to challenge the particular range of operational procedures and responsibilities that the Prince chose to label as 'institutional autonomy'. Simply to point out that the relationship between the university, government and society has evolved differently in those systems which actively functioned with reference to such a notion, the UK and the USA being the most obvious examples, is to invite the testy reply that 'circumstances alter cases'. Such rare instances as these, where a specific model of institutional autonomy held sway, do not mean that it is appropriate, still less applicable, elsewhere, though the label may provide a creative way to dress the package up.

That the Prince chose to use 'institutional autonomy' as bait to hoodwink Dame University is more a comment on his unavowable designs than on the *naïveté* of the lady herself!

15
Back to the Future

Introduction

Prophecy has no place in higher education. Non-negotiable though this stricture is, it does not completely absolve scholarship from the responsibility of exploring the implications that may flow from what has been found. True, the present does not predict the future. Still, the seeds of that future are nevertheless present with us today. It is not then always irrelevant to anticipate a little. Accordingly, this chapter will do precisely that. For, just as the Evaluative State was the product of crisis, so today it faces a new crisis. In the light of what we have learnt from the unfolding of the Evaluative State over the past two decades or more, further questions may be posed about the future and the part played by both the Evaluative State and institutional autonomy within it. Thus, in this final chapter, we return to the fundamental issue explored in this study: namely, the interplay between two key dimensions in policy – the instruments by which higher education is judged and the values that form the basis for this judgement.

Uncomfortable questions

Will the austerity that higher education along with the rest of society faces today be presented as saving the tattered remnants of neoliberalism – a first round in the process once described by a radical nineteenth-century German philosopher as history, and policy as a component in it, repeating itself? The first round, as Karl Marx once observed, carries with it all the trappings of tragedy. Farce characterizes the second round. However, at the time of writing, this does not seem overly distant! Will the same referential institutions – the large corporation as an analogue for 'best practice' in running the university, the boardroom as the archetype for governance overhauled, the notion of 'stakeholders' as the fundamental underpinning to the relationship between the universities and society – retain the slightest credibility? Will the rationale that governments derived from them to lever reform into higher education survive at all, given the amazing spectacle that these 'commanding heights' of finance capitalism have displayed across the face of Europe since September 2008? Do the organizational models, procedures, practices, forms and structures that the Prince and the Evaluative State have imposed on higher education remain robust outside the particular economic circumstances that set them up in the first place? Will the accompanying rhetoric of policy as remedy cling to the same attitude as that now displayed by the more obdurate denizens of Wall Street of 'business as usual' – a stance that leaves itself open to the same comment that contemporaries passed on the Bourbon dynasty, restored in 1815 by foreign arms to the throne of France: 'They forgot nothing and learnt nothing.'

Three timely reminders

Given the present pass, some timely reminders are not inappropriate.

The first reminder is simply to note that the origins of the reforming impulse, which has endured for the past 15 years, was itself born aloft on the wings of severe economic crisis, by structural changes in the economy and by major restrictions in the higher education budget. As this analysis has made clear, the rise of the Evaluative State was the considered response by governments to the earlier crisis of the 1980s. Substantial additions to the instrumentality of steering higher education created a further dimension to system steering through evaluating institutional performance, efficiency and achievement. The Evaluative State both complemented and supplemented the historic instrumentality grounded in legal codification and enactment in the shaping of higher education over the medium to long term. The Evaluative State provided system steering with focus only on the short term. It did not reduce regulation – quite the opposite in fact – though it may have reduced 'institutional response time'.

The second reminder emerges from the convergence of higher education's purpose and mission around the canons of one particular strand of economic thought, variously qualified as neoliberalism by its adepts or ultra-liberalism by its detractors (Neave, 2011a: 15–36).

The third reminder is that institutional autonomy, re-interpreted in the light of the demands of the knowledge economy, has as its specific purpose to expedite the institutional response to the express demands of external interests for knowledge that is useful and relevant to their purposes, and for the university to disseminate it. The instrumentalization of institutional autonomy reflects the unavoidable fact that, until the onset of the present troubles, the market in general was deemed to be the prime driving force in higher education. To an increasing extent, this instrumentalization of institutional autonomy also reflects the increasing dependence of universities on the state of the economy in which it is seen as an indispensable partner. The question the current crisis poses foursquare is 'which sector of the market – public or private – and in what proportions'?

The 1980s and the early 1990s saw Europe's universities weighed in the balance and found wanting. And whilst those who did the weighing were not necessarily proponents of neoliberalism, then known as 'supply-side economics', a decade later, this doctrine had become the all-pervasive main driver for re-engineering higher education. The onset of the current crisis will certainly test the viability and sustainability of those reforms if it does not also introduce similar heart-searching about the *bien fondé* of the doctrine itself. Will the tenets of neoliberalism figure as one of the many fallouts of the present queasiness in the economies of Europe? The place of the state is already a central issue for debate, though whether the spectre – and some of the remedies – of John Maynard Keynes will return to haunt London, Paris and Berlin is, to say the least, unlikely.

Even so, one feature on which both neoliberals and their opponents were in agreement was the need for higher education to *rapidly* adapt to what the former called 'change' and the latter called 'instability'. The present state of the world will, then, provide a modern edition of that medieval practice of 'trial by ordeal'. The experience ought to be enlightening. At the very least, it will give consultants and experts some insight into whether the assumptions behind managerialism and 'strong leadership' possess any operational depth or sustainability other than the inertia that comes from partially installed practice. The proof of sustainability will be clear and pragmatic. It will be seen in the capacity of the newly strengthened structures of governance, bolstered by 'strong leadership', to bear up under the strain, to think strategically, expeditiously – and to survive!

Marketization and some of its consequences

If most of Europe's governments have admitted the necessity of bailing out banks to fulfil short-term interests, can they deny the relevance of the same argument being applied to universities? To this, there is an additional argument, which drives in the same direction. By dint of the instrumentality of performance and output, which these same governments put in place, the university is itself increasingly focused on the short term. How is this to be reconciled with the other engagement that the universities are held to maintain: namely, a commitment that extends over the long term as well?

It is precisely because higher education today is more closely coupled to the market than ever before that it is more vulnerable than ever and more rapidly so to the vagaries and fortunes of that market. By the same logic, the university is very far from being invulnerable to serious recession. Seen from this angle, re-defining institutional autonomy as an instrument for expeditive managerialism takes on all the dimensions of a 'perverse effect'. It speeds up and amplifies the impact of the economic downturn on the groves of academia.

Equally disquieting is the possibility that those universities that have gone out of their way to diversify their financial base to the utmost and to place their fate on a continued stream of contracts with industry, business and information technology – the cream of the entrepreneurial universities – could suffer most. If business is laying off its own employees and management, what is the prospect that it will continue to back university research or to buy university services to the same degree, if at all? This does not bode well for those experimental foundations which, in Portugal, have as one of the prime conditions of being granted this status to raise half their annual income from non-public sources.[1] There is, however, evidence to suggest that the Prince is also prepared to indulge in a certain amount of creative accounting by allowing foundation universities in Portugal to count research contracts with public authorities as private-income sources, a device that allows both institutional honour and the legal fiction of more than half their income being derived from non-public sources to be sustained. Nor, it would seem, is the Prince's flexibility in assigning new heads and descriptors to income sources confined to Portugal. Similar juggling has been detected elsewhere in those establishments, anxious to show their successful sundering of their reliance on the largesse of the Prince and the public.

There is a further scenario that the current crisis, if prolonged, could open up. It entails a swing in the pendulum of policy fashion in the opposite direction: namely, that regulations put in place to elicit more initiative and responsiveness by higher education institutions are partly uncoupled and dissociated from the neoliberal agenda. Whether governments and the EU would contemplate 'guaranteeing' continued support to certain key areas of research and, in effect, creating a form of tightly defined and quasi-permanent 'pseudo markets' remains to be seen. It would certainly be one way to boost the European Research Area.

Lessons for higher education policy

If there is one lesson to be learnt from the experience of the past 20 years in comparative higher education policy, it is surely that economic crises spurred on reforms that were more radical by far and more sustained than was ever the case with economic prosperity. One has only to compare the 1960s with the 1980s and 1990s to see the assertion borne out. Whatever the contours and condition of higher education today, it is unlikely to emerge from the economic blizzard unblemished. Only time, the generosity of philanthropists and a remarkable forbearance by the banks can decide whether the blizzard will nip in the bud that part of the private sector in Western Europe which has emerged since 1990. The situation is more dramatic by far in Central and Eastern Europe. There, reliance on fees (Levy and Slancheva, 2007) and on a middle class whose existence, like the sector from which it derives its lifestyle and status, is both largely dependent on foreign investment places private sector higher education in those systems on an even more precarious footing.

Back to institutional autonomy

Despite the recession, there remain abiding questions that follow on from re-defining institutional autonomy as the central construct in higher education. The first is precisely how far and to what type of establishments is institutional autonomy to be applied? An alternative way to address this question is to ask whether the transition of institutional autonomy as a pervasive and universal *value* to being an operational *modus administrandi* is nearing completion.

There are two sides to this issue. Autonomy, whether institutional or positional, has served to identify and to confer status on institutions. It has also served to differentiate them. Thus, for instance, short-cycle higher education, whether in the form of French *Instituts Universitaires de Technologie*, German *Fachhochschulen* or polytechnics (whether British or Portuguese), tended, by and large, to come under closer control and more direct oversight from the central ministry (Pratt and Burgess, 1974; Doumenc and Gilly, 1977; Amaral and Carvalho, 2008). Differences in terms of the range and scope of autonomy between the university and non-university sectors were the source of much bad blood[2] as well as one of the root causes of 'academic drift' (Kyvik, 1981). Various remedies were advanced – for example, in the UK, the integration and nationalization of polytechnics as 'new universities' and in Portugal, under pressure from the polytechnic interest, the removal of pedagogical autonomy from the universities under the terms of Law 26/2000 and Law 1/2003 (Amaral and Carvalho, 2008).

Institutional autonomy for whom?

Yet, the issue of institutional autonomy as a programme to modernize and 'professionalize' higher education management tends to pay scant regard to the fact that over the past 20 years, the world of learning has passed through two changes in definition. Descriptors of the systems of post-school learning have moved from university to higher education and, more recently, from higher to tertiary education. The expanding provision of post-school education and training begs the question of where exactly are the lines to be drawn between post-school establishments where institutional autonomy is to apply and those where it does not, and why?

This is a delicate issue and falls fairly and squarely under the responsibility of the national authorities. Where are the boundaries of institutional autonomy to be set? On what criteria are they to be drawn up? Since this is a question present in all systems where a non-university, short-cycle higher education exists cheek by jowl with 'research universities', it also has (if only on geographical criteria) a 'European' dimension.

Institutional autonomy as a preliminary to institutional *triage*

This is not the only implication that follows on from re-defining institutional autonomy. Against what might be seen as an 'inclusive and maximalist' definition, explicitly upheld in the concept of tertiary education and training, there stands an 'exclusivist and minimalist' counterpart. The latter appears to be emerging in various forms in Germany (Kehm and Pasternak, 2009), France, Sweden (HSV, 2008) and the UK within the context of identifying, stimulating and preserving excellence. Crudely stated, such 'incentives' are nothing less than a policy of *triage*, well known to rescue services faced with major catastrophes. However, the search for excellence, together with the evident and well-advertised advantages that its recognition holds out, raises two other questions in turn. Are the excellent to be accorded separate status? Is the purpose of such public benediction a move to set aside a few 'super' or 'European' universities – say, 300 or so out of the 4,100 in Europe defined *sensu lato*?[3]

If the majority of higher education institutions are to be pressed towards private funding sources, which presumes those who have such largesse are willing to make it available, does this mean a form of guardian relationship based on public guarantees would apply only to a few universities? Certainly, these few do not always have, time after time, to be the same (Kehm and Pasternak, 2009). Performance does not always guarantee continuity in reward. In these circumstances, what would be the role of the Evaluative State?

The Evaluative State in times of crisis

These are very far from being idle questions. The Evaluative State, acting in its capacity of monitoring the performance and achievement of individual higher education institutions – and especially when its information results in ranking tables – is itself an instrument of *triage*. Whether that *triage* is to identify excellence or to pinpoint those underperforming, it rests on a reasonably objective base. What this suggests is that in times of sustained economic difficulty, the role of the Evaluative State becomes, if anything, more crucial still, precisely because governments now have information that is both detailed and reasonably up to date on which to graft such options as 'preserving excellence' – *triage par le haut* – or closing down those establishments that are manifestly not performing well – *triage par le bas*.

In both cases, irrespective of whether the financial limits are set by the Ministry of Education or by the Ministry of Finance, the 'track records' of private or public universities or polytechnics that fall into one of these categories are known to the government before the decision is taken. Being based on objective criteria, special pleading in the cases of the less fortunate loses much of its force. Seen from this standpoint, the role of the Evaluative State in times of crisis when drastic measures appear justified serves to amplify the capacity of central government to take strategic decisions. By the same token, however, reinforcement of the Evaluative State may, as the case of France has made clear, just as well serve to amplify the basis of debate and dissent that such decisions inevitably raise.[4]

Perverse potential

However, the reinforced Evaluative State may also have a 'perverse potential for mobilization'. Debate that begins by questioning the detailed and technical aspects of the validity and credibility of the procedures used to identify the good, the bad and the ugly can move on to question the underlying purpose, social viability and acceptability of the economic doctrine that underpins strategy, however that strategy is defined. Though the Evaluative State and its attendant instrumentality have as their specific purpose to 'expedite' institutional response by placing evaluation on a technical footing, the overflow of debate into the political and public domain cannot be ruled out, above all in times of widespread social tension. The boundaries of legitimacy that surround the Evaluative State are not impervious and certainly not when those who have to suffer its rigours perceive it less as an honest broker so much as the bludgeon of the Prince.

Yet, under a new guise of 'protecting excellence' or 'encouraging efficiency', the resurrection of what amounts to a 'publicly protected sector' of higher education poses issues that are crucial in determining the shape that higher education may assume in the near future. Rewarding excellence for the few may shelter them from the financial hurricane. It cannot but leave the formally less meritorious to struggle as best they can. What will be the consequences for the degree of institutional or positional discretion accorded to the excellent? Is 'the protection of excellence' to be taken at face value? For those held *not* to be excellent, is the other side of the same coin merely a feline form of 'benign neglect'? Will substantive differences arise as a result of the margin of real – as opposed to formal – institutional latitude enjoyed by the elect and that which is left to the remainder to fumble along with as best they can? In short, we return to the well-worn issue of whether variations in the degree of institutional latitude are to be considered a privilege – temporary, ephemeral and revocable – or whether the degree of self-determination granted to the majority is to be seen as a fundamental institutional right.

The guardian relationship resurrected?

This possibility is very far from a remote pipe dream. Certain Scandinavian governments are currently contemplating quite amazing reductions to their university base. This policy stands as a clear example of *triage*. Similar thrusts to protect 'excellence' gather pace in Germany (Kehm and Pasternak, 2009) and in more cautious and feline form in France. Both, however, open up another interesting prospect: namely, the return of a latter-day 'guardian relationship' for some of Europe's leading establishments whose recognized excellence is held to be outstanding or in the national interest – or both! Clearly, to let such establishments sink without trace would compromise the very visibility, not to mention the intellectual viability that Europe believes it ought to have, if the European adventure is itself to be taken seriously by students, parents, teachers and scholars – in short, by the citizens of Europe.

The revival of a post-modern version of the 'guardian relationship' raises two major questions. It also highlights the issue of the exact role that the Evaluative State may fulfil as an instrument for legitimizing them.

The possibility (which is purely speculative at the moment) that governments may move towards a highly focused and selective 'guardian relationship', resurrected and built around a few highly performing establishments, may not be in keeping with the strict canons of neoliberal doctrine. But life eternal is not granted to ideologies any more than it is to governments, and above all not in times of tension and social unrest, created by spiralling unemployment generally and by the spectre of youth unemployment in particular. Paradoxically, a return to the 'guardian relationship' may well be a way to sustain Europe's viability in a global economy. Seen in this light, such a scenario lends a further and no less interesting angle to the relationship between government, higher education and society.

Leaving aside whether the recognition of excellence is to be a passing or a permanent feature in terms of the advantages it secures, it is nevertheless a very clear example of extreme stratification. The new 'guardian relationship', assuming that it were to emerge, may well give rise to a system configuration that is not very different from the current profile found in Brazilian higher education. There, the elite universities form the public sector and mass universities the private sector (Schwartzman, 1998).

The implications of a resuscitated 'guardian relationship'

Given current developments, it is not too far-fetched to envisage one possible outcome in terms of a 'temporarily protected' sector consisting of highly performing research universities at the apex and a 'market-driven' mass sector at the base. The latter sector, whilst not private, would nevertheless compete ferociously for public funding and for whatever largesse could be obtained from private sector sources. Nor is it beyond the wit of humankind to see what such an arrangement would entail for the margin of institutional discretion – that is, what currently passes for institutional and positional autonomy.

The purpose of what is presented as institutional autonomy is to allow the individual higher education establishment to determine its best strategy to demonstrate performance, achievement and the fulfilment of its self-stated mission. From this it follows that positional autonomy is the reward for demonstrated achievement rather than a right that attaches unconditionally to the individual academic by the nature of his or her employment or level of seniority. Hence, positional autonomy is dependent on, and is conditioned by, the success that institutional autonomy may reap. In its turn, such a degree of conditionality and interdependence points to positional autonomy itself becoming a matter of privilege, which is conditional upon institutional success. Under such circumstances, positional autonomy is less a right attendant upon mere belonging to the Academic Estate, although, as we saw earlier, it was exactly this line of argument that French academia fought tooth and nail to maintain.[5]

A quizzical glance at the discourse of institutional autonomy

If the multiple dimensions involved in shifting the basis of authority within the university are analysed in terms of institutional autonomy alone, then certainly the issue is being debated in the very same ideological and political discourse that the Prince, his courtiers and his servants have themselves set. But the university is not the only axial institution to see the 'leadership principle' injected into the institutional tissue in the name of efficiency, largely construed in terms of cost savings, speed of response and enhanced output, however it is operationalized and irrespective of the criteria brought to bear on the process of operationalization itself.

The university is far from alone in having to submit to judgmentalism, which, whilst parading riotously under the flag of quality assured, is little more than quantity operationalized through output and performance at the undergraduate and most assuredly at the doctoral level (Lindqvist, 2006: 86–8). How far the Evaluative State has extended into the hospitals and the health services of our various nations deserves further development along these explicit lines of enquiry. The principle of 'leadership' in the person of professional managers is clearly evident in the UK just as current attempts are being made to extend the same performance-based managerial 'efficiency' in French hospitals at precisely the same time as the Prince seeks to thrust the very same principle down the craw of the university.

Smokescreens and presentational rhetoric

That the same broad strategy is being exerted – or, in other instances, has already been brought to bear – on two very different sectors shows how difficult it is to see the claims that the Prince makes for his version of institutional autonomy other than as a presentational rhetoric, an exercise in 'spin' by creating labels that are ostensibly designed to justify policy by drawing on historical, cultural and referential frameworks, which have great symbolic and real importance to the university. Whether the label corresponds to the content of the measures inserted under this terminological smokescreen raises the question of whether in reality what is presented corresponds to any degree of personal autonomy whatsoever.

That institutional autonomy is a rhetorical camouflage is evident from the fact that the same essential policy applied to hospitals makes not the slightest mention of autonomy at all. What, however, is common to both universities and hospitals in France emerges in two central ways: first, concentration around 'strong leadership'; and, second, the firm stamping upon, and rejection of, the basic professional ethic (*déontologie*) that earlier underpinned a distribution of authority, cohesion and engagement in the world of medicine and which performed the same function as collegiality in upholding a similar arrangement in the distribution of power and authority in the world of academia. Both professional ethics are deeply incompatible with corporate 'managerialism', though they are most certainly not incompatible with respect to either efficiency or equity. Manageralism demands performance and is prepared to have others pay the price by dispensing with ethics in the name of carrots for some and the stick for the rest.

Substituting procedures and techniques for values

The issue of power and authority, explored up to now within the specific terminology and values of higher education as an institution in transition from a social to an economic construct, takes on a rather broader significance. This it does when the particular contextual setting of higher education is itself placed against a yet broader panorama. There are many perspectives from which the broader issue may be addressed. One of these, and by no means the least interesting, is the way in which neoliberalism has attempted through the application of techniques commonly identified with New Public Management to convert the values to which the value-allocating bodies in society once voluntarily subscribed and perpetuated into non-negotiable techniques and procedures that are intended to enforce cost-effectiveness, financial benefit and productivity – or, for that matter, the consequences for higher education of the austerity that the Prince has decreed.

Such *technicité* is the natural creature of agencies of public purpose – perhaps unavoidably so. Its backwash into the value-allocating bodies, of which both the universities and the health services stand as prime examples, is a powerful dissolvent of the values that until recently accorded these two institutions their place in society. Thus, the cash nexus substitutes for values, despite the fact that the perverse effects of this latter-day monotheism are now so drastic that even the meanest intellect cannot fail to register them with all due amazement and horrified dismay.

The unenviable plight of the leadership principle

Political leadership has been forced to use that other key institution of value allocation – the tax system – in an effort as frantic as it is profligate to regulate and rein in the ravages of that self-same economic monotheism which the Prince was earlier pleased to embrace so heartily. Yet, the avidity and unchecked self-indulgence which strong corporate leadership has been graciously granted appears curiously impotent to come up with firm and resolute solutions to save itself from its own folly, other than extending the begging bowl and crying for public support as the price to be paid for demonstrating a leadership capacity that will hopefully become stronger still. Whether that strength betokens competence in any way that is viable remains the great unknown and as such now emerges 'in this night of doubt and sorrow' as the central article of faith amongst the neoliberal diehards. And doubtless, assessing leadership too could be made an explicit part of the business of the Evaluative State, along with administrative performance as an explicit rather than an assumed part of academic efficiency.

From there to conclude that the way in which universities have recently been organized – along corporate lines and according to corporate principles – is itself open to the same questioning as that now faced by the large industrial firms that influenced the reform of university governance is but one short step. To the testy, it raises the equally impertinent question of whether 'corporate management' as injected into universities is not just a further and more gigantic illustration of what the American scholar Robert Birnbaum termed 'management fads' in higher education (Birnbaum, 2000).

Envoi

Strong leadership in universities may be an excellent notion. However, the heart of the matter is whether that strength is defined as residing with the individual or with the collective, and, no less important, whether that strength stems from a balance between power and authority as opposed to its concentration and personification. So far, the general thrust in the systems examined here has been to flee the collective interpretation with scarcely disguised speed the better to embrace the individual.

Whether an impoverished citizenry in general or academia in particular can afford the consequences of 'strong leaders' and whether in practice individual leadership alone is sufficient to preserve the slightest semblance of equity, decency and social justice, let alone transparency and efficiency, above all in those symbols of business acumen and efficiency – the boardroom and the back office – is a very different matter indeed (Toynbee and Walker, 2008). And yet it is important that these values are not thrown to the four winds. They are perhaps the only means of preventing Anglo-Saxon corporatism from degenerating into an impervious economic oligarchy, and in doing so, summoning up the unwelcome ghosts of a very different corporative order that in the dim but not so distant past prided itself on its administrative efficiency, performance and ability to 'make its trains run on time', if not its universities.

Notes

1 Setting the Scene

1. '... if I extend the inquiry to the other colleges of Oxford and Cambridge, a silent blush, or a scornful frown, will be the only reply. The fellows or monks of my time were decent easy men, who supinely enjoyed the gifts of the founder; their days were filled by a series of uniform employments; the chapel and the hall, the coffee-house and the common room, till they retired, weary and well satisfied, to a long slumber' (Gibbon, *Memoires on My Life and Writings 1737–1794*).
2. 'This Place is the Devil or at least his principal residence. They call it the University, but any other Appellation would have suited it much better, for Study is the last pursuit of the Society; the Master eats, drinks, and sleeps; the Fellows drink, dispute and pun; the Employment of the Under graduates you will probably conjecture without my description' (letter from Byron to John Hanson, 23 November 1805, quoted in Prothero [2005]).
3. Founded in 1958, the CRE today brings together some 745 of Europe's leading universities. In 2002 it merged with the Liaison Committee of the Rectors of the Universities of the European Communities – a smaller body of presidents of universities within the then European Communities – and mutated into the EUA, having successfully extended its membership to universities in East and Central Europe and altered its official scope from being a conference of institutional leaders to becoming a mouthpiece for universities *tout court*.
4. Others of a more mischievous bent see this quality in terms of the rise of 'Caesearism' in academia. For this, see Fuller, 2006.
5. The assertion made by the main legal draftsman of Portugal's 2007 Higher Education Law that it was constructed with New Public Management in mind is one of the more interesting instances of claiming respectability by common association. However, as in supermarkets, it is not always the case that the label describes the goods well! See below, Chapter 11, pp. 145–7.
6. 'As a dog that returneth to his vomit, so is the fool that repeateth his folly' (Proverbs 26:11).

2 Autonomy and the Changing Contract between the State and Higher Education

1. This trend away from the organic and customary towards legal fiat in higher education policy has gathered weight fast and furiously in the UK since 1988. See below Chapter 3, p. 44, note 6.
2. The term 'pedagogical act' is taken from Portuguese legislation, more specifically from Law 108/88 of 24 September 1988 on University Autonomy. See below, Chapters 9–13.

3. See Chapters 5–7 below.
4. I am all too well aware that circumstances are very different in Eastern and Central Europe. But one has to draw a line somewhere. My knowledge of these systems deserves a little modesty as well as caution. I will avoid both by confining this analysis to the Western end of the European landmass.

3   The Evaluative State: A Formative Concept and an Overview

1. All too little attention has been paid to the often very specific connotations and *sous entendus* that accompany this term when transposed from one nation-state system of higher education to another. In part, this arises from the very nature of autonomy as the central 'taken for granted' feature in any one system of higher education. Matters are complicated yet further by the belief, which is largely unspoken even – or perhaps above all – amongst the denizens of academia itself, that because the same term is often shared across different systems, it carries with it the same operational outcomes or has been the result of similar experience. However, this is very rarely the case.

   Take for instance, the French rendition of university autonomy – *les libertés universitaires*. There is a world of difference, as any philosopher is aware, between freedom in the singular and liberties in the plural, the first being a quasi-permanent and inalienable condition, and the second a theoretically revocable privilege (Thorens, 2006; Neave, 2008a). The systematic exploration of the different connotations that attach to this term across different systems is very far from being a sterile exercise in comparative socio-linguistics. It merits further and sustained attention.
2. Humboldt saw the monarch as the best guarantor and through him the state apparatus. However, the elevation of the Prussian monarch as protector of universities was realized only in 1848 (Nybom, 2003).
3. For a more elaborate treatment, see Neave, 2001: 15–73.
4. Referential systems are those that have served as models or templates and/or whose practices were adopted elsewhere. Amongst the earlier examples have been Spain in the sixteenth century, England in the seventeenth century, Scotland in the eighteenth century, France and Germany in the nineteenth century and the USA and the USSR in the twentieth century. For this, see Neave, 1998b.
5. See below, Chapter 10, pp. 134–7.
6. The furious multiplication of such bodies on the British higher education landscape from 1992 onwards had never before been equalled. In addition to the four Higher Education Funding Councils for England, Scotland, Wales and Northern Ireland were the Quality Assurance Agency, the Adult Learning Inspectorate, the Teacher Training Agency, the Higher Education Staff Development Agency, the Institute of Learning and Teaching in Higher Education, not to mention the further division of the main research councils which alone constituted seven separate bodies. In addition to this, discussion in 2003–4 proposed Learning and Skills Councils and Sector Skills Councils dispersed at a regional level (for a more elaborate treatment of this curious phenomenon, see Neave, 2005: 17–22).

7. Juridification is an English take-over from the German term '*Verrechtligung*'. *Verrechtligung* is the process of having recourse to legal enactment as a means either of enforcing practice or, alternatively, of invoking formal legal judgment to settle inter-agency disputes rather than by agreement negotiated pragmatically by the two parties themselves. By extension, *Verrechtligung* may be seen as a particular form of extended bureaucratization. For a discussion of this process at the European level, see Mény, Mueller and Quermonne, 1996. For its form in higher education, see Neave, 1998a.

4   The Significance of Evaluative Homogeneity

1. For a more extended discussion of this point, see below, Chapter 14.
2. Being publicly responsible applies as much to publicly funded as to privately supported universities or polytechnics, regardless of whether their legal basis lies in public and/or administrative law or private/corporate legislation.
3. This point is developed further: see above, Chapter 3, pp. 39–40.
4. See above, Chapter 2, p. 33.

5   France: The Asterix Syndrome and the Exceptional Case

1. The use of this expression is deliberate. The French equivalent of 'academic freedom' (*les libertés universitaires*), quite apart from other connotations which were dealt with earlier (see above, Chapter 3, p. 36, note 1), makes no distinction between institutional and positional autonomy. The latter is largely defined in terms of the status of the individual academic as a public servant with the obligations and privileges that come with this (Chevaillier, 2003). In other words, institutional autonomy is held to be coterminous with the privileges accorded to its members.
2. As fans of Gosciny and Uzerdo cannot fail to recall, Asterix, the small, hot-tempered, quarrelsome but doughty warrior Gaul, together with his fellow villagers were the last to hold out against the might of Caesar's legions. Whether today this emblematic figure lives on in the French citizen's pronounced mistrust of capitalism and ultra-liberalism by extension must remain a matter of personal appreciation!
3. The distinction between higher education as a state – as opposed to a public – service may appear to be mere terminological quibbling. However, in the French context, it represents a fundamental difference in purpose between *Grandes Ecoles* and universities. The former may be seen as the way in which the state secures *for* itself its technical and political cadres at a very high level, sometimes qualified as 'a technocracy'. Public service, by contrast, may be seen in terms of a broader provision *by* the state for the education and training of its citizens, including the traditional 'liberal professions' of law, medicine and teaching, but not – except in Alsace – the Church, together with what is commonly alluded to as 'cadres' for both the public and private sectors of the economy.
4. In all, during the 100 years of its existence between 1881 and 1981, HEC produced some 19,000 qualified graduates. Even if one takes account of this institution's growth and drawing power, an average output of 190 per

annum is an impressive monument to excellence in its more Malthusian version! For this, see 'L'Histoire d'HEC', available at www.hec.fr/HEC-Paris/A-propos-d-HEC/L-histoire-d-HEC, date accessed 2 November 2011.

5. For the rationale of defining this as 'non-state' as opposed to 'private' higher education, see Neave, 2009b: 53–87.

6. There are some 470 *Classes Préparatoires aux Grandes Ecoles* (CPGEs) in Metropolitan France and overseas on the Ministry of Education's list. Located atop certain *Lycées*, they are selective and, as their name suggests, provide intense preparation over two or three years for the competitive examinations giving access to the *Grandes Ecoles*. If described in American terminology, they would correspond to Grades 13 and 14 (for recognized CPGEs, see 'Liste des Classes préparatoires aux Grandes Ecoles', Paris, Ministère de l'Education, available at www.sup.adc.education.fr/cpgelst, date accessed 2 November 2011).

7. As of 2009, there are some 116 IUTs enrolling some 134,000 students on specialized vocational courses (Ministère de l'Education nationale, 'IUT: le choix d'efficacité', available at www.iut-fr.com, date accessed 2 November 2011).

8. This emerged clearly in the composition of the *Conseil d'Administration* (Board of Management) of the individual university, which ranged from 30 to 60 members, with academic and research staff accounting for 40–45 per cent of the total, external representatives 20–30 per cent and students 20–25 per cent, with 10–15 per cent of places being assigned to the elected representatives of technical and support staff (Journal Officiel France, 1984: Article 28).

9. From an historical perspective, prime amongst them have been Italy and Spain – the former under the Casati Law of 1864 (Martinelli, 1992: 355–9) and the latter in the form of the *Ley Moyano* of 1854 (Garcia-Garrido, 1992: 663–76).

6   Strengthening the Evaluative State: Strategy, Values and Rhetoric

1. The complexity was impressive indeed, so much so that it inspired one Minister of Higher Education and Research to compare the relationship between various Directorates responsible for sectoral research with the writhing conduits of an oil refinery: '*(Ces Directions) sont reliées par une tuyauterie qui ferait pleurer de jalousie un constructeur de raffinerie de pétrole*' (Devacquet, 1988: 172). As both Minister and a chemist, Mr Devacquet was well qualified to make such a remark!

2. See above, Chapter 5, p. 64.

3. See above, Chapter 5, pp. 76–7.

4. For this point, see above, Chapter 5, pp. 71–3.

7   Discord Dissected: The 'New University' and some of its Discontents

1. For this, see above, Chapter 4, p. 58.

2. For this, see above, Chapter 5, p. 70.

3. For this, see above, Chapter 5, pp. 74–5.
4. See above, Chapter 6, p. 90.
5. The *Conseil National de l'Enseignement Supérieur et de la Recherche* is a consultative body with administrative and disciplinary responsibility covering the whole of higher education. Chaired by the Minister of Higher Education and Research and composed of some 62 members, the *Conseil* is a mixture of elected and nominated representatives. The formally elected element is made up of 22 members from the Academic Estate, 11 members of the Student Estate and 7 representatives of non-teaching staff. Nominated membership is drawn from the world of politics (one deputy and one senator), economics (one representative of the Social and Economic Council), culture and society. Non-elected members are nominated by the Minister of Higher Education and Research. With the exception of members from the student estate, whose mandate is for two years, members serve for four years. The CNESER meets three times a year, one of which is spent examining the budget proposed for higher education. Its oversight extends to all qualifications from the *Baccalauréat* through to the doctoral level. It may also be consulted on such matters as the four-year university contract with the government and service agreements between the university and firms. It has consultative status in the general area of higher education policy (FAGE, 2009).
6. Literally, 'a state corps'. Whilst usually translated into English as 'civil servant', this legal term has other associations that are redolent not merely of formal obligations to the state. Such obligations, rights and privileges form part of career-long conditions of service. Membership of '*le corps universitaire*' may not always, in the words of Benjamin Jowett (Master of Balliol College, Oxford in late-Victorian times), 'lead to high preferment'. However, being part of this official body most certainly carries with it 'high standing' (Kessler, 1986).

8 Spain: Defining Autonomy, Setting Up Evaluation

1. Today, Spain boasts 17 Autonomous Communities including two 'insular territories' (the Balearic Islands the and Canary Islands), the two city communities of Madrid and, in more limited form, Ceuta and Millila on the North African coast.
2. For the historical and contemporary significance of the dual hierarchy, see above, Chapter 3, p. 46.
3. See above, Chapter 7, p. 100.
4. Communication from José Gines Mora to Alberto Amaral, 18 July 2008.
5. See above, Chapter 8, p. 106.

9 Portugal: Laying out the Higher Education Landscape

1. See above, Chapter 2, pp. 27–32.
2. See above, Chapter 2, pp. 108–9.

10 The Dynamic in Portugal's Higher Education Policy

1. Conversation with A. Amaral, 19 January 2009.
2. The Law of Anticipated Results is one of the consequences that elsewhere in Europe have been identified amongst the major changes in institutional behaviour that follow from the national administration delegating key functions – for example, diversification of funding, contractualization, staff recruitment and promotion, and programme and course development – to the individual institution. With enhanced institutional initiative, universities are in a position to *anticipate* the will of the Prince so as to better secure for themselves those rewards that come with Princely approval. The Law of Anticipated Results is then a major consequence of performance-related budgeting and the shift in university finance from an *a priori* to an *a posteriori* mode.
3. This term – alas – is not original. It was first coined by the French political scientist François Goguel in his seminal book *Les Partis politiques sous la IIIè République* (1946).
4. See above, Chapter 2, pp. 31–2.
5. For this point, see above, Chapter 3, pp. 40–4.
6. See above, Chapter 3, pp. 41–3.
7. For an early attempt to explore this issue, see Barnett, 1994.
8. See above, Chapter 1, especially p. 6.
9. See above, Chapter 8.
10. See above, Chapter 10, p. 132.

11 Re-focusing Institutional Autonomy: the Portuguese Decree Law of 2007

1. This view has received corroboration from no less a source than the expert entrusted with drafting the law itself. In his opinion, New Public Management provided the basic architecture for shaping the law.
2. See above, Chapter 9, p. 124.
3. In the French context, see above, Chapter 5, p. 69.
4. A young Finnish colleague, visiting CIPES, pointed out in a presentation which compared higher education policy in Finland and Portugal that a similar suggestion for 'foundation universities' had been made by another OECD review team when it visited Finland in 2005.

   This is of more than passing interest. It hints at 'foundation universities' being less a creature of national policy review than an implanting of the OECD's programme into the tissues of its host's higher education system and as such a neat illustration of a post-modern version of that antique task otherwise known in the Church as proselytism. Whether such initiatives set the OECD within the ranks of the evangelists for neoliberalism is something that believers and sceptics must decide for themselves.
5. For a more extensive discussion of this general point, see above, Chapter 10, pp. 134–6.
6. See Chapter 10, pp. 124–5.
7. See above, Chapter 10, p. 128.

8. The 'experimental' nature of this policy is explicit in the Guideline Law. Universities opting for this status may, if they so wish, revert to their previous condition. They may also define how long they wish the initial period of 'experimentation' to last (Portugal, 2008: Article 129.4). By 2009, three universities had opted for foundation status: the University of Aveiro, the University of Porto and the Lisbon-based ISCTE (*Instituto Superior de Ciências do Trabalho e da Empresa*: the Higher Institute of Labour and Entrepreneurial Sciences).
9. Foundation universities are required to raise 50 per cent of their annual income from non-public sources.
10. CNAVES was closed down by Decree Law 369/2007 of 5 November 2007.
11. As an aside, league tables act as a powerful stimulant to that phenomenon noted earlier namely, the 'Law of Anticipated Results'. See above, Chapter 10, p. 129, note 2 (see p. 222).

12 Reform at the Cutting Edge: The Institutional Level

1. See above, Chapter 4, pp. 57–8.
2. Within the strict terms set out in the Higher Education Guideline Law, even the *existence* of the Senate as the main consultative body bringing together the representatives of organizational units, in effect, the highest organ of the ascending academic hierarchy, was made discretionary (Article 77).
3. See above, Chapter 7, p. 94.
4. Arguably, this is another 'perverse effect' of 'proceduralism'. For a more detailed discussion of the place, origins and consequences of proceduralism, see above, Chapter 1, pp. 17–19.
5. A slightly different perspective on the interplay between internal initiatives and external national administration is developed in Chapter 2, p. 30.
6. See above, Chapter 1, pp. 27–9.
7. One of the more disgraceful features of the British higher education system, which pioneered the theory and the grounded institutional consequences of both managerialism and 'leadership' as formal *managerial* functions, is that it remains in woeful and blissful ignorance of the exact size and boundaries of its Administrative Estate! For this, see Whitchurch, 2006.

   Alexander Pope, Poet Laureate and eighteenth-century master of the 'heroic couplet', would undoubtedly have had something highly appropriate to say on this curious condition.
8. As is the creation of professional associations by the denizens of the administrative estate in the Anglo-Saxon world: for example, the Conference of University Administrators in the UK, not to mention student counsellors and advisors, publicity cfficers, university press officers, international relations officers *et al.*, though sociologists tend to equate such moves with the emergence of *sub-professions*.
9. Whilst first developed, as we have seen (Chapter 5), in France, contractualization has also taken root in both Portugal and Spain.
10. For a discussion of ascending and descending hierarchies in Western European universities and their significance for leadership, see above, Chapter 3, pp. 46–7.

13 Portuguese Higher Education Reform: Four Key Dimensions

1. See above, Chapter 2, p. 30.
2. See above, Chapter 12, p. 161.
3. See above, Chapter 7, pp. 93–4.
4. See above, Chapter 4, p. 58.
5. See above, Chapter 12, pp. 165–7.
6. See above, Chapter 11, p. 152.
7. See above, Chapter 10, pp. 130–1.
8. See above, Chapter 12, pp. 106–7.
9. For the experimental nature of this initiative, see above, Chapter 11, p. 154.
10. My good colleague, Pedro Teixeira, suggests another possibility that echoes the aphorism hit upon in 1849 by the French journalist Alphonse Kahr: '*Il n'y a que le provisoire qui dure.*' Teixeira pointed out that one way of getting a controversial measure past obstinate colleagues is to suggest that it is only temporary and that they can get rid of it later. Thus, the provisional acts as a fig leaf to the *fait accompli*!
11. Another interpretation would see this provision as the legislator's implicit encouragement for what, following the argument developed by Gibbons *et al.* (1994), is referred to as the 'Mode 2' form of academic work. The 'Mode 2' concept starts from a standpoint that is rather different from the usual social sciences perspective of higher education policy. Its intellectual grounding lies in science policy. It claims that working in teams has become the predominant and necessary feature of present-day research and of academic endeavour generally. Gibbons *et al.* went so far as to assert that this pattern embraced the social sciences and humanities, although even in economics, grounded reality in both Norway and France, for example, does not always seems to bear this out (Heen, 2000; 2002: 77–95).
12. For this, see above, Chapter 11, p. 152.

14 A Flight over the Evolving Evaluative State

1. See above, Chapter 10, pp. 136–7.
2. See above, Chapter 8, pp. 112–13.
3. See above, Chapter 6, pp. 82–4.
4. See above, Chapter 7, pp. 85–6.
5. See above, Chapter 3, pp. 42–3.
6. See above, Chapter 12, p. 163.
7. Private universities and above all those remaining under Church control are a different matter. For Eastern and Central Europe, see Levy and Slancheva, 2007. For Western Europe, an excellent study is still Geiger, 1986.

15 Back to the Future

1. See above, Chapter 13, p. 181.
2. For Portugal, see above, Chapter 10, p. 136.

3. For those curious about how the number of 'super' universities is reached, suffice to say that in the USA, with some 3,600 colleges *à l'américaine* and universities, there were some 283 'Research Universities' in 2009 (Carnegie Foundation for the Advancement of Teaching, 2009). This does not mean, however, that we are under any obligation to apply a similar ratio. Still, it is a useful pointer to the shape of things that might still come and is useful as such!

4. Or to spark off an even more vehement response, as, for instance, did the Browne Report on Student Finance in December 2010 in the UK.

5. See above, Chapter 7, pp. 99–100.

Bibliography

AERES (2009) 'Communiqué de presse de l'AERES du 23 février 2009', available at: www.aeres-evaluation.frIMG/pdf/090223 CommuniquéAERES-2.pdf (date accessed 17 May 2009).

B. Alvarez and A. Alvarez (1992) 'Columbia', in B.R. Clark and G. Neave (eds), *The Encyclopedia of Higher Education*, vol. I, *National Systems of Higher Education* (Oxford: Pergamon).

A. Amaral (2008) *Políticas de Ensino Superior: quarto témas em debate* (Lisbon: Editorial del Ministério de Educação).

A. Amaral and T.A. Carvalho (2008) *Autonomy and Change in Portuguese Higher Education* (Matosinhos: CIPES).

A. Amaral and A. Magalhães (2007) 'Market Competition, Public Good and Institutional Governance', *Higher Education, Management and Policy* 19, 1: 63–76.

——. (2008) 'Market Competition, Social Accountability and Institutional Strategies', in A. Vaccaro, H. Horta and P. Madsen (eds), *Transparency, Information and Communication Technology – Social Responsibility in Business and Education* (Charlottesville, VA: Philosophy Documentation Center), pp. 205–26.

A. Amaral, P.A.M. Maassen, G. Neave and C. Musselin (eds) (2009) *European Integration and the Governance of Higher Education and Research* (Dordrecht: Springer).

A. Amaral and G. Neave (2008) 'The OECD and its Influence in Higher Education: A Critical Revision', in Roberta M. Bassett and Alma Maldonaldo-Maldonaldo (eds), *International Organizations and Higher Education Policy: Thinking Globally, Acting Locally* (London: Taylor & Francis).

A. Amaral and M.J. Rosa (2008), 'Evaluating Departments: Do They Contribute to Quality Improvement?', in A. Amaral, A. Rovio Johansson. M.J. Rosa and D. Westerheijden (eds), *Essays in Supportive Peer Review* (New York: Nova Science Publications), pp. 68–82.

ANECA (2007) *ANECA Self Evaluation Report according to the Standards and Guidelines for Quality Assurance in the European Higher Education Areas*, Madrid, available at: www.enqa_autoevaluación_eng_070328.pdf (date accessed 17 May 2009).

——. (2008) *ANECA Strategic Plan: Horizon 2010*, Madrid, available at: www.strategicplan_eng.pdf (date accessed 17 May 2009).

B. Askling, M. Bauer and S. Marton (1999) 'Swedish Universities Towards Self-Regulation: A New Look at Institutional Autonomy', *Tertiary Education and Management* 5, 2: 173–93.

R. Barnett (1994) 'Power, Enlightenment and Quality Evaluation', *European Journal of Education* 29, 2: 165–80.

T. Becher and M. Kogan (1991) *Structure and Process in Higher Education* (London: Heinemann).

J. Ben David (1978) *Centres of Learning: Britain, France, Germany, USA* (New York: McGraw-Hill for the Carnegie Foundation).

A.E. Berger (2007) 'La Loi Pécresse et le modèle américain', *Liberation*, 20 December 2007, available at: www.liberation.fr/rebonds/299182.FR.php (date accessed 15 November 2011).

A. Bladh (2007) 'Institutional Autonomy with Increasing Dependency on Outside Actors', *Higher Education Policy* 20, 4: 243–59.

I. Bleiklie (2007) 'Systematic Integration and Macro Steering', *Higher Education Policy* 20, 4: 291–313.

I. Bleiklie and M. Kogan (2007) 'Organization and Governance of Universities', *Higher Education Policy* 20, 4: 477–94.

R. Birnbaum (2000) *Management Fads in Higher Education: Where They Come From, What They Do, Why They Fail* (San Francisco, CA: Jossey Bass).

S. Boffo and R. Moscati (1998) 'Evaluation in the Italian Higher Education System: Many Tribes, Many Territories, Many Godfathers', *European Journal of Education* 33, 3: 349–60.

C. Boxer (1969) *The Portuguese Seaborne Empire 1415–1825* (London: Hutchinson).

Browne Report (2010) *Securing a Sustainable Future for Higher Education: An Independent Review of Higher Education Funding and Student Finance*, available at: www.bis.gov.uk/assets/biscore/corporate/docs/s/10-1208-securing-sustainable-higher-education-browne-report.pdf (date accessed 15 November 2011).

G. Brulin (2006) 'The Third Task of Universities: or How to Get Universities to Serve their Communities', in Peter Reason, and Hilary Bradbury (eds), *Handbook on Action Research: Participative Inquiry and Practice* (London: Sage).

G.G. Byron (1805) 'Letter to George Hanson, November 23rd 1805', quoted in R.E. Prothero (2005) *The Works Of Lord Byron, Letters and Journals*, vol. 1, available at: www.gutenberg.org/dirs/etext05/7blj110.txt (date accessed 15 November 2011).

Carnegie Foundation for the Advancement of Teaching (2009) 'Basic Classification Tables', *Classification of Institutions of Higher Education*, available at: www.carnegiefoundation.org/classifications/index.asp?key=805 (date accessed 15 November 2011).

M. Carrera Fernandes (2009) 'O Silêncio reina', *Journal de Noticias*, 6 February 2009, p. 23.

L. Cerych and P. Sabatier (1986) *Great Expectations: Implementing Reform in Europe's Higher Education* (Stoke-on-Trent: Trentham Books).

C. Charle (2004) 'Patterns', in W. Ruegg (ed.), *History of the University in Europe*, vol. 3, *Universities in the Nineteenth and Early Twentieth Centuries* (Cambridge University Press), pp. 34–5.

CHEPS (2007) *Issues in Higher Education Policy 2006: An Update on Higher Education Policy Issues in 2006 in 10 Western Countries* (Enschede: CHEPS).

T. Chevaillier (2001) 'French Academics between the Professions and the Civil Service', *Higher Education* 41, 1–2: 9–75.

——. (2002) 'University Governance and Finance: The Impact of Resource Allocation on Decision-making Structures', in A. Amaral, G.A. Jones and B. Karseth (eds), *Governing Higher Education: National Perspectives on Institutional Governance* (Dordrecht: Kluwer Academic Publishers), pp. 87–98.

———. (2004) 'The Changing Role of the State in French Higher Education: From Curriculum Control to Accreditation', in S. Schwartz-Hahn and D. Westerheijden (eds), *Accreditation and Evaluation in the European Higher Education Area* (Dordrecht: Kluwer Academic Publishers).

P. Clancy (2007) 'Resisting the Evaluative State: Irish Academics Win the Battle But Lose the War', in J. Enders and F.A. van Vught (eds), *Towards a Cartography of Higher Education Policy Change* (Enschede: CHEPS), pp. 111–18.

B.R. Clark (1960) 'The "Cooling Out" Function in Higher Education', *American Journal of Sociology* 65, 6: 569–76.

———. (1977) *Academic Power in Italy: Bureaucracy and Oligarchy in a National University System* (University of Chicago Press).

———. (1983) *The Higher Education System: Academic Organization in Cross-National Perspective* (Berkeley, CA: University of California Press).

———. (1994) *Places of Inquiry* (Berkeley, CA: University of California Press).

———. (1998) *Creating Entrepreneurial Universities: Organizational Pathways of Transformation* (Oxford: Elsevier).

———. (2004) *Sustaining Change in Universities: Continuities in Case Studies and Concepts* (Milton Keynes: Open University Press for SRHE).

CNRS (Centre National de la Recherche Scientifique) (2009) *CNRS dossier les frontières*, Paris, available at: www.sauvonslarecherche.fr/IMG/pdf/COM_32_global_32_20090605_32_V2.pdf (date accessed 15 November 2011).

Comité National d'Evaluation (1987) *Où va l'Université? Rapport du Comité national d'Evaluation* (Paris: Gaillimard).

———. (1989) *Priorités pour l'Université* (Paris: La Documentation française).

———. 'Les missions et les principes d'action', available at: www.cne-evaluation.fr/fr/present/som_mis.htm (date accessed 15 November 2011).

P. Coombes and J.A. Perkins (1989) *La Reforma Universitaria española: evaluación e informe* (Madrid: Consejo de Universidades).

M. Crozier (1987) *Etat modeste, état modern: stratégies pour un autre changement* (Paris: Fayard).

H. Daalder and E. Shils (1982) *Universities, Politicians and Bureaucrats* (Cambridge University Press).

U. Dahllöf, S. Lofgren and B. Willén (1979) *Evaluation, Recurrent Education and Higher Education Reform in Sweden* (Uppsala: Reports on Education No. 6).

M. Daxner (2006) 'Challenges to Academic Conduct and their Implications for University Development', *Higher Education in Europe* 31, 3: 231–40.

H. de Boer (2003) *Institutionele Verandering en professionele autonomie: een empirische verklarende studie naar de doorwerking van het Wet 'Modernisering Universitaire Bestuursorganisatie'* (MUB) (Enschede: CHOBS).

———. (2007) 'Change and Continuity in Dutch Internal University Governance and Management', in J. Enders and F.A. van Vught (eds), *Towards a Cartography of Higher Education Policy Change* (Enschede, CHEPS/UT), pp. 31–8.

H. de Boer, J. Enders and L. Leisyte (2009) 'New Public Management and the Academic Profession: The Rationalisation of Academic Work Revisited', in J. Enders and E. de Weert (eds), *The Changing Face of Academic Life: Analytical and Comparative Perspectives* (Basingstoke: Palgrave Macmillan), p. 44.

H. de Boer and L. Goedegebuure (2009) *'The Changing Nature of the Academic Deanship,'* Draft Report (Enschede/Melbourne: CHEPS, L.H. Martin Institute, University of Melbourne).

J. de Groof, G. Neave and J. Svec (1998) *Governance and Democracy in Higher Education*, vol. 2 in the Council of Europe series *Legislating for Higher Education in Europe* (Dordrecht: Kluwer Academic Publishers).

M. de Miguel Diaz (1999). *Calidad de la Enseñanza universitaria y excelencia academica* (Oviedo: Universidad de Oviedo, Servicio de Publicaciónes).

E. de Weert and L. van Vucht-Tijssen (1999) 'Academic Staff between Threat and Opportunity: Employment and Conditions of Service', in B. Jongbloed, P.A.M. Maassen and G. Neave (eds), *From the Eye of the Storm: Higher Education's Changing Institution* (Dordrecht: Kluwer Academic Publishers).

A. Devacquet (1988) *L'Amibe et l'Etudiant: Université et Recherche – l'Etat d'Urgence* (Paris: éditions Odile Jacob).

DfES (2004) Higher Education Act 2004 – Explanatory Notes, available at: www. legislation.gov.uk/ukpga/2004/8/notes/division/4 (date accessed 1 December 2011).

J-F. Dhainaut (2008) 'Universités: comment surmonter le syndrome d'Asterix', available at: www.aeres-evaluation.fr/Edito (date accessed 17 May 2009).

R. Diez Hochleitner (ed.) (1989) *La Educación postsecundaria: ante la sociedad del conocimiento y de las communicaciones. Documentos de un debate* (Madrid: Fundación Santillana).

D. Dill, B. Jongbloed, A. Amaral and P. Teixeira (eds) (2004) *Markets in Higher Education: Rhetoric or Reality?* (Dordrecht: Kluwer Academic Publishers).

Documentation française (2009a) 'L'évaluation de politiques publiques: les organismes independents', available at: www.ladocumentationfrancaise. fr/dossiers/evaluation-politiques-publiques/organismes-independants.shtml (date accessed 15 November 2011).

——. (2009b) 'L'évaluation de politiques publiques: chronologie', available at: www.ladocumentationfrançaise.fr/dossiers/evaluation-politiques-publiques/ chronologie.shtml (date accessed 17 May 2009).

M. Doumenc and J.C. Gilly (1977) *Les IUTs: ouverture et idéologie* (Paris: éditions du Seuil).

C. Durand-Prinborgne (1992) 'France', in B.R. Clark and G. Neave (eds), *The Encyclopedia of Higher Education*, vol. I, *National Systems of Higher Education* (Oxford: Pergamon), pp. 217–24.

D. Easton (1965) *A Framework for Political Analysis* (Englewood Cliffs, NJ: Prentice Hall).

J. Enders and O. Fulton (eds) (2002) *Higher Education in a Globalising World: International Trends and Mutual Observations* (Dordrecht: Kluwer Academic Publishers).

ENQA (European Network of Quality Assurance Agencies) (2006) 'Quality Assurance of Higher Education in Portugal: An Assessment of the Evaluation System and Recommendations for a Future System', *ENQAA Occasional Papers* No. 10, Helsinki, November 2006.

——. (2009a) 'ENQA History', available at: www.enqa.eu/history.lasso (date accessed 15 November 2011).

——. (2009b) 'ENQA Full Member Agencies', available at: www.enqa.eu/agencies. lasso (date accessed 15 November 2011).

——. (2009c) 'ENQA Candidate Members', available at: www.enqa.eu/candidates. lasso (date accessed 15 November 2011).

——. (2009d) 'Cooperation with Stakeholders', available at: www.enqa.eu/stakeholders.lasso (date accessed 15 November 2011).

EQAR (European Quality Assurance Register for higher Education) (2008) 'About EQAR', available at: www.eqar.eu/about/introduction.html (date accessed 15 November 2011).

European Commission (2006) 'Delivering the Modernisation Agenda for Universities: Education, Research and Innovation' (COM 2006 502).

——. (2007) 'Towards the European Higher Education Area: Responding to Challenges in a Globalized World', *Conference of European Higher Education Ministers; Contribution of the European Commission*, Brussels.

R. Eustace (1998) 'The United Kingdom', in T. Husén, T.N. Postlethwaite, B.R. Clark and G. Neave (eds), *The Complete Encyclopedia of Education* (Oxford: Elsevier Science), CD-ROM.

FAGE (*Fédération des Associations Générales Etudiante*) (2009) 'Qu'est-ce que le CNESER?', available at: http://cneser.fage.asso.fr/index.php?option=com_content&view=article&id=4&Itemid=15 (date accessed 17 May 2009).

S. Fuller (2006) 'Universities and the Future of Knowledge Governance from the Standpoint of Social Epistemology', in G. Neave (ed.), *Knowledge, Authority and Dissent: Critical Perspectives on Research into Higher Education and the Knowledge Society* (Paris: UNESCO), pp. 345–79.

M. Gallo (2009) 'Il suffit de quelques jours pour que la barbarie rejailisse', *Le Point*, 10 June 2009, available at: www.lepoint.fr/actualites-politique/2009-02-25/interview-max-gallo-il-suffit-de-quelques-jours-pour-que-la/917/0/320453 (date accessed 15 November 2011).

——. (2008) *La Révolution française. Tome 1 Le Peuple et le Roi* (Paris: XO editions).

J-L. Garcia-Garrido (1992) 'Spain', in B.R Clark and G. Neave (eds), *The Encyclopedia of Higher Education*, vol 1. *National Systems of Higher Education* (Oxford: Pergamon), pp. 663–76.

R. Geiger (1986) *Private Sectors in Higher Education: Structures, Function and Change in Eight Countries* (Ann Arbor: University of Michigan Press).

E. Gibbon. *Memoires on My Life and Writings 1737–1794*, available at: http://infomotions.com/etexts/gutenberg/dirs/etext04/gbnlw10.htm (date accessed 15 November 2011).

M. Gibbons, M. Trow, H. Nowotny, C. Limoges and P. Scott (1994) *The Production of Knowledge: The Dynamics of Science and Research in Contemporary Societies* (London: Sage)

F. Goguel (1946) *La Politique des partis sous la IIIè République* (Paris: éditions du Seuil).

A. Gornitzka (2005) 'Coordinating Policies for a "Europe of Knowledge": Emerging Practices of the "Open Method of Coordination" in Education and Research', *Working Paper No. 16* (Oslo: University of Oslo Centre for European Studies).

K.H. Gruber (1982) 'Higher Education and the State in Austria', *European Journal of Education* 27, 3: 259–70.

J. Guin (1990) 'The Re-awakening of Higher Education in France', *European Journal of Education* 25, 2: 123–45.

A.H. Halsey (1995) *Decline of Donnish Dominion: The British Academic Professions in the Twentieth Century* (Oxford: Clarendon).

G. Haug and C. Tausch (2001) *Towards the European Higher Education Area: A Survey of the Main Reforms from Bologna to Prague* (Geneva: Conférence des Recteurs Européens).

Hautes Etudes Commerciales (2009) 'L'Histoire d'HEC', available at: www.hec. fr/HEC-Paris/A-propos-d-HEC/L-histoire-d-HEC (date accessed 15 November 2011).

E. Heen (2000) 'The Research University: Quo Vadis?: Doctoral Research Training in Economics, Case Studies from France and Norway', PhD thesis, Stockholm: Institute of International Education.

———. (2002) 'Research Priorities and Disciplinary Cultures: Friends and Foes? A Cross-national Study on Doctoral Education', *Higher Education Policy* 15, 1: 77–95.

M. Heitor and H. Horta (2011) 'Science and Technology Policy in Portugal: From Late Awakening to the Challenge of Knowledge-integrated Communities', in G. Neave and A. Amaral (eds), *Higher Education in Portugal 1974–2009: A Nation, a Generation* (Dordrecht: Springer).

M. Henkel (1991) 'The New Evaluative State', *Public Administration* 69, 1: 121–36.

———. (2007) 'Can Academic Autonomy Survive in the Knowledge Society? A Perspective from Britain', *Higher Education Research and Development* 26, 1: 87–99.

W.Z. Hirsch and L.E. Weber (eds) (2001) *Governance in Higher Education: The University in a State of Flux* (London: Economica).

HSV (Hogskolverket) (2003) *The Third Report on the National Reviews of Swedish Higher Education by The International Advisory Board Report No. 2003:34* (Stockholm: Swedish National Agency for Higher Education).

———. (2005a) *Evaluation Activities of the National Agency for Higher Education in Sweden: A Final Report by the International Advisory Board*, Appendix: 'On Looking Forward to Innovation, Consolidation and Progress: A Short Saga of Organizational Anticipation', *Report No 2005:38R* (Stockholm: HSV).

———. (2005b) *The Evaluation Activities of the National Agency for Higher Education in Sweden. Final Report by the International Advisory Board Report 2005:38R* (Stockholm: HSV).

———. (2008) 'Centres of Excellence in Higher Education 2008', *Report 2008:38R* (Stockholm: HSV).

J. Huisman, P.A.M. Maassen and G. Neave (2001) *Higher Education and the Nation State* (Oxford: Elsevier-Pergamon for the IAU).

ICED (1989) *The Spanish University Reform: An Assessment and a Report* (Madrid: Consejo de Universidades).

Institute for International Education (2001) *Student Handbook* (Stockholm: IIE), available at: www.interped.su.se/pdfs/StudentHandbook2001.pdf (date accessed 17 May 2009).

M. Jeliaskova and D. Westerheijden (2002) 'Systematic Adaptation to a Changing Environment: Towards a Next Generation of Quality Assurance Models', *Higher Education* 44, 3–4: 433–48.

I. Jenniskens (1997) *Governmental Steering and Curriculum Innovations: A Comparative Study of the Relation between Governmental Steering Instruments and Innovations in Higher Education Curricula* (Utrecht: De Tijdstroom).

P. Jourde (2008) 'L'Université féodale de demain', *Le Monde Diplomatique*, April 2008.

Journal Officiel France (1984) *La Loi No 84-52 du 26 janvier 1984 sur l'Enseignement Supérieur*, available at: http://admi.net/jo/loi84-52.html (date accessed 15 November 2011).

———. (1985) *Decret 85 – 285 du 23 février 1985 relatif à l'organisation et au fonctionnement du Comité national d'évaluation des établissements publics à caractère scientifique, culturel et professionnel*, available at: www.cne-evaluation. fr/fr/present/loi210285.htm (date accessed 15 November 2011).

F. Kaiser and J. Huisman (2003) 'Expansion and Diversification in Higher Education', in R. Begg (ed.), *The Dialogue between Higher Education Research and Practices* (Dordrecht: Kluwer Academic Publishers).

J.P. Th. Kalkwijk (1998) 'On Dancing on a Slack Rope: An Introduction to the Consequences of Quality Assurance in Higher Education', in J.P Scheele P.A.M. Maassen and D. Westerheijden (eds), *To Be Continued...Follow Up of Quality Assurance in Higher Education* (Maarsen: Elsevier/De Tijdstroom), pp. 15–31.

D.B.T. Kallen *et al.* (eds) (1984) *Social Science Research and Public Policy-Making: A Reappraisal* (London: NFER Nelson).

B. Kehm (2007) 'The Evaluative State and Higher Education Policy in Germany', in J. Enders and F.A. van Vught (eds), *Towards a Cartography of Higher Education Policy Change* (Enschede: CHEPS), pp. 139–48.

B. Kehm and P. Pasternak (2009) 'The German "Excellence Initiative" and its Role in Re-structuring the National Higher Education Landscape', in D. Palfreyman and T. Tapper (eds), *Structuring Mass Higher Education: The Role of Elite Institutions* (Abingdon: Routledge), pp. 113–27.

B. Kehm and U. Teichler (1998) 'Germany', in T. Husén, T.N. Postlethwaite, B.R. Clark and G. Neave (eds), *The Complete Encyclopedia of Education* (Oxford: Elsevier Science), CD-ROM.

C. Kerr (2003) *The Blue and the Gold: A Personal Memoir of the University of California 1949–1967*, vol. 1, *Political Turmoil* (Berkeley, CA: University of California Press).

C. Kerr and M.L. Gade (1986) *The Many Lives of Academic Presidents: Time, Place, Character* (Washington DC: Association of Governing Boards of Universities and Colleges).

A-M. Kessler (1986) *Les Grands Corps de l'Etat* (Paris: Foundation nationale des sciences politiques).

M. Kogan (ed.) (2004) *Management and Evaluation in Higher Education, UNESCO Forum Occasional Paper Series, Paper No. 7* (Paris: UNESCO).

S. Kyvik (1981) *The Norwegian Regional Colleges: A Study of the Establishment and Implementation of a Reform in Higher Education* (Oslo: NIFU).

———. (2002) 'The Dynamics of Change in Higher Education', in A. Gornitzka, M. Kogan and A. Amaral (eds), *Reform and Change in Higher Education: Analysing Policy Implementation* (Dordrecht; Springer).

J-E. Lane (1982) 'Das Hochschulwesen in Skandanavien in einer vergleichenden Übersicht', in L. Hüber (ed.), *Europäischen Encyclopedie Erziehungswissenschaft* (Hamburg: Klett-Kotta Verlag).

———. (1992) 'Sweden', in B.R. Clark and G. Neave (eds), *The Encyclopedia of Higher Education*, vol. I, *National Systems of Higher Education* (Oxford: Pergamon).

Légifrance (2009a) *Décret n°2006-1334 du 3 novembre 2006 relatif à l'organisation et au fonctionnement de l'Agence d'évaluation de la recherche et de l'enseignement supérieur*, available at: www.legifrance.gouv.fr/affichTexte.do?cidTexte= JORFTEXT000000646922&dateTexte= (date accessed 15 November 2011).

——. (2009b) *Loi n°2006-450 du 18 avril 2006 de programme pour la recherche*, available at: www.legifrance.gouv.fr/affichTexte.do?cidTexte= JORFTEXT000000646922&dateTexte= (date accessed 15 November 2011).

Le Monde (2009a) 'Universités: l'évaluation au coeur de l'agitation', *Le Monde*, 4 February, available at: www.lemonde.fr/societe/article/2009/ 02/04/universites-l-evaluation-des-enseignants-au-coeur-de-l-agitation_ 1150518_3224.html (date accessed 15 November 2011).

——. (2009b) 'Enseignants-chercheurs: la fronde s'étend', *Le Monde*, 9 February, available at: www.lemonde.fr/societe/article/2009/02/09/enseignants- chercheurs-la-fronde-s-etend_1152743_3224.html (date accessed 15 November 2011).

A. Leparmentier (2009) 'Un exercise inédit du pouvoir, pas de réforme emblématique', in *Deux Ans à l'Elysée Dossier du Monde*, 5 May, p. 23.

L. Leslie and S.A. Slaughter (1997) 'The Development and Current Status of Market Mechanisms in U.S. Postsecondary Education', *Higher Education Policy* 10: 239–52.

D. Levy and S. Slancheva (eds) (2007) *Private Higher Education in East and Central Europe: The Quest for Legitimacy* (New York: Palgrave Macmillan).

S. Lindqvist (2006) 'The R&D Production Model: A Breug(h)elesque Alternative', in G. Neave, K. Blüchert and T. Nybom (eds), *The European Research University: An Historical Parenthesis* (Basingstoke: Palgrave Macmillan), pp. 77–90.

B. Little and M. Henkel (1999) *Changing Relationships between Higher Education and the State* (London: Jessica Kingsley).

LOU (2001) *Ley orgànica 6/2001 de Universidades de 21 de diciembro (BOE de 24 de diciembro)*, available at: www.educacion.gob.es/educacion/ universidades/educacion-superior-universitaria/titulos/homologacion-titulos/ convalidacion-parcial.html (date accessed 25 November 2011).

P. Maassen (2002) 'Changing Roles of Stakeholders in Dutch Universities', *European Journal of Education* 35, 4: 449–64.

P. Maassen and J. Olssen (2007) *European Integration and University Dynamics* (Dordrecht: Kluwer Academic Publishers).

A. Magalhães and A. Amaral (2007) 'Changing Values and Norms in Portuguese Higher Education', *Higher Education Policy* 20, 1: 1–24.

J. Markiewicz-Lagneau and P. Gruson (1983) *L'Enseignement supérieur et son efficacité: France, États-Unis, URSS, Pologne* (Paris: La Documentation française).

K. Martens and K.D. Wolf (2009) 'Boomerangs and Trojan Horses: The Unintended Consequences of internationalizing Education Policy through the EU and the OECD', in A. Amaral, G. Neave, P. Maassen and C. Musselin (eds), *European Integration and the Governance of Higher Education and Research* (London: Springer), pp. 81–108.

S. Marton (2007) 'University Autonomy under Threat? – A Case Study from Sweden', available at: www.flackattack.org/faw/index.php?title=University_ Autonomy_under_Threat%3F (date accessed 17 May 2009).

J-L. Mazet (2009) 'Open Letter to the Director General, CNRS', available at: www. sncs.fr/article.php37id_article=1819 (date accessed 17 May 2009).

J.E. McNair (1984) *Education for a Changing Spain* (Manchester University Press).

Y. Mény, P. Mueller and J-L. Quermonne (1996) *Adjusting to Europe: The Impact of the European Union on National Institutions and Policies* (London: Routledge).

W. Metzger (1987) 'The United States', in B.R. Clark (ed.), *The Academic Profession: Institutional, National and International Settings* (Berkeley, CA: University of California Press).

Ministère de l'Education (2009) 'Liste des Classes préparatoires aux Grandes Ecoles', Paris, Ministère de l'Education, available at: www.sup.adc.education.fr/cpgelst/ (date accessed 15 November 2011).

Ministério da Ciéncia, Tecnologia e Ensino Superior (2009) 'Governo cria Agência de Avaliação e Acreditação do Ensino Superior', available at: www.mctes.pt/?idc= 16&idi=285&idt= (date accessed 15 November 2011).

C. Montlaur-Creux (2007*) Loi n° 2007-1199 du 10 août 2007 relative aux libertés et responsabilités des universités* (Pau: Université de Pau et des Pays de l'Adour, Direction des Affaires juridiques).

G. Moodie (1986) 'The Disintegrating Chair: Professors in Britain Today', *European Journal of Education* 21, 1: 43–56.

J-G. Mora (1997) 'Market Trends in Spanish Higher Education', *Higher Education Policy* 10, 3–4: 187–98.

J-G. Mora and J. Vidal (2007) 'Two Decades of Change in Spanish Universities: Learning the Hard Way', in A. Amaral, A. Gornitzka and M. Kogan (eds), *Reform and Change in Higher Education: Renewed Expectations and Improved Performance* (Dordrecht: Springer), pp. 133–50.

C. Musselin (2004) 'Commentary on "The Bologna Process and the Evaluative State: a viticultural parable"', in M. Kogan (ed.), *Management and Evaluation in Higher Education, UNESCO Forum Occasional Paper Series, Paper No. 7* (Paris: UNESCO), pp. 35–8.

——. (2009) 'The Side-effects of the Bologna Process on Institutional Settings: The Case of France', in A. Amaral, G. Neave, C. Musselin and P. Maassen (eds), *European Integration and the Governance of Higher Education and Research* (London: Springer), pp. 181–206.

G. Neave (1987) *La Communidad Europea y la Educación* (Madrid: Fundación Universidad Empresa).

——. (1988a) 'On the Cultivation of Quality, Efficiency and Enterprise: An Overview of Recent Trends in Higher Education in Western Europe 1986–1988', *European Journal of Education* 23, 2–3: 7–23.

——. (1988b) 'Education and Social Policy: Demise of an Ethic or Change of Values?', *Oxford Review of Education* 14, 3: 273–83.

——. (1991) 'On the Procedures of Elevation: Or, How the Mantle of Elijah Falls upon the Shoulders of Elisha', in *Organisation und Management von Universitäten: Verhaltnis von Staat und Universität* (Vienna: Plenum), pp. 44–9.

——. (1993) 'Separation de Corps: The Training of Advanced Students and the Organization of Research in France', in B.R. Clark (ed.), *The Research Foundations of Graduate Education* (Berkeley, CA: University of California Press), pp. 159–91.

——. (1996a) 'The Evaluation of the Higher Education System in France', in Robert Cowen (ed.), *World Yearbook of Education 1966: The Evaluation of Systems of Higher Education* (London: Kogan Page), pp. 66–81.

——. (1996b) 'Homogenization, Integration and Convergence: The Cheshire Cats of Higher Education Analysis', in V. Lynn Meek, L. Goedegebuure, O. Kivinen and R. Rinne (eds), *The Mockers and Mocked: Comparative Perspectives* on *Differentiation, Convergence and Diversity in Higher Education* (Oxford, Pergamon), pp. 26–41.

——. (1998a) 'The Evaluative State Reconsidered', *European Journal of Education* 33, 3: 265–84.

——. (1998b) 'Quatre modèles pour l'Université', *Courrier de l'UNESO*, September, pp. 21–2.

——. (2002) 'The Stakeholder Perspective Historically Explored', in J. Enders and O. Fulton (eds), *Higher Education in a Globalising World: International Trends and Mutual Observations* (Dordrecht: Kluwer Academic Publishers), pp. 17–38.

——. (2002a) 'Vale Tudo – ou como a adaptação das universidades à integração europeia encerra contradiçãoes afinal inspiradoras', *Boletim universidade do Porto* 35: 9–18.

——. (2004a) 'The Bologna Process and the Evaluative State: A Viticultural Parable', in M. Kogan (ed.), *Management and Evaluation in Higher Education, UNESCO Forum Occasional Paper Series, Paper No. 7* (Paris: UNESCO), pp. 11–34.

——. (2004b) 'The Temple and its Guardians: An Excursion into the Rhetoric of Evaluating Higher Education', *Journal of Finance and Management in Colleges and Universities* (Tokyo) 1, 1: 212–27.

——. (2004c) 'Higher Education Policy as Orthodoxy: Being One Tale of Doxological Drift, Political Intention and Changing Circumstances', in D. Dill, B. Jongbloed, A. Amaral and P. Teixeira (eds), *Markets in Higher Education: Rhetoric or Reality?* (Dordrecht: Kluwer Academic Publishers).

——. (2005) 'The Super Marketed University: Reform, Vision and Ambiguity in British Higher Education', *Perspectives* 9, 1: 17–22.

——. (2006a) 'The Evaluative State and Bologna: Old Wine in New Bottles or Simply the Ancient Practice of "Coupage"?', in *Higher Education Forum*, vol. 3 (Hiroshima University Research Institute for Higher Education), pp. 27–46.

——. (2006b) 'Mapping the Knowledge Society Back into Higher Education', in T. Nybom, G. Neave and K. Blüchert (eds), *Knowledge, Authority and Dissent: Critical Perspectives on Higher Education and Research in Knowledge Society* (Paris: UNESCO), pp. 13–22.

——. (2007) 'A privatizaçao da Educaçao Superior e a Dinâmica do Estado Avaliador', in *ANAIS Educaçao Superior: questão de Estado prioridade social* (São Paulo: FNESP), pp. 109–92.

——. (2008) 'From Guardian to Overseer: Trends in Institutional Autonomy, Governance and Leadership', in A. Amaral (ed.), *Reforma do Ensino Superior: Quatro temas em Debate* (Lisbon: Conselho Nacional de Educação).

——. (2009a) 'The Evaluative State as Policy in Transition: An Anatomical Study', in R. Cowen and A. Kazamias (eds), *International Handbook of Comparative Education*, vol. 1 (London: Springer), pp. 551–68.

——. (2009b) 'Now You See It, Now You Don't: Privatization as the Will o' the Wisp in the Higher Education Policies of Western Europe', in N. Liron and C. Diamant (eds), *Privatization in Higher Education: Proceedings of the International Conference*, the Samuel Neaman Institute, Technion – Israel Institute of Technology (Haifa, Israel: S. Neaman Press), CD-ROM, pp. 53–87, available at: www.neaman.org.il/Neaman/publications/publication_item.asp? fid=899&parent_fid=489&iid=7765 (date accessed 15 November 2011).

——. (2009c) 'The Bologna Process as Alpha or Omega or, On Interpreting History and Context as Inputs to Bologna, Prague, Berlin and Beyond', in

A. Amaral, G. Neave, C. Musselin and P. Maassen (eds), *European Integration and the Governance of Higher Education and Research* ((London: Springer), pp. 17–58.

——. (2009d) 'Institutional Autonomy 2010–2020. A Tale of Elan – Two Steps Back to Make One Very Large Leap Forward', in J. Huisman, B. Stensaker and B.M. Kehm (eds), *The European Higher Education Area: Perspectives on a Moving Target* (Rotterdam: Sense Publishers), pp. 3–22.

——. (2011a) 'The Changing "Vision Thing"': Academia and the Changing Mission of Higher Education', *Educação, Sociedade, Cultura* 33: 15–36.

——. (2011b) 'El Estudio de la gobernanza en la educación superior: vaciamento, re-construcción y re-ingeniería del significado', in R. Grediago Kuri and R. López Zárate (eds), *Aportaciones a la agenda de investigación subre educación superior 2010–2020* (Mexico: Universidad Autónomia Metropolitana, Unidad Azcapotzalco), pp. 261–98.

——. (forthcoming) 'Change, Leverage, Suasion and Intent: An Historical Excursion across Three Decades of Change in Higher Education in Western Europe', in C. Sarrico, J. Valimaa and B. Stensaker (eds), *Managing Reform in Universities: The Dynamics of Culture, Identity and Organizational Change* (Basingstoke: Palgrave Macmillan).

G. Neave and A. Amaral (2008) 'On Process, Progress, Success and Methodology; Or, the Unfolding of the Bologna Process as it Appears to Two Reasonably Benign Observers', *Higher Education Quarterly* 62, 1–2: 40–62.

——. (eds) (2011) *Higher Education in Portugal 1974–2009: A Nation, a Generation* (Dordrecht: Springer).

G. Neave and R. Edelstein (1987) 'The Research Training System in France: A Microstudy of Three Academic Disciplines', in B.R. Clark (ed.), *The Research Foundations of Graduate Education* (Berkeley, CA: University of California Press), pp. 192–220.

G. Neave and G. Rhoades (1987) 'The Academic Estate in Western Europe', in B.R. Clark (ed.), *The Academic Profession: National, Disciplinary and Institutional Settings* (Berkeley, CA: University of California Press), pp. 211–70.

G. Neave and F.A. van Vught (1994a) *Prometeo Encadenado: estado y educación superior en Europa* (Barcelona: Gedisa).

——. (1994b) *Government and Higher Education Relationships across Three Continents: The Winds of Change* (Oxford: Elsevier/Pergamon).

M. Neave (2009) 'From Soldier of the King to Soldier of the Republic: The French Fighting Man 1783–1795. A Study in Standing, Status, Motivation, Conditions and Effectiveness', unpublished BA dissertation, University of Exeter, Department of Politics.

Nederlands Vlaams Accreditatieorganisatie (NVAO) (2009) 'Historie NVAO', available at: www.qrossroads.eu/quality-assurance-and-accreditation/netherlands—nvao-20/legal-framework (date accessed 26 November 2011).

NQA (Netherlands Quality Agency) (2009) www.linkedin.com/companies/netherlands-quality-agency (date accessed 15 November 2011).

T. Nybom (2003) 'The Humboldtian Legacy: Reflections on the Past, Present and Future of the European University', *Higher Education Policy* 16, 2: 141–69.

——. (2007) 'University Autonomy and Academic Freedom: Political Rhetoric or Institutional Reality?', keynote presentation to the *Transition to Mass Higher*

Education Systems: International Comparisons and Perspectives conference, Haifa, Israel, the Technion Israel Institute of Technology, 4–6 December.

OECD (1969) *The Development of Secondary Education* (Paris: OECD)

——. (2006) 'Portugal Needs to Overhaul its Higher Education System, OECD Says', Press Release, 13 December 2006, available at: www.oecd. org/document/21/0,3343,en_2649_37455_37827989_1_1_1_1,00.html (date accessed 15 November 2011).

——. (2007) *Review of the Portuguese Higher Education System* (Paris: OECD).

——. (2008) *Tertiary Education for the Knowledge Society: OECD Thematic Review of Tertiary Education: Synthesis Report, vol. 1* (Paris: OECD).

H. Perkin (1969) *Key Profession: The History of the Association of University Teachers* (London: Routledge & Kegan Paul).

H. Peschar (2003) 'In Search of a New Profession', in A. Amaral, V. Lynn Meek and M. Larsen (eds), *Higher Education's Managerial Revolution* (Dordrecht: Kluwer Academic Publishers), pp. 103–9.

M. Pollack (1994) 'Creeping Competence, the Expanding Agenda of the European Community', *Journal of Public Policy* 14, 2: 95–145.

——. (2000) 'The End of Creeping Competence? EU Policy-making since Maastricht', *Journal of Common Market Studies* 38, 3: 519–38.

C. Pollitt (1995) 'Justification by Works or by Faith? Evaluating the New Public Management', *Evaluation* 1: 133–54.

C. Pollitt and G. Bouckaert (2004) *Public Management Reform: A Comparative Analysis*, 2nd edn (New York: Oxford University Press).

T. Porter and M. Webb (2007) 'The Role of the OECD in the Orchestration of Global Knowledge Networks', *Presentation to the Canadian Political Science Association Annual Meeting*, Saskatoon, Saskatchewan, Canada, 30 May.

Portugal (1988) *Assembly of the Republic Law 108/88 September 24th University Autonomy* (Lisbon: Centro de Informações sobre a Reconhecimento Académico de Diplomas).

——. (2007) *Law 38/2007 August 16th 2007 Legal Framework for the Evaluation of Higher Education*, Lisbon (English translation).

——. (2008) *Decree Law 62/ 2007 September 10th 2007: The Legal Framework of Higher Education Institutions*, Lisbon (English translation).

J. Pratt and T. Burgess (1974) *The Polytechnics* (London: Pitmans).

R. Premfors (1981) 'National Policy Style and Higher Education in France, Sweden and the United Kingdom', *European Journal of Education* 16, 2: 253–62.

——. (1989) 'Vitality of Basic Units in Universities', *Higher Education in Europe* 14, 3: 5–22.

J.L. Pressman and A.B. Wildavsky (1984) *Implementation: How great expectations in Washington are dashed in Oakland: or, why it's amazing that federal programs work at all, this being a saga of the Economic Development Administration as told by two sympathetic observers who seek to build morals on a foundation of ruined hopes*, 3rd edn (Berkeley, CA: University of California Press).

R.E. Prothero (2005). *The Works Of Lord Byron, Letters and Journals*, vol. 1, available at: www.gutenberg.org/dirs/etext05/7blj110.txt (date accessed 15 November 2011).

L. Purser and D. Crozier (2007) 'Trends V: Key Messages', *4th Convention of European Higher Education Institutions*, Lisbon, March (PowerPoint presentation).

QANU (Quality Assurance Agency Netherlands Universities) (2009) www.qanu. nl/index.aspx?contentid=227 (date accessed 15 November 2011).

Y.M. Rabkin (1992) 'Academies: The Soviet Union', in B.R. Clark and G. Neave (eds), *The Encyclopedia of Higher Education*, vol. 2, *Analytical Perspectives, Section ii: The Institutional Fabric of the Higher Education System* (Oxford: Pergamon), pp. 1049–54.

F.T. Read (2000) 'The Unique Role of the American Law School Dean: Academic Leader or Embattled Juggler?', *University of Toledo Law Review* 31, 4: 715–24.

G. Rhoades (1998) *Managed Professionals: Unionized Faculty and Restructuring Academic Labour* (Albany, NY: SUNY Press).

I. Richter (1992) 'Law', in B.R. Clark and G. Neave (eds), *The Encyclopedia of Higher Education*, vol. 3, *Analytical Perspectives, Section v: Disciplinary Perspectives on Higher Education* (Oxford: Pergamon), pp. 1834–46.

S.L. Robertson and R. Dale (2009) *The World Bank, the IMF and the Possibilities of Critical Education* (London: Routledge).

S. Rothblatt (1997) *The Modern University and its Discontents: The Fate of Newman's Legacies in Britain and America* (Cambridge University Press).

L. Sanchez-Ferrer (1997) 'From Bureaucratic Centralism to Self-regulation: The Reform of Higher Education in Spain', *Western European Politics* 20, 3: 164–84.

R. Santiago, T.A. Carvalho, A. Amaral and V.L Meek (2006) 'Changing Patterns in the Middle Management of Higher Education Institutions: The Case of Portugal', *Higher Education* 52: 215–50.

P. Savidan (2007) *Repenser l'égalité des chances* (Paris: Grasset).

S. Schwartz-Hahn and D. Westerheijden (eds) (2004) *Accreditation and Evaluation in the European Higher Education Area* (Dordrecht: Kluwer Academic Publishers).

S. Schwartzman (1998) 'Brazil', in T. Husén, T.N. Postlethwaite, B.R Clark and G. Neave (eds), *Education: The Complete Encyclopedia* (updated edition) (Oxford: Elsevier), CD-ROM.

P. Scott (1998) *The Globalization of Higher Education* (Milton Keynes: Open University Press).

M. Shattock (2003) 'Re-balancing Modern Concepts of University Governance', *Higher Education Quarterly* 56, 3: 235–44.

D. Smith, J. Adams and D. Mount (2007) *UK Universities and Executive Officers: The Changing Role of Pro Vice Chancellors: Final Report* (London: Leadership Foundation for Higher Education).

S. Sorlin and H. Vessuri (2007) *Knowledge Society vs. Knowledge Economy: Knowledge, Power and Politics* (Basingstoke: Palgrave Macmillan).

A. Soulier (1939) *L'Instabilité ministerielle sous la Troisième République 1871–1939* (Paris: éditions Sirey).

A. Staropoli (1987) 'The Comité National d'Evaluation: Preliminary Results of a French Experiment', *European Journal of Education* 22, 2: 123–31.

B. Stensaker (2004) *The Transformation of Organisational Identities: Interpretations of Policies Concerning the Quality of Teaching and Learning in Norwegian Higher Education* (Enschede: CHEPS).

R. Stichweh (1994) *Wissenschaft, Universität, Professionen* (Frankfurt am Main: Suhrkamp).

SVR (Svensk Vetenskapsradet) (2008) 'The Linnaeus Grant Programme: An Organizational Evaluation', *Report of the International Evaluation Panel to the Swedish Research Council, Stockholm* (mimeo).

L. Svensson (1982) 'The State and Higher Education: A Sociological Critique from Sweden', *European Journal of Education* 27, 3: 295–306.

U. Teichler (2007) *Higher Education Systems: Conceptual Frameworks, Comparative Perspectives, Empirical Findings* (Rotterdam: Sense Publications).

P. Teixeira and D. Dill (2011) 'The Many Faces of Marketisation', in P. Teixeira and D. Dill (eds), *Public Vices, Private Virtues? Assessing the Effects of Marketization in Higher Education* (Rotterdam: Sense Publications).

J. Thorens (2006) 'Liberties, Freedom and Autonomy: A Few Reflections on Academia's Estate', *Higher Education Policy* 19, 1: 87–110.

A. Tjeldvoll (1998) A *Service University in Scandinavia?* (Oslo: University Institute for Educational Research).

P. Toynbee and D. Walker (2008) *Unjust Rewards: Exposing Greed and Inequality in Britain Today* (London: Granta Publications).

M. Trow (1974) *The Transition from Elite to Mass Higher Education* (Paris: OECD) 2 vols.

——. (1975) 'The Public and Private Lives of Higher Education', *Daedalus,* 104: 113–27.

——. (1996) 'Trust, Markets and Accountability in Higher Education: A Comparable Perspective', *Higher Education Policy* 9, 4: 309–24.

M. Twain (1889) *A Connecticut Yankee at King Arthur's Court* (New York: Charles L Webster).

W. Ullman (1961) *Principles of Government and Politics in the Middle Ages* (New York: Barnes & Noble).

M. van Keulen and J.Q.T. Rood (2003) 'The Netherlands Presidency of 1997: Between Ambition and Modesty', in O. Engstrom (ed;) *European Union Council Presidencies: A Comparative Perspective* (London: Routledge), pp. 71–86.

F.A. van Vught (1989) *Governmental Strategies and Innovation in Higher Education* (London: Jessica Kingsley).

——. (1997) 'To Innovate for Quality', in *Quality Assurance as Support for Processes of Innovation: The Swedish Model in Comparative Perspective* (Stockholm: HSV), pp. 80–104.

——. (ed.) (2009) *Mapping the Higher Education Landscape: Towards a European Classification of Higher Education* (Dordrecht: Springer).

F.A. van Vught and P.A.M. Maassen (1988) 'An Intriguing Janus Head: The Two Faces of the New Governmental Strategy for Higher Education in the Netherlands', *European Journal of Education* 23, 1–2: 65–76.

L. van Welie (2000) 'Walk on Air Do We?', in S. Janosik, D.G. Creamer and A.M. David (eds), *International Perspectives on Quality in Higher Education* (Virginia Polytechnic Institute, Education Policy Institute) (mimeo), pp. 8–15.

VSNU (Vereeniging der Samenwerkende Nederlandse Universiteiten) (2009) 'Association of Universities in the Netherlands', available at: http://english.vsnu.nl/web/show/id=88879/langid=42 (date accessed 17 May 2009).

R. in 't Veldt, H-P. Füssel and G. Neave (eds) (1996) *The Relations between State and Higher Education,* vol. 1 in the Council of Europe *Legislating for Higher Education in Europe* series (Dordrecht: Kluwer Academic Publishers).

J. Verger (1986) *Histoire des universités en France* (Toulouse: Privat).

J.C. Verhoeven and G. Devos (2002) 'Integration of Merged Colleges and Decentralization of Decision-making in Flanders, Belgium', in A. Amaral, G.A. Jones and B. Karseth (eds), *Governing Higher Education: National Perspectives on Institutional Governance* (Dordrecht: Kluwer Academic Publishers).

C. Weiss (1977) 'Bridging Research and Policy. Research for Policy's Sake: The Enlightenment Function of Social Research', *Policy Analysis* 3, 4: 531–45.

G. Weisz (1983) *The Emergence of Modern Universities in France 1863–1914* (Princeton University Press).

C. Whitchurch (2006) *Professional Managers in UK Higher Education. Preparing for Complex Futures: Interim Report* (London: Leadership Foundation for Higher Education).

———. (2009) 'Some Implications of "Public/Private Space" for Professional Identities in Higher Education', *Presentation to the 21st CHER Conference*, 10–12 September, Porto, Portugal (mimeo).

White Paper (1983) *Taakverdeling en Concentratie in het Wetenschappelijk Onderwijs* (The Hague: Ministerie van Onderwijs en Wetenschapen).

———. (2003) *The Future of Higher Education* (London: Department for Education and Skills).

W. Wielemans and W.G.M. Roth van der Werf (1997) *Onderwijs en de Europese Unie: eenheid en verschillenheid* (Appeldorn/Antwerp: Garant).

G. Williams (1996) 'The Many Faces of Privatization', *Higher Education Management* 8, 3: 39–56.

———. (2004) 'The Higher Education Market in the UK', in D. Dill, B. Jongbloed, A. Amaral and P. Teixeira (eds), *Markets in Higher Education: Rhetoric or Reality?* (Dordrecht: Kluwer Academic Publishers), pp. 241–70.

Index